I0121350

John Pagen White

Lays and Legends of the English Lake Country

With Copious Notes

John Pagen White

Lays and Legends of the English Lake Country
With Copious Notes

ISBN/EAN: 9783337151300

Printed in Europe, USA, Canada, Australia, Japan

Cover: Foto ©Thomas Meinert / pixelio.de

More available books at **www.hansebooks.com**

Lays and Legends

OF THE

English Lake Country,

WITH COPIOUS NOTES.

BY

JOHN PAGEN WHITE, F.R.C.S.

> " In early date,
> When I was beardless, young, and blate,
> E'en then a wish, I mind its power,
> A wish that to my latest hour
>   Shall strongly heave my breast ;
> That I for poor auld *Cumbria's* sake,
> Some usefu' plan or beuk could make,
>   Or sing a sang at least."

LONDON: JOHN RUSSELL SMITH.
CARLISLE: G. & T. COWARD.
MDCCCLXXIII.

PREFACE.

The English Lake District may be said, in general terms, to extend from Cross-Fell and the Solway Firth, on the east and north, to the waters of Morecambe and the Irish Sea; or, more accurately, to be comprised within an irregular circle, varying from forty to fifty miles in diameter, of which the centre is the mountain Helvellyn, and within which are included a great portion of Cumberland and Westmorland and the northern extremity of Lancashire.

After the conquest of England by the Normans, the counties of Cumberland and Westmorland, the ancient inheritance of the Scottish Kings, as well as the county of Northumberland, were placed by William under the English crown. But the regions thus alienated were not allowed to remain in the undisturbed possession of the strangers. For a long period they were disquieted by the attempts which from time to time were made by successive kings of Scotland to re-establish their supremacy over them.

Supporting their pretensions by force of arms, they
carried war into the disputed territory, and conducted
it with a rancour and cruelty which spared neither
age or sex. The two nations maintained their cause,
just or unjust, with unfaltering resolution; or if they
seemed to hesitate for a moment, and a period of
settlement to be at hand, their frequent compromises
only ended in a renewal of their differences. Thus
these northern counties continued to pass alternately
under the rule of both the contending nations, until
the Scottish dominion over them was finally termin-
ated by agreement in the year 1237; Alexander of
Scotland accepting in lieu lands of a certain yearly
value, to be holden of the King of England by the
annual render of a falcon to the Constable of the
Castle of Carlisle, on the Festival of the Assump-
tion.

The resumption, at no distant period, of the
manors which had been granted to Alexander,
renewed in all their strength the feelings of ani-
mosity with which the Scots had been accustomed
to regard their southern neighbours, and the feuds
between the two kingdoms continued with unabated
violence for more than three centuries longer. The
dwellers in the unsettled districts lying along the
English and Scottish borders, being originally
derived from the same Celtic stock, had been
gradually and progressively influenced as a race by
the admixture of Saxon and Danish blood into the
population; and although much of the Celtic char-

acter was thereby lost, they seem to have retained in their mountains and forests much of the spirit, and many of the laws and manners, of the ancient Britons. They continued to form themselves into various septs, or clans, according to the Celtic custom; sometimes banded together for the attainment of a common end; and as often at feud, one clan with another, when some act of personal wrong had to be revenged upon a neighbouring community. Thus a state of continual restlessness, springing out of mutual hatred and jealousies, existed among the borderers of either nation. The same feelings of enmity were fostered, and the same system of petty warfare was carried on, between the borderers of the two kingdoms. Cumberland and Westmorland, from their position, were subject to the frequent inroads of the Scots; by whom great outrages were committed upon the inhabitants. They drove their cattle, burned their dwellings, plundered their monasteries, and even destroyed whole towns and villages. A barbarous system of vengeance and retaliation ensued. Every act of violence and bloodshed was perpetrated; whilst the most nefarious practices of free-booting became the common occupation of the marauding clans; and a *raid* into a neighbouring district had for them the same sort of charm and excitement which their descendants find in a modern fox chase. Even after the union of the two kingdoms under one sovereign, when the term " Borders " had been changed to " Middle Shires," as being

more suitable to a locality which was now nearly in
the centre of his dominions, the long cherished dis-
tinctions and prejudices of the inhabitants were
maintained in all their vigour; and it required a
long period of conflict with these to be persevered
in, before the extinction of the border feuds could
be completely effected. These distractions have
now been at an end for more than two centuries.
The mountains look down upon a peaceful domain;
the valleys, everywhere the abode of quiet and
security, yield their rich pasturage to the herds, or
their corn-fields redden, though coyly, to the harvest;
and the population, much of it rooted in the soil,
and attached by hereditary ties to the same plots of
ancestral ground in many instances for six or seven
hundred years, is independent, prosperous, and
happy.

Some evidences of the old troublous times remain,
in the dismantled Border Towers, and moated or
fortified houses called Peles, which lie on the more
exposed parts of the district; in the ruins of the
conventual retreats; and in the crumbling strong-
holds of the chiefs, which still retain something of a
past existence in the names which even yet cling
about their walls, as if the spirits of their former
possessors were reluctant to depart entirely from
them. Whilst a few traditions and recollections
survive of those stirring periods which have left
their mark upon the nation's history, and are
associated for ever with images of those illustrious

persons whose familiar haunts were within the shadows of the hills.

But the great charm of this region, which is not without attractions also of a superstitious and romantic character, lies in the variety of the aspects of nature which it presents; exhibiting, on a diminutive scale, combinations of the choicest features of the scenery of all those lands which have a name and fame for beauty and magnificence. Mr. West, a Roman Catholic clergyman, long resident in the district, and the author of one of the earliest Guides to the Lakes, thus expresses himself : " They who intend to make the continental tour should begin here; as it will give in miniature, an idea of what they are to meet with there, in traversing the Alps and Appenines : to which our northern mountains are not inferior in beauty of line, or variety of summit, number of lakes, and transparency of water; not in colouring of rock or softness of turf; but in height and extent only. The mountains here are all accessible to the summit, and furnish prospects no less surprising, and with more variety than the Alps themselves." Wordsworth also, who could well judge of this fact, and none better; he who for fifty years

> " Murmured near *these* running brooks
> A music sweeter than their own,"

and looked on all their changing phases with a superstitious eye of love; after he had become acquainted with the mountain scenery of Wales,

Scotland, Switzerland, and Italy, gave his judgment that, as a whole, the English Lake District within its narrow limits is preeminent above them all. He thus speaks: " A happy proportion of component parts is indeed noticeable among the landscapes of the North of England; and, in this characteristic essential to a perfect picture, they surpass the scenes of Scotland, and, in a still greater degree, those of Switzerland. . . . On the score even of sublimity, the superiority of the Alps is by no means so great as might hastily be inferred; and, as to the *beauty* of the lower regions of the Swiss mountains, their surface has nothing of the mellow tone and variety of hues by which our mountain turf is distinguished. . . . The Lakes are much more interesting than those of the Alps; first, as is implied above by being more happily proportioned to the other features of the landscape; and next, as being infinitely more pellucid, and less subject to agitation from the winds." And again, " The water of the English Lakes being of a crystalline clearness, the reflections of the surrounding hills are frequently so lively, that it is scarcely possible to distinguish the point where the real object terminates, and its unsubstantial duplicate begins."

It is therefore not to be wondered at, that during the greater part of a century, where the old Border *raids* of violence have ceased, excursions of a very different character should have taken their place. Every summer brings down upon the valleys clouds of visitors from every corner of our island, and from many countries of Europe and America, eager to enjoy their freshness and beauty, and breathe a new life in the companionship of the lakes and hills. And if in a spirit somewhat more akin to the moss-trooping Borderer of an earlier time, an occasional intruder has scoured the vales in search of their traditions ; and in the pursuit of these has ransacked their annals, plundered their guides, and levied a sort of black-mail upon even casual and anonymous contributors to their history ; it may in some degree extenuate the offence to remember that such literary free-booting makes no one poorer for what it takes away ; and that the *opima spolia* of the adventurer are only so much gathered to be distributed again. More especially to the Notes which constitute so large a portion of the present Volume may this remark be applied. Scenery long outlasts all traditional and historical associations. To revive these among their ancient haunts, and to awaken yet another interest in this land of beauty, has been the aim and end of this modern *Raid* into the valleys of the North, and the regions that own the sovereignty of the "mighty Helvellyn."

CONTENTS.

THE PAST.

(IN SIGHT OF DACRE CASTLE.)

Through yon old archway grey and broken
Rides forth a belted knight;
Upon his breast his true-love's token
And armour glittering bright.

His arm a fond adieu is waving,
And answering waves a hand
From one whose love her grief is braving—
The fairest of the land.

The trumpet calls, and plain and valley
Give forth their armed men;
And round the red-cross flag they rally,
From every dale and glen.

And she walks forth in silent sorrow,
Who was so blest to-day,
And thinks on many a lone to-morrow
In those old towers of grey.

1

From many a piping throat so mellow
    The joyful song bursts forth ;
On many a field the corn so yellow
    Makes golden bright the earth.

And mountains o'er the green woods frowning
    Close round the banner'd walls ;
While mid-day sunshine, all things crowning,
    In summer splendour falls.

But ours is not the age they walk in ;
    It is the years of yore :
And ours is not the tongue they talk in ;
    'Tis language used no more.

Yet many an eye in silence bending
    O'er this unmurmur'd lay,
Beholds that knight the vale descending,
    And feels that summer's day.

Lives it then not ?   Yes ; and when hoary
    Beneath our years we stand,
That scene of summer, love, and glory,
    Shall still be on the land.

Truth from the earth itself shall perish
    Ere that shall be no more ;
The heart in song will ever cherish
    What has been life of yore.

THE BANNER OF BROUGHTON TOWER.

The knight looked out from Broughton Tower ;
   The stars hung high o'er Broughton Town ;
" There should be tidings by this hour,
   From Fouldrey Pile or Urswick Down ! "

Far out the Duddon roll'd its tide
   Beneath ; and on the verge afar,
The Warder through the night descried
   The beacon, like a rising star.

It told that Fouldrey by the sea
   Was signall'd from the ships that bore,
With Swart's Burgundian chivalry,
   The false King from the Irish shore.

And Lincoln's Earl, and Broughton's Knight,
   And brave Lord Lovel, wait the sign
To march their hosts to Urswick's height,
   To hail him King, of Edward's line.

Brave men as ever swerv'd aside !
   But faithful to their ancient fame,
The white Rose wooed them in her pride
   Once more ; and foremost forth they came.

The Knight looked out beneath his hand;
    The Warder pointed to the glow;
" Now droop my banner, that my band
    May each embrace it! then we'll go.

" And if we fall, as fall we may,
    Thus resolute the wronged to raise,
The banner that we bear to-day,
    Shall be our monument and praise!"

One look into his lady's bower;
    One step into his ancient hall;
And then adieu to Broughton Tower,
    Till blooms the white Rose over all!

High o'er the surge of many a fight,
    That banner, for the Rose, had led
The liegemen of the Broughton knight
    To victory's smiles, or glory's bed.

And 'twas a glorious sight to see
    That break of day, from tower and town,
Pour forth his martial tenantry,
    To swell the array on Urswick Down:

To see the glancing pennons wave
    Above them, and the banner borne
All joyously by warriors, brave
    As ever hailed a battle morn.

And 'twas a stirring sound to hear,
　Uprolling from the camp,—the drum,
The music, and the martial cheer,
　That told the chiefs, "We come, we come!"

Then in that sunny time of June,
　When green leaves burdened every spray,
With all the merry birds in tune,
　They marched upon their southward way.

And, as through channel'd sands afar
　The tides with steady onward force
Push inland, roll'd their wave of war
　To Trent, its unresisted course.

And spreading wide its crest where Stoke
　O'erlook'd the Royal lines below,
Spent its long gathering strength, and broke,
　And plung'd in fury on the foe.

For three long hours that summer morn
　King Henry by his standard rode,
Through onset and repulse upborne,
　A tower of strength where'er it glowed.

For three long hours the fated band
　Of chiefs, that summer morning waged
A desperate battle, hand to hand,
　Where'er the thickest carnage raged,

Till midst four thousand liegemen slain,
   The flower of that misguided host,
Borne down upon the fatal plain,
   Fame, honour, life, and cause were lost.

Turn ye, who high in hall and tower
   Sit waiting for your lords, and burn
To wrest the tidings of that hour
   From lips that never may return :

Turn inwards from the news that flies
   Through England's summer groves, and close
The circlets of your asking eyes
   Against the coming cloud of woes !

Wild rumour, like the wind that wings,
   None knows or how or whence, its way,
Storm-like on Broughton's turret rings
   The dire disaster of that day.

Storm-like through his dislorded halls
   And farmsteads lone, the rumour breaks ;
And far by Witherslack's grey walls,
   And hamlet cots, despair awakes.

And all old things meet shock and change,
   Since Broughton, down-borne in his pride
On that red field, no more shall range
   By Duddon's rocks, or Winster's side.

And while the hills around rejoiced,
    And in the triumph of their King
Old strains of peace sang trumpet-voiced,
    And bade the landscapes smile and sing ;

Far stretching o'er the land, his sign
    The King from Broughton's charters tore ;
And the old honours of his line
    In his old tower were known no more.

His halls, his manors, his fair lands,
    Pass'd from his name ; round all he'd loved,
And all that loved him, power's dread hands
    In shadow through the noontide moved :

E'en to those cottage homes apart,
    His poor men's huts by lonely ways—
To crush from out the humblest heart
    Each pulse that dared to throb his praise !

But when old feuds had all been healed,
    And England's long lost smiling years
Returned, and tales of Stoke's red field
    Fair eyes had ceased to flood with tears ;

'Twas whispered 'mid the fields and farms,
    That once were Broughton's free domain,—
His *banner*, saved from strife of arms,
    Was somewhere 'mid those homes again.

That o'er the hills afar, where lies
    Lone Witherslack by moorland roads,
His own old liegemen true the prize
    Held fast within their safe abodes.

Thrice honour'd in that matchless zeal
    To brave proscription, death and shame ;
Thus rescued by their hearths to feel
    The symbol of his ancient fame !

So for old faithfulness renowned,
    The tenants of that knightly race
Their age-long acts of service crowned
    With that last deed of loyal grace.

Last ? Nay ! for on one Sabbath morn,
    An old man, blanch'd by years and cares,
Gave up his spirit, tired and worn,
    Amidst those humble liegemen's prayers.

Gave up a long secreted life
    'Mid hinds and herds, by peasant maids
Nurtured and soothed, while shadows rife
    With death's stern edicts, stalked the glades.

He pass'd while Cartmel's monks sang dole,
    As for a brave man gone to rest ;
And men sighed, "Glory to his soul !"
    And wrapt the banner round his breast :

And placed the tassell'd bridle reins
And spurs that, by his lattice, led
His thoughts so oft to far off plains,
Beside him in his narrow bed :

And borne on high their arms above,
As hinds are borne to churchyard cells,
With kindly speech of truth and love,
Mix'd with the sound of mournful bells,

They laid him in a tomb, engraved
With no memorial, date, or name ;
But one dear relic round him, saved
To whisper in the earth his fame.

And when that age had all gone down
To mingle with its native dust,
And time his deeds had overgrown,
His banner yielded up its trust ;

And told from one low chancel's shade
Where good men sang on holy days—
" Here Broughton's Knight in earth was laid.
Peace ! To his tenants, endless praise ! "

NOTES TO "THE BANNER OF BROUGHTON TOWER."

Broughton Tower, the ancient part of which is all that remains of the residence of the unfortunate Sir Thomas Broughton, stands a little to the eastward of the town of that name, upon the neck of a wooded spur of land, which projects from the high ground above the houses towards the river Duddon, about a mile distant. The towered portion, as it rises from the wood, has much of the appearance of a church; but is in reality part of the ancient building, now connected with a modern mansion. It has a southern aspect, with a slope down to the river, being well sheltered in the opposite direction. "It commands an extensive view, comprising in a wonderful variety hill and dale, water, wooded grounds, and buildings; whilst fertility around is gradually diminished, being lost in the superior heights of Black Comb, in Cumberland, the high lands between Kirkby and Ulverston, and the estuary of the Duddon expanding into the sands and waters of the Irish sea." ·

The Broughtons were an Anglo-Saxon family of high antiquity, in whose possession the manor of Broughton had remained from time immemorial, and whose chief seat was at Broughton, until the second year of the reign of Henry the Seventh. At this period the power and interest of Sir Thomas Broughton were so considerable, that the Duchess of Burgundy, sister to the late King and the Duke of Clarence, relied on him as one of the principal confederates in the attempt to subvert the government of Henry by the pretensions of Lambert Simnel.

Ireland was zealously attached to the house of York, and held in affectionate regard the memory of the Duke of Clarence, the Earl of Warwick's father, who had been its lieutenant. No sooner, therefore, did the impostor Simnel present himself to Thomas Fitz-Gerald, Earl of Kildare, and claim his protection as the unfortunate Warwick, than that credulous nobleman paved the way for his reception, and furthered his design upon the throne, till the people in Dublin with one consent tendered their allegiance to him as the true Plantagenet. They paid the pretended Prince attendance as their sovereign, lodged him in the Castle of Dublin, crowned him with a diadem taken from a statue of the Virgin, and publicly proclaimed him King, by the appellation of Edward the Sixth.

In the year 1487 Lambert, with about two thousand Flemish troops under the command of Colonel Martin Swart, a man of noble family in Germany, an experienced and valiant soldier, whom the Duchess of Burgundy had chosen to support the pretended title of Simnel to the crown of England, and a number of Irish, conducted by Thomas Gerardine their captain from Ireland, landed in Furness at the Pile of Fouldrey. The army encamped in the neighbourhood of Ulverston, at a place now known by the name of Swart-Moor. Sir Thomas Broughton joined the rebels with a small body of English. The army, at this time about eight thousand strong, proceeded to join the Earl of Lincoln, Lord Lovel, and the rest of the confederates, passing on through Cartmel to Stoke field, near Newark-upon-Trent, where they met and encountered the King's forces on the 5th of June, 1487.

The day being far advanced before the King arrived at Stoke, he pitched his camp and deferred the battle till the day following. The forces of the Earl of Lincoln also encamped at a little distance from those of the King, and undismayed by the superior numbers they had to encounter, bravely entered the field the next day, and arranged themselves for battle, according to the directions of Colonel Swart and other superior officers. The charge being sounded, a desperate conflict was maintained with equal valour on both sides for three hours. The Germans were in every respect equal to the English, and none surpassed the bravery of Swart their commander. For three hours each side contended for victory, and the fate of the battle remained doubtful. The Irish soldiers, however, being badly armed, and the Germans being overpowered by numbers, the Lambertines were at length defeated, but not before their principal officers, the Earl of Lincoln, Lord Lovel, *Sir Thomas Broughton*, Colonel Swart, and Sir Thomas Gerardine captain of the Irish, and upwards of four thousand of their soldiers were slain.

Young Lambert and his tutor were both taken prisoners. The latter, being a priest, was punished with perpetual imprisonment ; Simnel was too contemptible to be an object either of apprehension or resentment to Henry. He was pardoned, and made a scullion in the King's kitchen, whence he was afterwards advanced to the rank of falconer, in which employment he ended his days.

Sir Thomas Broughton is said to have fallen on the field of

battle : but there remains a tradition, that he returned and
lived many years amongst his tenants in Witherslack, in West-
morland ; and was interred in the Chapel there ; but of this
nothing is known for certain at present, or whether he returned
or where he died.   Dr. Burn, speaking of the grant of Wither-
slack to Sir Thomas, on the attainder of the Harringtons in
the first year of Henry's reign for siding with the house of
York, and of its subsequent grant to Thomas Lord Stanley,
the first Earl of Derby, on the attainder of Sir Thomas for
having been concerned in this affair of Lambert Simnel, goes
on to say—"And here it may not be amiss to rectify a mistake
in Lord Bacon's history of that King, (Henry VII.) who saith
that this Sir Thomas Broughton was slain at Stoke, near
Newark, on the part of the counterfeit Plantagenet, Lambert
Simnell ; whereas Sir Thomas Broughton escaped from that
battle hither into Witherslack, where he lived a good while
incognito, amongst those who had been his tenants, who were
so kind unto him as privately to keep and maintain him, and
who dying amongst them was buried by them, whose grave Sir
Daniel Fleming says in his time was to be seen there."
    The erection of the new chapel of Witherslack by Dean
Barwick, in 1664, at a considerable distance from where the
ancient chapel stood, has obliterated the memory of his once
well-known grave.   With this unhappy gentleman the family
of Broughton, which had flourished for many centuries and
had contracted alliances with most of the principal families in
these parts, was extinguished in Furness.
    After these affairs the King had leisure to revenge himself
on his enemies, and made a progress into the northern parts
of England, where he gave many proofs of his rigorous dis-
position.   A strict inquiry was made after those who had
assisted or favoured the rebels, and heavy fines and even
sanguinary punishments, were imposed upon the delinquents
in a very arbitrary manner.   The fidelity therefore of Sir
Thomas Broughton's tenants to their fallen master was not
without its dangers, and is a pleasing instance of attachment
to the person of a leader in a rude and perilous age.
    In the wars of the Roses the Broughtons had always
strenuously supported the House of York.   It is however
remarkable that, the manor of Witherslack having been
granted to Sir Thomas by Henry the Seventh in the first
year of his reign, he should have joined the Pretender in arms
against that monarch in the following year.
    Methop and Ulva, though distinctly named in the title
and description of this manor, yet make but a small part of it.

They are all included within a peninsula, as it were, between Winster Beck, Bryster Moss, and Lancaster Sands.

The fate of Lord Lovel, another of the chiefs in this disastrous enterprise, is also shrouded in mystery. It has often been told that he was never seen, living or dead, after the battle.

The dead bodies of the Earl of Lincoln and most of the other principal leaders, it was said, were found where they had fallen, sword-in-hand, on the fatal field ; but not that of Lord Lovel. Some assert that he was drowned when endeavouring to escape across the river Trent, the weight of his armour preventing the subsequent discovery of his body. Other reports apply to him the circumstances similar to those which have been related above as referring to Sir Thomas Broughton ; namely, that he fled to the north where, under the guise of a peasant, he ended his days in peace. Lord Bacon, in his History of Henry the Seventh, says "that he lived long after in a cave or vault." And his account has been partly corroborated in modern times. William Cowper, Esquire, Clerk of the House of Commons, writing from Herlingfordbury Park in 1738, says—"In 1708, upon the occasion of new laying a chimney at Minster Lovel, there was discovered a large vault or room underground in which was the entire skeleton of a man, as having been sitting at a table which was before him, with a book, paper, pen, etc. ; in another part of the room lay a cap, all much mouldered and decayed ; which the family and others judged to be this Lord Lovel, whose exit has hitherto been so uncertain."

A tradition was rife in the village in the last century to the effect that, in this hiding place, which could only be opened from the exterior, the insurgent chief had confided himself to the care of a female servant, was forgotten or neglected by her, and consequently died of starvation.

The ancient Castle or Pile of Fouldrey, (formerly called Pele of Foudra, or Futher,) stands upon a small island near the southern extremity of the isle of Walney ; and is said by Camden to have been built by an Abbot of Furness, in the first year of King Edward the Third (A.D. 1327). It was probably intended for an occasional retreat from hostility ; a depository for the valuable articles of the Monastery of Furness ; and for a fortress to protect the adjoining harbour ; all which intentions its situation and structure were well calculated to answer at the time of its erection.

It seems to have been the custom in the northern parts of the kingdom, for the monasteries to have a fortress of this kind, in which they might lodge with security their treasures and records on the approach of an enemy ; of this the Castle on Holy Island, in Northumberland, and Wulstey Castle, near the Abbey of Holm Cultram, in Cumberland, are examples. It has even been said that an underground communication existed between Furness Abbey and the Pele of Fouldrey.

The harbour alluded to, appears to have been of considerable importance to the shipping of that period, when the relations of Ireland with the monks had become established. In the reign of Henry the Sixth, it is mentioned as being found a convenient spot for the woollen merchants to ship their goods to Erne-mouth, in Zealand, without paying the duty ; and in Elizabeth's days as "the only good haven for great shippes to londe or ryde in" between Scotland and Milford Haven, in Wales.

It was apprehended that the Spanish Armada would try to effect a landing in this harbour.

GILTSTONE ROCK;

OR, THE SLAVER IN THE SOLWAY.

The Betsey-Jane sailed out of the Firth,
As the Waits sang "Christ is born on earth"—
The Betsey-Jane sailed out of the Firth,
    On Christmas-day in the morning.
The wind was East, the moon was high,
Of a frosty blue was the spangled sky,
And the bells were ringing, and dawn was nigh,
    And the day was Christmas morning.

In village and town woke up from sleep,
From peaceful visions and slumbers deep—
In village and town woke up from sleep,
    On Christmas-day in the morning,
The many that thought on Christ the King,
And rose betimes their gifts to bring,
And "peace on earth and good will" to sing,
    As is meet upon Christmas morning.

The Betsey-Jane pass'd village and town,
As the Gleemen sang, and the stars went down—
The Betsey-Jane pass'd village and town,
    That Christmas-day in the morning;

And the Skipper by good and by evil swore,
The bells might ring and the Gleemen roar,
But the chink of his gold would chime him o'er
    Those waves, next Christmas morning.

And out of the Firth with his reckless crew,
All ready his will and his work to do—
Out of the Firth with his reckless crew
    He sailed on a Christmas morning !
He steer'd his way to Gambia's coast ;
And dealt for slaves ; and Westward cross'd ;
And sold their lives, and made his boast
    As he thought upon Christmas morning.

And again and again from shore to shore,
With his human freight for the golden ore—
Again and again from shore to shore,
    Ere Christmas-day in the morning,
He cross'd that deep with never a thought
Of the sorrow, or wrong, or suffering wrought
On souls and bodies thus sold and bought   ·
    For gold, against Christmas morning !

And at length, with his gold and ivory rare,
When the sun was low and the breeze was fair—
At length with his gold and ivory rare
    He sailed, that on Christmas morning
He might pass both village and town again
When the bells were ringing, as they rung then,
When he pass'd them by in the Betsey-Jane,
    On that lást bright Christmas morning.

The Betsey-Jane sailed into the Firth,
As the bells rang "Christ is born on earth"—
The Betsey-Jane sailed into the Firth,
 And it *was* upon Christmas morning !
The wind was west, the moon was high,
Of a hazy blue was the spangled sky,
And the bells were ringing, and dawn was nigh,
 Just breaking on Christmas morning.

The Gleemen singing of Christ the King,
Of Christ the King, of Christ the King—
The Gleemen singing of Christ the King,
 Hailed Christmas-day in the morning ;
When the Betsey-Jane with a thundering shock
Went ripping along on the Giltstone Rock,
In sound of the bells which seemed to mock
 Her doom on that Christmas morning.

With curse and shriek and fearful groan,
On the foundering ship, in the waters lone—
With curse and shriek and fearful groan,
 They sank on that Christmas morning !
The Skipper with arms around his gold,
Scared by dark spirits that loosed his hold,
Was down the deep sea plunged and roll'd
 In the dawn of that Christmas morning :—

While village and town woke up from sleep,
From peaceful visions and slumbers deep—
While village and town woke up from sleep,
 That Christmas-day in the morning !

And many that thought on Christ the King,
Rose up betimes their gifts to bring,
And, "peace on earth and good will to sing,"
Went forth in the Christmas morning !

NOTE.

The rock thus named, lies off the harbour at Harrington, on the coast of Cumberland, and is only visible at low water during spring tides.

The Gleemen, or Waits, as the Christmas minstrels are called, still keep up their annual rounds, with song and salutation, and with a heartiness and zeal, which have been well described by the great Poet of the Lake district in those feeling and admirable verses to his brother, Dr. Wordsworth, prefixed to his Sonnets on the River Duddon.

In the parish of Muncaster, on the eve of the new year, the children go from house to house, singing a ditty, which craves the bounty, "*they were wont to have, in old king Edward's days.*" There is no tradition whence this custom arose ; the donation is two-pence or a pie at every house. Mr. Jefferson suggests, may not the name have been altered from Henry to Edward ? and may it not have an allusion to the time when King Henry the sixth was entertained at Muncaster Castle in his flight from his enemies ?

CRIER OF CLAIFE.

A wild holloa on Wynander's shore,
'Mid the loud waves'splash and the night-wind's roar !
Who cries so late with desperate note,
Far over the water, to hail the boat ?

'Tis night's mid gloom ; the strong rain beats fast :
Is there one at this hour will face the blast,
And the darkness traverse with arm and oar,
To ferry the Crier from yonder shore ?

A mile to cross, and the skies so dread ;
With a storm around that would wake the dead ;
And fathoms of boiling depths below ;
The ferry is hailed, and the boat must go.

Snug under that cliff, whence over the Mere,
When summer is merry and skies are clear,
In holiday times hearts light and gay
Look over the hills and far away—

At the Ferry-house Inn, sat warm beside
The bright wood-fire and hearth-stone wide,
A rollicking band of jovial souls
With tinkling cans and full brown bowls.

Without, the sycamores' branches rode
The storm, as if fiends the roof bestrode;
Yet stout of heart, to that wild holloa
The ferryman smiled—"The boat must go."

His comrades followed out into the dark,
As the young man strode to the tumbling bark;
And, wishing him luck in the perilous storm,
With a shudder went back to the fireside warm.

An hour is gone! against wind and wave
Well struggled and strove that heart so brave.
Another! they crowd to the whistling door,
To welcome the guide and his freight to shore.

But pallid, and stunn'd, aghast, alone,
He stood in the boat, and speech had none :
His lips were locked, and his eyes astare,
And blanched with terror his manly hair.

What thing he had seen, what utterance heard,
What horror that night his senses stirr'd,
Was frozen within him, and choked his breath,
And laid him, ere morning, cold in death.

But what that night of horror revealed,
And what that night of horror concealed
Of spirits and powers in storms that roam,
Lies hid with the monk in St. Mary's Holm.

Still, under the cliff—whence over the Mere,
When summer was merry and skies were clear,
In holiday times hearts light and gay
Looked over the hills and far away—

When the rough winds blew amid rain and cold,
The Ferry-house gathered its hearts of old,
Who sat at the hearth and o'er the brown ale,
Oft talked of that night and its dismal tale.

And often the Crier was heard to wake
The night's foul echoes across the lake;
But never again would a hand unmoor
The boat, to venture by night from shore:

Till they sought the good monk of St. Mary's Holm,
With relics of saints and beads from Rome,
To row to the Nab on Hallowmas night,
And bury the Crier by morning's light.

With Aves muttered, and spells unknown,
The monk rows over the Mere alone;
Like a feather his bark floats light and fast;
When the Crier's loud hail sweeps down the blast.

Speed on, bold heart, with gifts of grace!
He is nearing the wild fiend-blighted place.
Now heed thee, foul spirit! the priest has power
To bind thee on earth till the morning hour.

He rests his oars ; and the faint blue gleam
From a marsh-light sheds on the ground its beam.
There's a stir in the grass; and there's ONE on a knoll,
Unearthly and horrid to sight and soul.

That horrible cry rings through the dark,
As the monk steps out of the grounding bark ;
And he charms a circle around the knoll,
Wherein he must sit till the mass-bell toll.

Then over the lake, with the fiend in tow,
To the quarry beyond the monk will go,
And bury the Crier with book and bell,
While the birds of morning sing him farewell.

The morn awoke.   As the breezy smile
Of dawn played over St. Mary's Isle,
The tinkling sound of the mass-bell rose,
And startled the valleys from brief repose.

Then, like a speck from afar descried,
The monk row'd out on the waters wide—
From the Nab row'd out, with the fiend in his wake,
To lay him in quiet, across the lake.

And fear-struck men, and women that bore
Their babes, beheld from height and shore,
How he reached the wood that hid the dell,
Where he laid the Crier with book and bell.

"For the ivy green" the spell was told;
"For the ivy green" his knell was knoll'd;
That as long as by wall and greenwood tree
The ivy flourished, his rest might be.

So did the good monk; and thus was laid
The Crier in ground by greenwood shade.
In the quarry of Claife the wretched ghost
To human ear for ever was lost.

And country folk in peace again
Went forth by night through field and lane,
Nor dreaded to hear that terrible note
Cry over the water, and hail the boat.

And still on that cliff, high over the Mere,
When summer is merry, and skies are clear,
In holiday times hearts light and gay
Look over the hills and far away.

But what that night of horror revealed,
And what that night and morrow concealed,
Of spirits so wicked and given to roam,
Lies hid with the monk in St. Mary's Holm.

Peace be with him, peaceful soul!
Long his bell has ceased to toll.
Green the Isle that folds his breast;
Clear the Lake that lull'd his rest.

Though the many ages gone
Long have left his place unknown ;
Yet where once he kneel'd and pray'd,
By his altar long decay'd,
Stranger to this Island led !
Humbly speak and softly tread ;
Catching from the ages dim
This, the burden of his hymn :—

" Ave, Thou before whose name
   Wrath and shadows swiftly flee !
Arm Thy faithful bands with flame,
   Earth from foulest foes to free.

" Peace on all these valleys round,
   Breathe from out this Islet's breast ;
Wafting from this holy ground
   Seeds of Thy eternal rest.

" Wrath and Evil, then no more
   Here molesting, all shall cease.
Peace around ! From shore to shore—
   Peace ! On all Thy waters—peace !"

NOTES TO "CRIER OF CLAIFE."

The little rocky tree-decked islet in Windermere, called St. Mary's, or the Ladye's Holme, hitherto reputed to have formed part of the conventual domains of the Abbey at Furness, had its name from a chantry dedicated to the Virgin Mary, which was standing up to the reign of King Henry the Eighth, but of which no traces are now remaining. "When," says an anonymous writer, "at the Reformation, that day of desolation came, which saw the attendant priests driven forth, and silenced for ever the sweet chant of orison and litany within its walls; the isle and revenues of the institution were sold to the Philipsons of Calgarth. By them the building was suffered to fall into so utter a state of ruin, that no trace even of its foundations is left to proclaim to the stranger who meditates upon the fleeting change of time and creed, that here, for more than three centuries, stood a hallowed fane, from whence at eventide and prime prayers were wafted through the dewy air, where now are only heard the festal sounds of life's more jocund hours." Lately renewed anti-quarian investigation has, however, disclosed the erroneousness of the generally received statement respecting the early owner-ship of this tiny spot; as in Dodsworth's celebrated collection of ancient evidences there is contained an Inquisition, or the copy of one, taken at Kendal, so far back as the Monday after the feast of the Annunciation, in the 28th Edward the Third, which shews that this retreat, amid the waters of our English Como, appertained not to Furness Abbey, but to the house of Segden, in Scotland, which was bound always to provide two resident chaplains for the service of our Ladye's Chapel in this island solitude. For the maintenance and support of those priests, certain lands were given by the founder, who was either one of that chivalrous race, descended from the Scottish Lyndseys "light and gay," whose immediate ancestor in the early part of the thirteenth century had married Alice, second daughter and co-heiress of William de Lancaster, eighth Lord of Kendal; and with her obtained that moiety of the Barony of Kendal, whose numerous manors are collectively known as the Richmond Fee; or the chantry may have owed its foundation to the pious impulses of Ingelram de Guignes, Sire de Couci, one of the grand old Peers of France, whose house, so renowned in history and romance, proclaimed its independence and its pride in this haughty motto :—

"Je ne suis Roy ni Prince aussi,
Je suis Le Seignhor de Courci."

And which Ingelram in 1285 married Christiana, heiress of the last de Lyndsey, and in her right, besides figuring on innumerable occasions as a feudal potentate, both in England and Scotland, he became Lord of the Fee, within which lies St. Mary's Isle.

On an Inquisition taken after the death of Johanna de Coupland, in the 49th Edward the Third, it was found that she held the advowson of the Chapel of Saint Mary's Holme, within the lake of Wynandermere, but that it was worth nothing, because the land which the said Chapel enjoyed of old time had been seized into the hands of the King, and lay within the park of Calgarth. It is on record, however, that in 1492, an annual sum of six pounds was paid out of the revenues of the Richmond Fee, towards the support of the Chaplains ; and in the returns made by the ecclesiastical Commissioners in Edward the Sixth's reign, "the free Chapel of Holme and Wynandermere" is mentioned, shortly after which it was granted, as aforesaid, to the owners of Calgarth.

The singular name of the "Crier of Claife" is now applied to an extensive slate or flag quarry, long disused, and overgrown with wood, on the wildest and most lonely part of the height called Latter-barrow, which divides the vales of Esthwaite and Windermere, above the Ferry. In this desolate spot, by the sanctity and skill of holy men, had been exorcised and laid the apparition who had come to be known throughout the country by that title ; and the place itself has ever since borne the same name. None of the country people will go near it after night fall, and few care to approach it even in daylight. Desperate men driven from their homes by domestic discord, have been seen going in its direction, and never known to return. It is said the Crier is allowed to emerge occasionally from his lonely prison, and is still heard on very stormy nights sending his wild entreaty for a boat, howling across Windermere. Mr. Craig Gibson, in one of his graphic sketches of the Lake country, says that he is qualified to speak to this, for he himself has heard him. "At least," says he, "I have heard what I was solemnly assured by an old lady at Cunsey must have been the Crier of Claife. Riding down the woods a little south of the Ferry, on a wild January evening, I was strongly impressed by a sound made by the wind as, after gathering behind the hill called Gummershow for short periods of comparative calm, it came rushing up and across the lake with a sound startlingly suggestive of the cry of a human being in extremity, wailing for succour. This sound lasted till the squall it always preceded struck the western shore, when it was lost in the louder rush of the wind through the leafless woods. I am induced to relate this," he continues, "by the belief I entertain that the phenomenon described thus briefly and imperfectly, may account for much of the legend, and that the origin of many similar traditional superstitions may be found in something equally simple."

The late Mr. John Briggs, in his notes upon "Westmorland as it was," by the Rev. Mr. Hodgson, has furnished his readers with some curious information upon the "philosophy of spirits," which he collected from those ancient sages of the dales who were supposed to be best acquainted with the subject. Many of these superstitions are now exploded : but the marvellous tales at one time currently believed, still furnish conversation for the cottage fireside. According to the gravest authorities, he says, no spirit could appear before twilight had vanished in the evening, or after it had appeared in the morning. On this account, the winter nights were peculiarly dangerous, owing to the long revels which ghosts, or dobbies, as they were called, could keep at that season. There was one exception to this. If a man had murdered a woman who was with child by him, she had power to haunt him at all hours ; and the Romish priests (who alone had the power of laying spirits,) could not lay a spirit of this kind with any certainty, as she generally contrived to break loose long before her stipulated time. A culprit might hope to escape the gallows, but there was no hope of escaping being haunted. In common cases, however, the priest could "lay" the ghosts; "while ivy was green," was the usual term. But in very desperate cases, they were laid in the "Red Sea," which was accomplished with great difficulty and even danger to the exorcist. In this country, the most usual place to confine spirits was under Haws Bridge, a few miles below Kendal. Many a grim ghost has been chained in that dismal trough !

According to the laws to which they were subject, ghosts could seldom appear to more than one person at a time. When they appeared to the eyes, they had not the power of making a noise ; and when they saluted the ear, they could not greet the eyes. To this, however, there was an exception, when a human being spoke to them in the name of the Blessed

Trinity. For it was an acknowledged truth, that however wicked the individual might have been in this world, or however light he might have made of the Almighty's name, he would tremble at its very sound, when separated from his earthly covering.

The causes of spirits appearing after death were generally three. Murdered persons came again to haunt their murderers, or to obtain justice by appearing to other persons likely to see them avenged. Persons who had hid any treasure, were doomed to haunt the place where that treasure was hid ; as they had made a god of their wealth in this world, the place where their treasure lay was to be their heaven after death. If any person could speak to them, and give them an opportunity of confessing where their treasure was hid, they could then rest in peace, but not otherwise. Those who died with any heavy crimes on their consciences, which they had not confessed, were also doomed to wander on the earth at the midnight hour.

Spirits had no power over those who did not molest them ; but if insulted, they seem to have been extremely vindictive, and to have felt little compunction in killing the insulter. They had power to assume any form, and to change it as often as they pleased ; but they could neither vanish nor change, while a human eye was fixed upon them.

Midway on Windermere, below the range of islands which intersect the lake, extends the track along which ply the Ferry boats between the little inn on the western side and the wooded promontory on the opposite shore. The Ferry House, with its lawn in front and few branching sycamores, occupies a jutting area between the base of a perpendicular cliff and the lake. Few finer prospects can be desired than that afforded from the summit which overhangs the Mere at this point. The summer house, which has been built for the sake of the views it commands of the surrounding country, is a favourite resort of lovers of the beautiful in nature, whence they may witness, in its many aspects afar, the grandeur of the mountain world ; and near and below, the beauty of the curving shores and wooded isles of this queen of English lakes. From the Ferry House to the Ferry Nab, as the promontory is called, on the western shore, is barely half a mile. It was from thence that in the dark stormy night the Evil voice cried "Boat !" which the poor ferryman obeyed so fatally. No passenger was there, but a sight which sent him back with bloodless face and dumb, to die on the morrow.

THE CUCKOO IN BORRODALE.

Far within those rocky regions
Where old Scawfell's hoary legions,
   Robed and capped with storms and snow,
Here like rugged Vikings towering,
There like giants grimly cowering,
   Look into the vales below;

Once where Borrhy wild and fearless,
Once where Oller brave and peerless,
   Hew'd the forest, cleared the vale,
Gave their names to cling for ever
Round thy dells by crag and river,
   Dark and wintry Borrodale!

In that dreariest of the valleys,
Strifes for evermore, and malice
   Without end the dalesmen vexed.
Neighbour had no heart for neighbour.
Never side by side to labour
   Went or came they unperplex'd.

Cheerless were the fields and houses.
Gloomily the sullen spouses
   Moved about the hearths and floors.
Sunshine was an alms from Heaven
That not one day out of seven
   God's bright beams brought to their doors.

And 'mid discontent and anguish
Every virtue seem'd to languish;
   Every soul groan'd with its load.
Lingering in his walks beside them,
Oft their friendly Pastor eyed them,
   And his heart with pity glow'd.

"Ah!" he thought, "that looks of kindness
Could but enter here! the blindness
   Of this life, could it but seem
To them the death it is!—but listen!"—
And his eyes began to glisten:
   Spring was round him like a dream.

"'Tis the Cuckoo!"—In the hollow
Up the valley seem'd to follow
   Spring's fair footsteps that sweet throat.
All the fields put off their sadness;
Trees and hills and skies with gladness
   Answering to the Cuckoo's note.

Then on that still Sabbath-morrow,
Spake the Pastor—" Let us borrow
   Gladness from this new-born Spring.
Hark, the bird that brings the blossoms !
Brings the sunshine to our bosoms !
   Makes with joy the valleys ring !

" Coming from afar to cheer us,
Could we always keep him near us,
   'All these heavenly skies from far,
All this blessed morn discovers,
All this Spring that round us hovers,
   Would be still what now they are !

" Let us all go forth and labour,
Sire, and son, and wife, and neighbour,
   First the bread, the life, to win :
Then by yonder stream we'll rally,
Build a wall across the valley,
   And we'll close the Cuckoo in.

" So this Spring time, never failing,
While it hears his music hailing
   From the wood and by the rill,
Shall, its new-born life retaining,
Till our mortal hours are waning,
   Warm and light and cheer us still."—

Flush'd the morn; and all were ready.
Sowers sowed with paces steady;
    Plough'd the ploughers in the field;
Delved the gardeners; planters planted;
Then to their great work, undaunted
    Forth they fared their wall to build.

Stone by stone, the wall beside them
Rose.   Their Pastor came to guide them,
    Day by day, and spake to cheer;
While each labouring hand the others
Helped, and one and all like brothers
    Wrought along the ripening year.

Then they gathered in their houses,
Men and maidens, sires and spouses,
    Talking of their wall.   And when
Soon the long bright day returning
Called them, every heart was yearning
    To resume its task again.

And on every eve they parted
At their thresholds, kindlier-hearted,
    Looking forth again to meet.
All had something good or gladdening
On their lips; the only saddening
    Sounds were those of parting feet.

So their wall, extending ever,　·
Spann'd at length the vale and river;
　Grasp'd the mountains there and here :
Reached towards the blue of heaven;
Touched the light cloud o'er it driven;
　And the end at length was near.

June had come; and all was vernal :
Seemed secure their Spring eternal :
　Eyes were bright, and skies were blue :
When—at Nature's call—unguided—
Out the voice above them glided,
　"Cuckoo!"—far away, "Cuckoo!"

"Gone!" a hundred tongues in chorus
Shouted; "Gone! the bird that bore us
　Spring with all things bright and good!"
While, in stupor and amazement,
Vacantly from cope to basement
　Glowering at their wall, they stood.—

But though all forgot, while building
Up their wall, that months were yielding
　Each in turn to others' sway,
With their leaves and landscapes changing;
And, to skies more constant ranging,
　Fled the Cuckoo far away!

Winter from their hearts had perished ;
Spring in every heart was cherished ;
    Every charm of life and love—
Love for wife and home and neighbour—
Sprang from out that genial labour ;
    Peace around, and Heaven above.

Faith into their lives had entered ;
Joy and fellowship were centred
    Wheresoe'er a hearth was found.
While the calm bright hope before them
Temper'd even the rains, and o'er them
    Charmed to rest the tempests' sound.

NOTES TO "THE CUCKOO IN BORRODALE."

If the traditions of the past, and the estimate formed of them by their distant neighbours, bear rather hardly upon the people of Borrodale, it must be remembered that the relations of that dale to the world without were very different a hundred years ago from what they are now. It was a recess, approached by a long and winding valley, from the vale of Keswick, with the lake extending between its entrance and the town. The highest mountains of the district closed round its head. Its entrance was guarded by a woody hill, on which had formerly stood a Roman fortress, afterwards occupied by the Saxons, and which in later times was maintained in its military capacity by the monks of Furness. For here one of their principal magazines was established, and the holy fathers had great possessions to defend from the frequent irruptions of the Scots in those days. Besides their tithe corn, they amassed here the valuable minerals of the country; among which salt, produced from a spring in the valley, was no inconsiderable article.

In this deep retreat the inhabitants of the villages of Rosthwaite and Seathwaite, having at all times little intercourse with the country, during half the year were almost totally excluded from all human commerce. The surrounding hills attract the vapours, and rain falls abundantly; snow lies long in the valleys; and the clouds frequently obscure the sky. Upon the latter village, in the depth of winter, the sun never shines. As the spring advances, his rays begin to shoot over the southern mountains; and at high noon to tip the chimney tops with their light. That radiant sign shows the cheerless winter to be now over; and rouses the hardy peasants to the labours of the coming year. Their scanty patches of arable land they cultivated with difficulty; and their crops late in ripening, and often a prey to autumnal rains, which are violent in this country, just gave them bread to eat. Their herds afforded them milk; and their flocks supplied them with clothes: the shepherd himself being often the manufacturer also. No dye was necessary to tinge their wool: it was naturally a russet brown; and sheep and shepherds were clothed alike, both in the simple livery of nature. The procuring of fuel was among their greatest hardships. Here the inhabitants were obliged to get on the tops of the mountains; which abounding with mossy grounds, seldom found in the valleys below, supplied them with peat. This, made into bundles, and fastened upon sledges, they guided down the precipitous sides of the mountains, and stored in their outbuildings. At the period to which we refer, a hundred years ago, the roads were of the rudest construction, scarcely passable even for horses. A cart or any kind of wheeled carriage was totally unknown in Borrodale. They carried their hay home upon their horses, in bundles, one on each side: they made no stacks. Their manure they carried in the same manner, as also the smaller wood for firing: the larger logs they trailed. Their food in summer consisted of fish and small mutton; in winter, of bacon and hung mutton. Nor was their method of drying their mutton less rude: they hung the sheep up by the hinder legs, and took away only the head and entrails. In this situation, I myself, says Clarke, have seen seven sheep hanging in one chimney.   ·

The inhabitants of Borrodale were a proverb, even among their unpolished neighbours, for ignorance; and a thousand absurd and improbable stories are related of their stupidity; such as mistaking a red-deer, seen upon one of their mountains, for a horned horse; at the sight of which they assembled in considerable numbers, and provided themselves with ropes, thinking to take him by the same means as they did their horses when wild in the field, by running them into a strait, and then tripping them up with a cord. A chase of several hours proved fruitless; when they returned thoroughly convinced they had been chasing a witch. Such like is the story of the mule, which, being ridden into the dale by a stranger bound for the mountains, was left in the care of his host at the foot of a pass. The neighbours assembled to see the curious animal, and consulted the wise man of the dale as to what it could be. With his book, and his thoughts in serious deliberation, he was enabled to announce authoritatively that the brute was a peacock! So when a new light broke into Borrodale, and lime was first sent for from beyond Keswick; the carrier was an old dalesman with horse and sacks. Rain falling, it began to smoke: some water from the river was procured by him to extinguish the unnatural fire; but the evil was increased, and the smoke grew worse. Assured at length that he had got the devil in his sacks, as he must be in any fire which was aggravated by water, he tossed the whole load over into the river. The tale of the stirrups is perhaps a little too absurd even for Borrodale. A "'statesman" brought home from a distant fair or sale, what had never before been seen in the dale, a pair of stirrups. Riding home in them, when he reached his own door, his feet had become so fastened in them, that they could not be got out ; so as there was no help for it, he patiently sat his horse in the pasture for a day or two, his family bringing him food, then it was proposed to bring them both into the stable, which was done ; his family bringing him food as before. At length it occurred to some one that he might be lifted with the saddle from the horse, and carried thereupon into the house. There the mounted man sat spinning wool in a corner of the kitchen, till the return of one of his sons from St. Bees school, whose learning, after due consideration of the case, suggested that the good man should draw his feet out of his shoes : when to the joy of his family he was restored to his occupation and to liberty. But the story of the Cuckoo has made its local name the "Gowk" synonymous with an inhabitant of the vale. There the Spring was very charming, and the voice of the bird rare and gladsome. It occurred to the natives that a wall built across the entrance of their valley, at Grange, if made high enough, would keep the cuckoo among them, and make the cheerful Spring-days last for ever. The plan was tried, and failed only because, according to popular belief from genera-tion to generation, the wall was not built one course higher.

The wetness of the weather in Borrodale is something more than an occasional inconvenience. It may be judged of by observations which show the following results. The average quantity of rain in many parts of the south of England does not exceed 20 inches, and sometimes does not even reach that amount. The mean rain fall for England is 30 inches. Kendal and Keswick have been considered the wettest places known in England ; and the annual average at the former place is 52 inches. It was found by experiments made in 1852, that while 81 inches were measured on Scawfell Pike ; 86 at Great Gable ; 124 at Sty Head ; 156 were measured at Seathwaite in Borrodale ; shewing, with the exception of that at Sprinkling Tarn, between Scawfell, and Langdale Pikes, and Great Gable, where it measured 168 inches nearly, the greatest rainfall in the Lake District to be at the head of Borrodale. Taking a period of ten years, the average annual rainfall at Seathwaite in that dale was over 126 inches ; for the rest of England it was 29 inches.

KING EVELING.

King Eveling stood by the Azure River,
　When the tide-wave landward began to flow;
And over the sea in the sunlight's shiver,
　He watch'd one white sail northward go.

" Twice has it pass'd; and I linger, weary :
　How I long for its coming, my life to close !
My lands forget me, my halls are dreary,
　And my age is lonely; I want repose.

" If rightly I read the signs within me,
　The tides may lessen, the moon may wane,
And then the Powers I have serv'd will win me
　A pathway over yon shining plain.

" It befits a King, who has wisely spoken,
　Whose rule was just, and whose deeds were brave,
To depart alone, and to leave no token
　On earth but of glory—not even a grave.

" And now I am going.　No more to know me,
　My banners fall round me with age outworn.
I have buried my crown in the sands below me ;
　And I vanish, a King, into night forlorn.

" What of mine is good will endure for ever,
  Growing into the ages on earth to be,
When—Eveling dwelt by the Azure River,
  A King—shall be all that is told of me."

For days the tides with ebbing and flowing
  Grew full with the moon ; and out of the dim,
On the ocean's verge came the white sail growing,
  And anchor'd below on the shoreward rim.

His people slept.   For to them descended,
  In that good time of the King, their rest,
While the lengthening shades of the eve yet blended
  With the golden sunbeams low in the west.

No banded host on his footsteps waited,
  No child nor vassal from bower or hall :
He look'd around him like one belated
  On a lonely wild ; and he went from all.

Slowly he strode to the ship ; and for ever
  Sailed out from the land he had ruled so well ;
And the name of the King by the Azure River
  Is all that is left for the bards to tell.

NOTES TO "KING EVELING."

The ancient, but now insignificant town and seaport of
Ravenglass, six miles from Bootle and about sixteen from
Whitehaven, is situated on a small creek, at the confluence
of the rivers Esk, Mite, and Irt, which form a large sandy
harbour.   Of this place the Editor of Camden, Bishop Gibson,
says—"The shore, wheeling to the north, comes to Raven-
glass, a harbour for ships, and commodiously surrounded with
two rivers; where, as I am told, there have been found Roman
inscriptions.   Some will have it to have been formerly called
Aven-glass, i.e. (Cœruleus) an azure sky-coloured river ; and
tell you abundance of stories about King Eveling, who had
his palace here."
   Ravenglass appears from Mr. Sandford's M.S. to have been
of old of some importance as a fishing town.   He says—"Here
were some salmons and all sorts of fish in plenty ; but the
greatest plenty of herrings, (it) is a daintye fish of a foot long ;
and so plenteous a fishing thereof and in the sea betwixt and
the ile of man, as they lie in sholes together so thike in the
sea at spawning, about August, *as a ship cannot pass thorow :*
and the fishers go from all the coast to catch them."
   There was also formerly a considerable pearl-fishery at this
place : and Camden speaks of the shell-fish in the Irt pro-
ducing pearls.   Sir John Hawkins obtained from government
the right of fishing for pearls in that river.   The pearls were
obtained from mussels, by the inhabitants of the neighbourhood,
who sought for them at low water, and afterwards sold them
to the jewellers.   About the year 1695, a patent was granted
to some gentlemen, for pearl-fishing in the Irt ; but how the
undertaking prospered is uncertain.   The pearl-mussels do not
appear to have been very plentiful for many years.   Nicolson
and Burn observe, that Mr. Thomas Patrickson, of How in
this County, is said to have obtained as many from divers
poor people, whom he employed to gather them, as he
afterwards sold in London for £800.
   Tacitus in the "Agricola" describes the pearls found in
Britain as being of a dark and livid hue.   Pliny also :—"In

Britain some pearls do grow, but they are small and dim, not clear and bright." And again :—"Julius Cæsar did not deny, that the breast-plate which he dedicated to Venus Genitrix, within the temple, was made of British pearls." So that it is not at all improbable that our little northern stream even may have contributed in some degree to the splendour of the imperial offering.

The manor in which Ravenglass is included is dependent on the barony of Egremont; and King John granted to Richard Lucy, as lord paramount, a yearly fair to be held here on St. James's day, and a weekly market every Saturday; and at the present time the successor to the Earls of Egremont, Lord Leconfield, holds the fair of Ravenglass, on the eve, day, and morrow of St. James. Hutchinson thus describes it :—"There are singular circumstances and ceremonies attending the proclamation of this fair, as being anciently held under the maintenance and protection of the Castle of Egremont. On the first day, the lord's steward is attended by the sargeant of the Borough of Egremont, with the insignia (called the bow of Egremont), the foresters, with their bows and horns, and all the tenants of the forest of Copeland, whose special service is to attend the lord and his representative at Ravenglass fair, and abide there during its continuance ; anciently, for the protection of a free-trade, and to defend the merchandise against free-booters, and a foreign enemy : such was the wretched state of this country in former times, that all such protection was scarce sufficient. For the maintenance of the horses of those who attend the ceremony, they have by custom, a portion of land assigned in the meadow, called, or distinguished, by the name of two Swaiths of grass in the common field of Ravenglass. On the third day at noon, the earl's officers; and tenants of the forest depart, after proclamation ; and Lord Muncaster (as mesne lord) and his tenants take a formal repossession of the place ; and the day is concluded with horse races and rural diversions."

A genuine specimen of feudal observances is preserved in the custom of riding the boundaries of manors, which, in the mountain district, where the line of division is not very distinct, is performed perhaps once during each generation, by the representatives of the lord of the manor, accompanied by an immense straggling procession of all ages,—the old men being made useful in pointing out important or disputed portions of the boundary, and the young in having it impressed on their memories, so that their evidence or recollection may be made available in future peregrinations. In older times, when the interests of the lords outweighed farther than in our own day the rights of the peasantry, certain youthful members of the retinue, in order to deepen the impression and make it more enduring, were severely whipped at all those points which the stewards were most anxious to have held in remembrance. The occasions always wind up with a banquet, provided on a most liberal scale by the lord of the manor, and open to all who take part in the business of the day.

Another local usage connected with the landed interest, and long observed with notable regularity, was the following. When salmon was plentiful in the Cumberland rivers, and formed a very important element in the ordinary living of the occupants of adjoining lands, the tenants of the manor of Ennerdale and Kinniside claimed "a free stream" in the river Ehen, from Ennerdale lake to the sea, and assembled once a year to "ride the stream." If obstructions were found, such as weirs and dams, they were at once destroyed. Refreshments were levied or provided at certain places on the river for the cavalcade. This custom has long ceased to be observed.

About a quarter of a mile to the south east of this place is an old ivy-mantled ruin, designated Wall Castle. It is said to have been the original residence of the Penningtons, but in all probability it dates from a much remoter period. Stone battle-axes and arrow-heads have been found around it, and coins of different people, principally Roman and Saxon. The building is strongly cemented with run lime.

This old castle stands at no great distance from the second cutting through which the railroad passes after leaving Ravenglass : adjoining to which, a little below the surface of the ground, an ancient fosse and several foundations of walls have been laid bare by the owner of the estate, and large quantities of building stone removed from them at various times. In making this cutting, the workmen laid open an ancient burial place, which was of great depth, and contained a quantity of human remains, with several bones of animals. The sides were secured by strong timber and stone work. The buried bodies were very numerous, and the place was evidently of very great antiquity. From the presence of oak leaves and acorns, charred wood, etc., it has been supposed to have been the tomb of the victims in some Druidical sacrifice : it being known that the Druids immolated their criminals, by placing them collectively in the interior of a large image of wicker-work, and then setting fire to it ; and that various animals were sacrificed along with them by way of expiation.

About five miles to the east of Ravenglass is the small lake of Devoke Water, near the foot of which, on the summit of a considerable hill, stand the ruins of another interesting piece of antiquity, the so-called city of Barnscar or Bardscar. Its site is so elevated, as to command a wide extent of country, and an ancient road from Ulpha to Ravenglass passes through it. The name is purely Scandinavian, and tradition ascribes it to the Danes. A well known popular saying in the locality refers to the manner in which this city is said to have been peopled by its founders, who gathered for inhabitants the men of Drigg and the women of Beckermet. The original help-mates of the latter place are supposed to have fallen in battle : what had become of the wives and daughters of the former place is not averred. But the saying continues—"Let us gang togidder like t' lads o' Drigg, an' t' lasses o' Beckermet."

The description of this place given by Hutchinson at the latter end of last century is as follows :—"This place is about 300 yards long, from east to west ; and 100 yards broad, from north to south ; now walled round, save at the east end, near three feet in height ; there appears to have been a long street, with several cross ones : the remains of housesteads, within the walls, are not very numerous, but on the outside of the walls they are innumerable, especially on the south side and west end ; the circumference of the city and suburbs is near three computed miles ; the figure an oblong square." It is added that about the year 1730, a considerable quantity of silver coin was found in the ruins of one of the houses, concealed in a cavity, formed in a beam ; none of which unfortunately has been preserved, to throw light upon the name, the race, or character and habits of its possessors.

From the Pow to the Duddon innumerable objects of interest lie scattered between the mountains and the sea coast, of which little more can be said than was stated, as above, by Camden's editor— "Some tell you abundance of stories about them "—as well as "about King Eveling, who had his palace here."

SIR LANCELOT THRELKELD.

The widows were sitting in Threlkeld Hall;
   The corn stood green on Midsummer-day ;
Their little grand-children were tossing the ball ;
And the farmers leaned over the garden wall ;
   And the widows were spinning the eve away.

They busily talk'd of the days long gone,
   While the corn stood green on Midsummer-day ;
How old Sir Lancelot's armour had shone
On the panels of oak by the broad hearth-stone,
   Where the widows sat spinning that eve away.

For, Threlkeld Hall of his mansions three—
   Where the corn stood green on Midsummer-day—
Was his noblest house ; and a stately tree
Was the good old Knight, and of high degree ;
   And a braver rode never in battle array.

Now peaceful farmers think of their corn—
   The corn so green on Midsummer-day—
Where once, at the blast of Sir Lancelot's horn,
His horsemen all mustered, his banner was borne ;
   And he went like a Chief in his pride to the fray.

And there the good Clifford, the Shepherd-Lord,
  When the corn stood green on Midsummer-day,
Sat, humbly clad, at Sir Lancelot's board ;
And tended the flocks, while rusted his sword
  In the hall where the widows were spinning away;

Till the new King called him back to his own—
  When the corn stood green on Midsummer-day—
To his honours and name of high renown ;
When Sir Lancelot old and feeble had grown ;
  From his rude shepherd-life called Lord Clifford
    away.

And sad was that morrow in Threlkeld Hall—
  And the corn was green on that Midsummer-day—
When the Clifford stood ready to part from all ;
And his shepherd's staff was hung up on the wall,
  In that room where the widows sat spinning away.

And Sir Lancelot mounted, and called his men—
  While the corn stood green on Midsummer-day—
And he gazed on Lord Clifford again and again ;
And Sir Lancelot rode with him over the plain ;
  And at length with strong effort his silence gave
    way.

"I am old," Sir Lancelot said; "and I know—
  When the corn stands green on Midsummer-day—
There will wars arise, and I shall be low,
Who ever was ready to arm and go!"—
  For he loved the war tramp and the martial array.

"If ever a Knight might revisit this earth—
  While the corn stands green on Midsummer-day"—
Said the Clifford—"When troubles and wars have
      birth,
Thou never shalt fail from Threlkeld's hearth!"
  From that hearth where the widows were spinning
      away.

And so, along Souter-fell side they press'd—
  While the corn stood green on Midsummer-day,—
And then they parted—to east and to west—
And Sir Lancelot came and was laid to his rest.
  Said the widows there spinning the eve away.

And the Shepherd had power in unwritten lore:
  The corn stands green on Midsummer-day:
And although the Knight's coffin his banner hangs
      o'er,
Sir Lancelot yet can tread this floor;
  Said the widows there spinning the eve away.—

Thus gossip'd the widows in Threlkeld Hall,
    While the corn stood green on Midsummer-day :
When the sound of a footstep was heard to fall,
And an arm'd shadow pass'd over the wall—
    Of a Knight with his plume and in martial array.

With a growl the fierce dogs slunk behind the huge
    chair,
    While the corn stood green on that Midsummer-
    day ;
And the widows stopt spinning ; and each was aware
Of a tread to the porch, and Sir Lancelot there—
    And a stir as of horsemen all riding away.

They turned their dim eyes to the lattice to gaze—
    While the corn stood green on Midsummer-day—
But before their old limbs they could feebly raise,
The horsemen and horses were far on the ways—
    From the Hall, where the widows were spinning
    away.

And far along Souter-fell side they strode,
    While the corn stood green on that Midsummer-
    day.
And the brave old Knight on his charger rode,
As he wont to ride from his old abode,
    With his sword by his side and in martial array.

Like a chief he galloped before and behind—
　While the corn stood green on Midsummer-day—
To the marshalled ranks he waved, and signed ;
And his banner streamed out on the evening wind,
　As they rode along Souter-fell side away.

And to many an eye was revealed the sight,
　While the corn stood green that Midsummer-day;
As Sir Lancelot Threlkeld the ancient Knight
With all his horsemen went over the height :
　O'er the steep mountain summit went riding away.

And then as the twilight closed over the dell—
　Where the corn stood green that Midsummer-day—
Came the farmers and peasants all flocking to tell
How Sir Lancelot's troop had gone over the fell !
　And the widows sat listening, and spinning away.

And the widows looked mournfully round the old
　　hall ;
　And the corn stood green on Midsummer-day ;
" He is come at the good Lord Clifford's call !
He is up for the King, with his warriors all ! "—
　Said the widows there spinning the eve away.

" There is evil to happen, and war is at hand—
   Where the corn stands green this Midsummer-
     day—
Or rebels are plotting to waste the land ;
Or he never would come with his armed band "—
   Said the widows there spinning the eve away.

" Our old men sleep in the grave.   They cease :
   While the corn stands green on Midsummer-day—
They rest, though troubles on earth increase ;
And soon may Sir Lancelot's soul have peace ! "
   Sighed the widows while spinning the eve away.

" But this was the Promise the Shepherd-Lord—
   When the corn stood green that Midsummer-day—
Gave, parting from Threlkeld's hearth and board,
To the brave old Knight—and he keeps his word ! "
   Said the widows all putting their spinning away.

NOTES TO "SIR LANCELOT THRELKELD."

The little village of Threlkeld is situated at the foot of Blencathra about four miles from Keswick, on the highroad from that town to Penrith. The old hall has long been in a state of dilapidation, the only habitable part having been for years converted into a farm house. Some faint traces of the moat are said to be yet discernible. This was one of the residences of Sir Lancelot Threlkeld, a powerful knight in the reign of Henry the Seventh, step-father to the Shepherd Lord. His son, the last Sir Lancelot, was wont to say that he had "three-noble houses—one for pleasure, Crosby in Westmorland, where he had a park full of deer; one for profit and warmth, wherein to reside during winter, namely, Yanwath, near Penrith ; and the third, Threlkeld, on the edge of the vale of Keswick, well stocked with tenants to go with him to the wars." Sir Lancelot is said to have been a man of a kind and generous disposition, who had either taken the side of the White Rose in the great national quarrel, or at least had not compromised himself to a ruinous extent on the other side ; and has long had the reputation of having afforded a retreat to the Shepherd Lord Clifford, on the utter ruin of his house, after the crushing of the Red Rose at Towton, when the Baron (his late father) was attained in parliament, and all his lands were seized by the crown.

The Cliffords, Lords of Westmorland, afterwards Earls of Cumberland, were a family of great power and princely possessions, who for many generations occupied a position in the North West of England, similar to that held by the Percies, Earls of Northumberland, in the north-east.

Their blood was perhaps the most illustrious in the land. Descended from Rollo first Duke of Normandy, by alliances in marriage it intermingled with that of William the Lion, King of Scotland, and with that of several of the Sovereigns of England.

Their territorial possessions corresponded with their illustrious birth. These comprised their most ancient stronghold, Clifford Castle, on the Wye, in Herefordshire ; the lordship of the barony of Westmorland, including the seigniories and Castles of Brougham and Appleby; Skipton Castle in the West Riding of Yorkshire, with its numerous townships, and important forest and manorial rights, their most princely, and apparently favourite residence; and the Hall and estates of Lonsborrow in the same County.

The Cliffords are said to be sprung from an uncle of William the Conqueror. The father of William had a younger brother, whose third son, Richard Fitz-Pontz, married the daughter and heiress of Ralph de Toni, of Clifford Castle, in Herefordshire. Their second son, Walter, succeeding to his mother's estates, assumed the name of Clifford, and was the father of the Fair Rosamond, the famous mistress of King Henry the Second. He died in 1176. His great-grandson, Roger de Clifford acquired the inheritance of the Veteriponts or Viponts, Lords of Brougham Castle in Westmorland, by his marriage with one of the co-heiresses of Robert de Vipont, the last of that race. It was their son Robert who was first summoned to sit in parliament, by a writ dated the 29th of December, 1299, as the Lord Clifford.

The Cliffords were a warlike race, and engaged in all the contests of the time. For many generations the chiefs of their house figure as distinguished soldiers and captains; and most of them died on the field of battle.

Roger, the father of the first lord, was renowned in the wars of Henry III. and of Edward I., and was killed in a skirmish with the Welsh in the Isle of Anglesey, on St. Leonard's day, 1283.

His son Robert, the first Lord Clifford, a favourite and companion in arms of Edward I., was one of the guardians of Edward II. when a minor, and Lord High Admiral in that monarch's reign. He fell at the battle of Bannockburn, in 1314.

Roger, his son, the second lord, was engaged in the Earl of Lancaster's insurrection, and had done much to deserve political martyrdom in that rebellious age : but a feeling of humanity, such as is seldom read of in civil wars, and especially in those times, saved him from execution, when he was taken prisoner with Lancaster and the rest of his associates. He had received so many wounds in the battle (of Borough bridge), that he could not be brought before the judge for the summary trial, which would have sent him to the hurdle and the gallows. Being looked upon, therefore, as a dying man, he was respited from the course of law : time enough elapsed, while he continued in this state, for the heat of resentment to abate, and Edward of Carnarvon, who, though a weak and most misguided prince, was not a cruel one, spared his life ; an act of mercy which was the more graceful, because Clifford had insulted the royal authority in a manner less likely to be forgiven than his braving it in arms.   A pursuivant had served a writ upon him in the Barons' Chamber, and he made the man eat the wax wherewith the writ was signed, "in contempt, as it were, of the said King."

He was the first Lord Clifford that was attainted of treason. His lands and honours were restored in the first year of Edward III., but he survived the restoration only a few weeks, dying in the flower of his age, unmarried ; but leaving "some base children behind him, whom he had by a mean woman who was called Julian of the Bower, for whom he built a little house hard by Whinfell, and called it Julian's Bower, the lower foundation of which standeth, and is yet to be seen," said the compiler of the family records, an hundred and fifty years ago, "though all the walls be down long since.   And it is thought that the love which this Roger bore to this Julian kept him from marrying any other woman."

Roger de Clifford was succeeded in his titles and estates by his brother Robert, the third baron, who married Isabella de Berkeley, sister to Thomas, Lord Berkeley, of Berkeley Castle ; in which Castle, two years after it had rung with "shrieks of death," when the tragedy of Edward II. was brought to its dreadful catastrophe there, the marriage was performed.

This Robert lived a country life, and "nothing is mentioned of him in the wars," except that he once accompanied an army into Scotland.   It is, however, related of him, that when Edward Baliol was driven from Scotland, the exiled king was "right honourably received by him in Westmorland, and entertained in his Castles of Brougham, Appleby, and Pendragon;" in acknowledgement for which hospitality Baliol, if he might at any time recover the kingdom of Scotland out of his adversaries' hands, made him a grant of Douglas Dale, which had been granted to his grandfather who fell in Wales. The Hart's Horn Tree in Whinfell Park, well known in tradition, and in hunters' tales, owes its celebrity to this visit. He died in 1340.

Robert, his son, fourth lord, fought by the side of Edward the Black Prince at the memorable battles of Cressy and Poictiers.

Roger, his brother, the fifth lord, styled "one of the wisest and gallantest of the Cliffords," also served in the wars in France and Scotland, in the reign of Edward III.

Thomas, his son, sixth lord Clifford, one of the most chivalrous knights of his time, overcame, in a memorable passage of arms, the famous French knight, "le Sire de Burjisande," and, at the age of thirty, was killed in the battle at Spruce in Germany.

John, his son, the seventh lord, a Knight of the Garter, carried with him to the French wars three knights, forty-seven esquires, and one hundred and fifty archers. He fought under the banner of Henry V. at the battle of Agincourt, attended him at the sieges Harfleur and Cherbourg, and was eventually slain, at the age of thirty-three, at the siege of Meaux in France.

Thomas, his son, eighth lord Clifford, described as "a chief commander in France," was grandson on his mother's side to the celebrated Hotspur, Harry Percy, and gained renown by the daring and ingenious stratagem which he planned and success-fully executed for taking the town of Pontoise, near Paris, in 1438. The English had lain for some time before the town, with little prospect of reducing it, when a heavy fall of snow suggested to Lord Clifford the means of effecting its capture. Arraying himself and his followers with white tunics over their armour, he concealed them during the night close to the walls of the town, which at daybreak he surprised and carried by storm. Two years afterwards he valiantly defended the town of Pontoise against the armies of France, headed by Charles VII. in person.

In the Wars of the Roses they were not less prominent. The last mentioned Thomas, though nearly allied by blood to the house of York, took part with his unfortunate sovereign, Henry VI., and fell on the 22nd of May, 1455, at the first battle of St. Albans, receiving his death-blow from the hands of Richard Duke of York, at the age of forty.

John, his son, the next and ninth lord, called from his complexion the Black-faced Clifford, thirsting to revenge the fate of his father, perpetrated that memorable act of cruelty, which for centuries has excited indignation and tears, the murder of the young Earl of Rutland, brother of Edward IV., in the pursuit after the battle of Wakefield, on the 30th December, 1460. The latter, whilst being withdrawn from the field by his attendant chaplain and schoolmaster, a priest, called Sir Robert Aspall, was espied by Lord Clifford; and being recognised by means of his apparel, "dismayed, had

not a word to speak, but kneeled on his knees imploring
mercy and desiring grace, both with holding up his hands and
making dolorous countenance, for his speech was gone for
fear. 'Save him,' said his chaplain, 'for he is a prince's son,
and peradventure may do you good hereafter.' With that
word, the Lord Clifford marked him and said, 'By God's
blood, thy father slew mine, and so will I do thee and all thy
kin ;' and with that word stuck the earl to the heart with his
dagger, and bade his chaplain bear the earl's mother and
brother word what he had done and said."

The murder in cold blood of this unarmed boy, for he was
only twelve or at most seventeen years old, while supplicating
for his life, was not the only atrocity committed by Lord
Clifford on that eventful day. "This cruel Clifford and
deadly blood-supper," writes the old chronicler, "not content
with this homicide or child-killing, came to the place where
the dead corpse of the Duke of York lay, and caused his head
to be stricken off, and set on it a crown of paper, and so fixed
it on a pole and presented it to the queen, not lying far from
the field, in great spite and much derision, saying, 'Madam,
your war is done ; here is your king's ransom ;' at which
present was much joy and great rejoicing."

Lord Clifford fought at the second battle of St. Albans, on
the 17th of February, 1461. It was in his tent, after the
Lancastrians had won the victory, that the unfortunate
Henry VI. once more embraced his consort Margaret of
Anjou, and their beloved child.

Lord Clifford is usually represented as having been slain at
the battle of Towton. He fell, however, in a hard fought
conflict which preceded that engagement by a few hours, at a
spot called Dittingale, situated in a small valley between
Towton and Scarthingwell, struck in the throat by a headless
arrow, discharged from behind a hedge.

A small chapel on the banks of the Aire formerly marked
the spot where lay the remains of John Lord Clifford, as well
as those of his cousin, Henry Percy, Earl of Northumberland,
who perished later in the day upon Towton Field, on the 29th
of March, 1461.

For nearly a quarter of a century from this time, the name
of Clifford remained an attainted one ; their castles and
seigniories passed into the hands of strangers and enemies.
The barony of Westmorland was conferred by Edward IV.
upon his brother Richard Duke of Gloucester ; the castle and
manor of Skipton he bestowed, in the first instance, upon Sir

William Stanley; but in the fifteenth year of his reign he
transferred them to his "dear brother," which lordly appan-
age he retained till his death on Bosworth Field.*

The young widow left by the Black-faced Clifford, was
Margaret daughter and sole heiress of Henry de Bromflete,
Baron de Vesci. She had borne her husband three children,
two sons and a daughter, now attainted by parliament,
deprived of their honours and inheritance, and their persons
and lives in hourly jeopardy from the strict search which was
being made for them. The seat of her father at Lonsborrow
in Yorkshire, surrounded by a wild district, offered a retreat
from their enemies; and thither, as soon as the fate of her
lord was communicated to her, driven from the stately halls
of Skipton and Appleby, of which she had ceased to be
mistress, flew the young widow with her hunted children, and
saved them from the rage of the victorious party by conceal-
ment.

Henry, the elder son, at the period of their flight to
Lonsborrow was only seven years old. He was there placed
by his mother, in the neighbourhood where she lived, with a
shepherd who had married one of her inferior servants, an
attendant on his nurse, to be brought up in no better condition
than the shepherd's own children. The strict inquiry which
had been made after them, and the subsequent examination
of their mother respecting them, at length led to the conclu-
sion that they had been conveyed beyond the sea, whither in
truth the younger boy had been sent, into the Netherlands,
and not long after died there. The daughter grew up to
womanhood, and became the wife of Sir Robert Aske, from
whom descended the Askes of Yorkshire, and the Lord
Fairfax of Denton in the same county.

When the high born shepherd boy was about his fourteenth
year, his grandfather, Lord de Vesci being dead, and his
mother having become the wife of Sir Lancelot Threlkeld, a
rumour again arose and reached the court that the young
Lord Clifford was alive; whereupon his mother, with the
connivance and assistance of her husband, had the shepherd
with whom she had placed her son, removed with his wife
and family from Yorkshire to the more mountainous country

* Whitaker gives the terms of this grant: "The king, in cons'on of
ye laudable and commendable service of his dere b'r Richard Duke of
Gloucester, as *for the encouragement of piety and virtue* in the said duke,
did give and grant, etc., the honor, castle, manors, and demesnes of
Skipton, with the manor of Marton, etc., etc." Pat: Rolls, 15 Edw. IV.

of Cumberland. In that wild and remote region, the persecuted boy was "kept as a shepherd sometimes at Threlkeld amongst his step-father's kindred, and sometimes upon the borders of Scotland, where they took land purposely for those shepherds who had the custody of him, where many times his step-father came purposely to visit him, and sometimes his mother, though very secretly."

In this obscurity the heir of the Cliffords passed the remainder of his boyhood, all his youth, and his early manhood ; haunting, in the pursuit of pastoral occupations, the lofty moorland wastes at the foot of Blencathra, or musing in the solitude of the stupendous heights of that "Peak of Witches ;" at other times, ranging amid the lonesome glens of Skiddaw Forest, or on the bleak heath-clad hills of Caldbeck and Carrock.

Thus being of necessity nurtured much in solitude, and, habited in rustic garb, bred up to man's estate among the simple dalesmen, to whom, as well as to himself, his rank and station were unknown, he was reared in so great ignorance that he could neither read nor write ; for his parents durst not have him instructed in any kind of learning, lest by it his birth should be discovered ; and when subsequently he was restored to his title and estates, and took his place among his peers, he never attained to higher proficiency in the art of writing than barely enabled him to sign his name.

One of the first acts of Henry VII. was to restore the lowly Clifford to his birthright and to all that had been possessed by his noble ancestors. And his mother, who did not die till the year 1493, lived to see him thus suddenly exalted from a poor shepherd into a rich and powerful lord, at the age of one and thirty.

In his retirement he had acquired great astronomical knowledge, watching, like the Chaldeans of old time, the stars by night upon the mountains, as is current from tradition in the village and neighbourhood of Threlkeld at this day. And when, on his restoration to his estates and honours, he had become a great builder and repaired several of his castles, he resided chiefly at Barden Tower, in Yorkshire, to be near the Priory of Bolton ; "to the end that he might have opportunity to converse with some of the canons of that house, as it is said, who were well versed in astronomy ; unto which study having a singular affection (perhaps in regard to his solitary shepherd's life, which gave him time for contemplation,) he fitted himself with diverse instruments for use therein."

Whitaker, in like manner, represents the restored lord as having brought to his new position "the manners and education of a shepherd," and as being "at this time, almost, if not altogether, illiterate." But it is added that he was "far from deficient in natural understanding, and, what strongly marks an ingenuous mind in a state of recent elevation, depressed by a consciousness of his own deficiencies." If it was on this account, as we are also told, that he retired to the solitude of Barden, where he seems to have enlarged the tower out of a common keeper's lodge, he found in it a retreat equally favourable to taste, to instruction, and to devotion. The narrow limits of his residence show that he had learned to despise the pomp of greatness, and that a small train of servants could suffice him, who had lived to the age of thirty a servant himself.

Whitaker suspects Lord Clifford, however, "to have been sometimes occupied in a more visionary pursuit, and probably in the same company," namely, the canons of Bolton, from having found among the family evidences two manuscripts on the subject of Alchemy, which may almost certainly be referred to the age in which he lived. If these were originally deposited with the MSS. of the Cliffords, it might have been for the use of this nobleman. If they were brought from Bolton at the Dissolution, they must have been the work of those canons with whom he almost exclusively conversed.

In these peaceful employments Lord Clifford spent the whole reign of Henry VII., and the first years of that of his son. His descendant the Countess of Pembroke describes him as a plain man, who lived for the most part a country life, and came seldom either to court or London, excepting when called to Parliament, on which occasion he behaved himself like a wise and good English nobleman. But in the year 1513, when almost sixty years old, he was appointed to a principal command over the army which fought at Flodden, and showed that the military genius of the family had neither been chilled in him by age, nor extinguished by habits of peace.

He survived the battle of Flodden ten years, and died April 23rd, 1523, aged about 70; having by his last will appointed his body to be interred at Shap, if he died in Westmorland; or at Bolton, if he died in Yorkshire. "I shall endeavour," says Whitaker, "to appropriate to him a tomb, vault, and chantry, in the choir of the Church of Bolton, as I should be sorry to believe that he was deposited, when dead, at a distance from the place which in his life time he loved so well." There

exists no memorial of his place of burial. The broken floors
and desecrated vaults of Shap and Bolton afford no trace or
record of his tomb. It is probable, however, that in one of
these sanctuaries he was laid to rest among the ashes of his
illustrious kindred.

The vault at Skipton Church was prepared for the remains
of his immediate descendants. Thither, with three of their
wives, and a youthful scion of their house, the boy Lord
Francis, were borne in succession the five Earls of Cumber-
land of his name; when this their tomb finally closed over
the line of Clifford: the lady Anne choosing rather to lie
beside "her beloved mother," in the sepulchre which she had
erected for herself at Appleby, than with her martial ancestors
at Skipton.

Having thus been wonderfully preserved—says a writer
whose words have often been quoted in these pages—and
after twenty years of secretness and seclusion, having been
restored in blood and honours, to his barony, his lands, and
his castles; he, the Shepherd Lord, came forth upon the
world with a mind in advance of the age, a spirit of know-
ledge, of goodness, and of light, such as was rarely seen in
that time of ignorance and superstition; averse to courtly
pomp, delighting himself chiefly in country pursuits, in re-
pairing his castles, and in learned intercourse with such
literate persons as he could find. He was the wisest of his
race, and falling upon more peaceful times, was enabled to
indulge in the studies and thoughtful dispositions which his
early misfortunes had induced and cultured. Throughout a
long life he remained one, whose precious example, though it
had but few imitators, and even exposed him to be regarded
with dread, as dealing in the occult sciences, and leagued with
beings that mortal man ought not to know, was nevertheless
so far appreciated by his less enlightened countrymen, that
his image was always linked in their memories and affections
with whatever was great and ennobling, and caused him to
be recorded to this, our day, by the endearing appellation of
the "Good Lord Clifford."

This nobleman was twice married,—first to Anne, daugh-
ter of Sir John St. John of Bletsoe, cousin-germain to King
Henry the Seventh, by whom. he had two sons and five
daughters. Lady Clifford was a woman of great goodness
and piety, who lived for the most part a country life in her
husband's castles in the North, during the twenty-one years
she remained his wife. His second wife was Florence,

daughter of Henry Pudsey, of Bolton, in Yorkshire, Esquire, grandson of Sir Ralph Pudsey, the faithful protector of Henry the Sixth after the overthrow of the Lancastrian cause at Hexham. By her he had two or three sons, and one daughter, Dorothy, who became the wife of Sir Hugh Lowther, of Lowther, in Westmorland, and from whom the Earls of Lonsdale are descended.

It is said that, towards the end of the first Lady Clifford's life, her husband was unkind to her, and he had two or three base children by another woman.

Lord Clifford was unfortunate in having great unkindness and estrangement between himself and his oldest son Henry. Early habits of friendship, on the part of the latter, with King Henry VIII. and a strong passion for parade and greatness, seem to have robbed his heart of filial affection. The pure simplicity and unequivocal openness of his father's manners had long been an offence to his pride ; but the old man's alliance with Florence Pudsey provoked his irreconcilable aversion. By his follies and vices, also, the latter years of his father were sorely disturbed. That wild and dissolute young nobleman, attaching himself to a troop of roystering followers, led a bandit's life, oppressed the lieges, harassed the religious houses, beat the tenants, and forced the inhabitants of whole villages to take sanctuary in their churches. He afterwards reformed, and was employed in all the armies sent into Scotland by Henry the Seventh and his successor, where he ever behaved himself nobly and valiantly ; and subsequently became one of the most eminent men of his time, and within two years after his father's death, having been through life a personal friend and favourite of Henry the Eighth, was elevated by that partial monarch to the dignity of Earl of Cumberland, which title he held till his decease in 1542. It has been conjectured, but on no sufficient grounds, that he was the hero of the ballad of "The Nut-Brown Maid."

In addition to the members of this distinguished family who have already been enumerated as attaining to great personal distinction, may be named George, the third of the five Earls of Cumberland, the favourite of Queen Elizabeth, called the "Great Sea-faring Lord Clifford," an accomplished courtier as well as naval hero,* one of those to whom England is indebted

* A notable example of the piety of our ancestors is recorded in a MS. Journal of a Voyage to India, still preserved in Skipton Castle, made under the auspices of this Earl of Cumberland. It gives an account of the proceedings of the Expedition on a Saturday and Sunday.
"Nov. 5. Our men went on shor and fet rys abord, and burnt the

for her proud title of "the Ocean Queen." And lastly, his daughter, the Lady Anne Clifford, Countess of Dorset, Pembroke, and Montgomery, of famous memory, one of the most celebrated women of her time.

About three miles from Threlkeld, the ancient home of Sir Lancelot Threlkeld and his noble step-son, stands as the eastern barrier of the Blencathra group of mountains, that part of it which is known as Souter Fell ; whose irregular and precipitous summit, everywhere difficult of access, rises to a height of about 2,500 feet. It is on the south of Bowscale Fell, leaning westward from the Hesketh and Carlisle road, by which its eastern base is skirted. This mountain is celebrated in local history as having several times been the scene of those singular aerial phenomena known as mirages. A tradition of a spectral army having been seen marching over these mountains had long been current in the neighbourhood, and this remarkable exhibition was actually witnessed in the years 1735, 1737, and 1745, by several independent parties of the dalesmen ; and, as may well be supposed, excited much attention in the north of England, and long formed a subject of superstitious fear and wonder in the surrounding district. A sight so strange as that of the whole side of the mountain appearing covered with troops, both infantry and cavalry, who after going through regular military evolutions for more than an hour, defiled off in good order, and disappeared over a precipitous ridge on the summit, was sure to be the subject of much speculation and enquiry. Many persons at a distance hearing of the phenomenon, proceeded to the places where it was witnessed, purposely to examine the spectators who asserted the fact, and who continued positive in their assertions as to the appearances. Amongst others, one of the contributors to Hutchinson's History of Cumberland went to inquire into the subject ; and the following is the account of the information he obtained, given in his own words.

"On Midsummer Eve 1735, William Lancaster's servant related that he saw the east side of Souter Fell, towards the top, covered with a regular marching army for above an hour together ; he said they consisted of distinct bodies of troops,

rest of the houses in the negers towne ; and our bot went downe to the outermoste pointe of the ryver, and burnt a towne, and brout away all the rys that was in the towne.   The 6th day we servyd God, being Sunday."

In what manner they served God on the Sunday, after plundering and burning two towns on the Saturday, the writer has not thought it necessary to relate.

which appeared to proceed from an eminence in the north end, and marched over a nitch in the top, but as no other person in the neighbourhood had seen the like, he was discredited and laughed at.

"Two years after, on Midsummer Eve also, betwixt the hours of eight and nine, William Lancaster himself imagined that several gentlemen were following their horses at a distance, as if they had been hunting, and taking them for such, paid no regard to it, till about ten minutes after, again turning his head to the place, they appeared to be mounted, and a vast army following, five in rank, crowding over at the same place, where the servant said he saw them two years before. He then called his family, who all agreed in the same opinion ; and what was most extraordinary, he frequently observed that some one of the five would quit the rank, and seem to stand in a fronting posture, as if he was observing and regulating the order of their march, or taking account of the numbers, and after some time appeared to return full gallop to the station he had left, which they never failed to do as often as they quitted their lines, and the figure that did so was one of the middlemost men in the rank. As it grew later they seemed more regardless of discipline, and rather had the appearance of people riding from a market, than an army, though they continued crowding on, and marching off, as long as they had light to see them.

" This phenomenon was no more seen till the Midsummer Eve, which preceded the rebellion, when they were determined to call more families to witness this sight, and accordingly went to Wiltonhill and Soutra-Fell side, till they convened about twenty-six persons, who all affirm that they saw the same appearance, but not conducted with the usual regularity as the preceding ones, having the likeness of carriages interspersed ; however it did not appear to be less real, for some of the company were so affected with it as in the morning to climb the mountain, through an idle expectation of finding horse shoes, after so numerous an army, but they saw not a vestige or print of a foot.

" William Lancaster, indeed, told me, that he never concluded they were real beings, because of the impracticability of a march over the precipices, where they seemed to come on ; that the night was extremely serene ; that horse and man, upon strict looking at, appeared to be but one being, rather than two distinct ones ; that they were nothing like any clouds or vapours, which he had ever perceived else-

where ; that their number was incredible, for they filled
lengthways near half a mile, and continued so in a swift
march for above an hour, and much longer he thinks if night
had kept off."

The writer adds,—"This whole story has so much the air
of a romance, that it seemed fitter for *Amadis de Gaul,* or
Glenvilles System of Witches, than the repository of the learned;
but as the country was full of it, I only give it verbatim from
the original relation of a people, that could have no end in
imposing upon their fellow-creatures, and are of good repute
in the place where they live."

Not less circumstantial is the account of this remarkable
phenomenon gathered from the same sources by Mr. James
Clarke, the intelligent author of the Survey of the Lakes ;
and which account, he says, "perhaps can scarcely be par-
alleled by history, or reconciled to probability ; such, how-
ever, is the evidence we have of it," he continues, "that I
cannot help relating it, and then my readers must judge for
themselves. I shall give it nearly in the words of Mr. Lan-
caster of *Blakehills,* from whom I had the account ; and
whose veracity, even were it not supported by many concur-
rent testimonies, I could fully rely upon. The story is as
follows :

"On the 23rd of June 1744 (Qu. 45 ?), his father's servant,
Daniel Stricket (who now lives under Skiddaw, and is an
auctioneer), about half past seven in the evening was walking
a little above the house. Looking round him he saw a troop
of men on horseback riding on *Souther fell-side,* (a place so
steep that an horse can scarcely travel on it at all,) in pretty
close ranks and at a brisk walk. Stricket looked earnestly at
them some time before he durst venture to acquaint any one
with what he saw, as he had the year before made himself
ridiculous by a visionary story, which I beg leave here also to
relate : He was at that time servant to John Wren of *Wilton-
hill,* the next house to *Blakehills,* and sitting one evening
after supper at the door along with his master, they saw a
man with a dog pursuing some horses along Southerfell-side ;
and they seemed to run at an amazing pace, till they got out
of sight at the low end of the Fell. This made them resolve to
go next morning to the place to pick up the shoes which they
thought these horses must have lost in galloping at such a
furious rate ; they expected likewise to see prodigious grazes
from the feet of these horses on the steep side of the moun-
tain, and to find the man lying dead, as they were sure he run

so fast that he must kill himself. Accordingly they went, but, to their great surprise, found not a shoe, nor even a single vestige of any horse having been there, much less did they find the man lying dead as they had expected. This story they some time concealed ; at length, however, they ventured to tell it, and were (as might be expected) heartily laughed at. Stricket, conscious of his former ridiculous error, observed these aerial troops some time before he ventured to mention what he saw ; at length, fully satisfied that what he saw was real, he went into the house, and told Mr. Lancaster he had something curious to show him. Mr. Lancaster asked him what it was, adding, " I suppose some bonefire," (for it was then, and still is a custom, for the shepherds, on the evening before St. John's day, to light bonefires, and vie with each other in having the largest.) Stricket told him, if he would walk with him to the end of the house he would show him what it was. They then went together, and before Stricket spoke or pointed to the place, Mr. Lancaster himself discovered the phenomenon, and said to Stricket, " Is that what thou hast to show me ?" " Yes, Master," replied Stricket : " Do you think you see as I do ?" They found they did see alike, so they went and alarmed the family, who all came, and all saw this strange phenomenon.

" These visionary horsemen seemed to come from the lowest part of Souther-Fell, and became visible first at a place called KNOTT : they then moved in regular troops along the side of the Fell, till they came opposite *Blakehills*, when they went over the mountain : thus they described a kind of curvilineal path upon the side of the Fell, and both their first and last appearance were bounded by the top of the mountain.

" Frequently the last, or last but one, in a troop, (always either the one or the other,) would leave his place, gallop to the front, and then take the same pace with the rest, a *regular*, *swift walk :* these changes happened to every troop, (for many troops appeared,) and oftener than once or twice, yet not at all times alike. The spectators saw, *all alike*, the same changes, and at the same time, as they discovered by asking each other questions as any change took place. Nor was this wonderful phenomenon seen at Blakehills only, it was seen by *every* person at *every cottage* within the distance of a mile ; neither was it confined to a momentary view, for from the time that Stricket first observed it, the appearance must have lasted at least two hours and a half, viz. from half past seven, till the night coming on prevented the farther view ; nor yet was the distance such as could impose rude resemblances on the eyes of credulity : *Blakehills* lay not half a mile from the place where this astonishing appearance *seemed* to be, and many other places where it was likewise seen are still nearer."

This account is attested by the signatures of William Lancaster and Daniel Stricket, and dated the 21st day of July 1785.

"Thus I have given," continues Mr. Clark, "the best account I can procure of this wonderful appearance ; let others determine.what it was. This country, like every other where cultivation has been lately introduced, abounds in the *aniles fabellæ* of fairies, ghosts, and apparitions; but these are never even *fabled* to have been seen by more than one or two persons at a time, and the view is always said to be momentary. Speed tells of something indeed similar to this as preceding a dreadful intestine war. Can something of this nature have given rise to Ossian's grand and awful mythology ? or, finally, Is there any impiety in supposing, as this happened immediately before that rebellion which was intended to subvert the liberty, the law, and the religion of England ; that though immediate prophecies have ceased, these visionary beings might be directed to warn mankind of approaching *tumults ?* In short, it is difficult to say what it was, or what it was not."

Sir David Brewster, in his work on *Natural Magic,* after quoting this narrative from Mr. James Clark, which he describes as "one of the most interesting accounts of aerial spectres with which we are acquainted," continues—"These extraordinary sights were received not only with distrust, but with absolute incredulity. They were not even honoured with a place in the records of natural phenomena, and the philosophers of the day were neither in possession of analagous facts, nor were they acquainted with those principles of atmospherical refraction upon which they depend. The strange phenomena, indeed, of the *Fata Morgana,* or the *Castles of the Fairy Mor-Morgana,* had been long before observed, and had been described by Kircher, in the 17th century, but they presented nothing so mysterious as the aerial troopers of Souter Fell ; and the general characters of the two phenomena were so unlike, that even a philosopher might have been excused for ascribing them to different causes."

The accepted explanation of this appearance now is, that on the evenings in question, the rebel Scotch troops were performing their military evolutions on the west coast of Scot-

land, and that by some peculiar refraction of the atmosphere
their movements were reflected on this mountain. Phenomena
similar to these were seen near Stockton-on-the-Forest, in
Yorkshire, in 1792 ; in Harrogate, on June 28th, 1812 ;
and near St. Neot's, in Huntingdonshire, in 1820. Tradition
also records the tramp of armies over Helvellyn, on the eve
of the battle of Marston Moor. To these may be added the
appearance of the Spectre of the Brocken in the Hartz Moun-
tains ; and an instance mentioned by Hutchinson, that in the
spring of the year 1707, early on a serene still morning, two
persons who were walking from one village to another in
Leicestershire, observed a like appearance of an army march-
ing along, till, going behind a great hill, it disappeared. The
forms of pikes and carbines were distinguishable, the march
was not entirely in one direction, but was at first like the
junction of two armies, and the meeting of generals.

Aerial phenomena of a like nature are recorded by Livy,
Josephus, and Suetonius ; and a passage in Sacred History
seems to refer to a similar circumstance. See Judges ix. 36.

Many in this country considered these appearances as
ominous of the great waste of blood spilt by Britain in her
wars with America and France. Shakespeare says, in *Julius
Cæsar*,

> " When these prodigies
> Do so conjointly meet, let not men say,
> ———————— they are natural ;
> For, I believe, they are portentous things
> Unto the climate that they point upon."

PAN ON KIRKSTONE.

Not always in fair Grecian bowers
Piped ancient Pan, to charm the hours.
Once in a thousand years he stray'd
Round earth, and all his realms survey'd.

And fairer in the world were none
Than those bright scenes he look'd upon,
Where Ulph's sweet lake her valleys woo'd,
And Windar all her isles renew'd,

For, long ere Kirkstone's rugged brow
Was worn by mortal feet as now,
Great Pan himself the Pass had trod,
And rested on the heights, a God !

Who climbs from Ulph's fair valley sees,
Still midway couched on Kirkstone-Screes,
Old as the hills, his Dog on high,
At gaze athwart the southern sky.

A rock, upon that rocky lair,
It lives from out the times that were,
When hairy Pan his soul to cheer
Look'd from those heights on Windermere.

There piped he on his reed sweet lays,
Piped his great heart's delight and praise;
While Nature, answering back each tone,
Joy'd the glad fame to find her own.

"Could I, while men at distance keep,"
Said Pan, "in yon bright waters peep,
And watch their ripples come and go,
And see what treasures hide below!

"Rivall'd is my fair Greece's store,
My own Parnassian fields and shore!
I will delight me, and behold
Myself in yon bright Mere of gold."

Like thought, his Dog sprang to yon lair
To watch the heights and sniff the air:
Like thought, on Helm a Lion frown'd,
To guard the northern Pass's bound:

And with his mate a mighty Pard
On Langdale-head, kept watchful ward :—
That great God Pan his soul might cheer,
Glass'd in the depths of Windermere.

Then down the dell from steep to steep,
With many a wild and wayward leap,
The God descending stood beside
His image on the golden tide.

His shaggy sides in full content
He sunn'd, and o'er the waters bent ;
Then hugg'd himself the reeds among,
And piped his best Arcadian song.

What was it, as he knelt and drew
The wave to sip, that pierced him through?
What whispered sound, what stifled roar,
Has reached him listening on the shore?

He shivers on the old lake stones ;
He leans, aghast, to catch the groans
Which come like voices uttering woe
Up all the streams, and bid him go.

Onward the looming troubles roll,
All centring towards his mighty soul.
He shriek'd ! and in a moment's flight,
Stunn'd, through the thickets plunged from sight.

Plunged he, his unking'd head to hide
With goats and herds in forests wide?
Or down beneath the rocks to lie,
Shut in from leaves, and fields, and sky?

Gone was the great God out from earth !
Gone, with his pipe of tuneful mirth !
Whither, and wherefore, men may say
Who stood where Pilate mused that day.

And with that breath that crisp'd the rills,
And with that shock that smote the hills,
A moment Nature sobb'd and mourn'd,
And things of life to rocks were turned.

Stricken to stone in heart and limb,
Like all things else that followed him,
Yonder his Dog lies watching still
For Pan's lost step to climb the hill.

And those twin Pards, huge, worn with time,
Stretch still their rocky lengths sublime,
Where once they watched to guard from man
The sportive mood of great God Pan.

And craggy Helm's grey Lion rears
The mane he shook in those old years,
In changeless stone, from morn to morn
Awaiting still great Pan's return.

Could he come back again, to range
The earth, how much must all things change !
Not Nature's self, even rock and stone,
Would deign her perished God to own.

The former life all fled away—
No custom'd haunt to bid him stay—
No flower on earth, no orb on high,
No place, to know him—Pan must die.

Down with his age he went to rest ;
His great heart, stricken in his breast
By tidings from that far-off shore,
Burst—and great Pan was King no more !

NOTES TO "PAN ON KIRKSTONE."

The sudden trouble and annihilation of Pan have reference to a passage in Plutarch, in his *Treatise on Oracles*, in which he relates that at the time of the Crucifixion, a voice was heard by certain mariners, sweeping over the Egean Sea, and crying " Pan is dead" ; and the Oracles ceased. This idea, so beautifully expressing the overthrow of Paganism, and the flight of the old gods, at the inauguration of Christianity, Milton has finely elaborated in his sublime " Hymn on the Morning of the Nativity."

Many of the mountains in the North of England derive their name from some peculiarity of form : as *Helm-Crag* in Grasmere, *Saddle-Back* near Keswick, *Great Gable* at the head of Wast-Water, *The Pillar* in Ennerdale, *The Hay Stacks*, *The Haycocks*, *High Stile*, *Steeple*, &c.

There are also very marked resemblances to animate ob- jects, well known to those familiar with the Lake District, as the *Lion and the Lamb* on the summit of Helm-Crag ; the *Astrologer*, or *Old woman cowering*, on the same spot when seen from another quarter ; the rude similitude of a female colossal statue, which gives the name of *Eve's Crag* to a cliff in the vale of Derwentwater. An interesting and but little known Arthurian reminiscence is found in the old legend that the recumbent effigy of that great king may be traced from some parts of the neighbourhood of Penrith in the outlines of the mountain range of which the peaks of Saddleback form the most prominent points. From the little hill of Castle Head or Castlet, the royal face of George the Third with its double chin, short nose, and receding forehead, can be quite made out in the crowning knob of Causey Pike. From under Barf, near Bassenthwaite Water, is seen the form which gives name to the *Apostle's Crag*. At a particular spot, the solemn shrouded figure comes out with bowed head and reverent mien, as if actually detaching itself from the rock—a vision seen by the passer by only for a few yards, when the magic ceases, and the Apostle goes back to stone. The massy forms of the Langdale Pikes, as seen from the south east, with the sweeping curve of Pavey Ark behind, are strikingly suggestive of two gigantic lions or pards, crouching side by side, with their breasts half turned towards the spectator. And a remarkable figure of a shepherd's dog, but of no great size, may be seen stretched out on a jutting crag, about half way up the precipice which overhangs the road, as the summit of Kirkstone Pass is approached from Brother's Water. It is not strictly, as stated in the foregoing verses, on the part of Kirkstone Fell called Red Screes, but some distance below it on the Patterdale side.

Among the freaks of Nature occasionally to be found in these hilly regions, is the print of the heifer's foot in Borrowdale, shown by the guides ; and on a stone near Buck-Crag in Eskdale, the impressions of the foot of a man, a boy, and a dog, without any marks of tooling or instrument ; and the remarkable precipices of Doe-Crag and Earn-Crag, whose fronts are polished as marble, the one 160 yards in perpendicular height, the other 120 yards.

On the top of the Screes, above Wastwater, stood for ages a very large stone called Wilson's Horse ; which about a century ago fell down into the lake, when a cleft was made one hundred yards long, four feet wide, and of incredible depth.

ST. BEGA AND THE SNOW MIRACLE.

The seas will rise though saints on board
Commend their frail skiff to the Lord.
And Bega and her holy band
Are shipwrecked on the Cumbrian strand.

" Give me," she asked, " for me and mine,
O Lady of high Bretwalda's line !
Give, for His sake who succoured thee,
A shelter for these maids and me."—

Then sew'd, and spun, and crewl-work wrought,*
And served the poor they meekly taught,
These virgins good ; and show'd the road
By blameless lives to Heaven and God.

They won from rude men love and praise ;
They lived unmoved through evil days ;
And only longed for a home to rise
To store up treasures for the skies.

That pious wish the Lady's bower
Has reached ; and forth she paced the tower ;—
" My gracious Lord ! of thy free hand
Grant this good Saint three roods of land.

* See Note on page 80.

" Three roods, where she may rear a pile,
To sing God's praise through porch and aisle ;
And, serving Him, us too may bless
For sheltering goodness in distress."

The Earl he turned him gaily near,
Laughed lightly in his Lady's ear—
" By this bright Eve of blessed St. John !
I'll give—what the snow to-morrow lies on."

His Lady roused him at dawn with smiles—
" The snow lies white for miles and miles !"
From loop-hole and turret he stares on the sight
Of Midsummer-morning clothed in white.

"—Well done, good Saint ! the lands are thine.
Go, build thy church, and deck thy shrine.
I 'bate no jot of my plighted word,
Though lightly spoken and lightly heard.

" If mirth and my sweet Lady's grace
Have lost me many a farm and chace,
I know that power unseen belongs
To holy ways and Christian songs.

" And He, who thee from wind and wave
Deliverance and a refuge gave,
When we must brave a gloomier sea,
May hear thy prayers for mine and me."

NOTES TO "ST. BEGA AND THE SNOW MIRACLE."

The remains of the Monastery of St. Bees, about four miles south of Whitehaven, stand in a low situation, with marshy lands to the east, and on the west exposed to storms from the Irish Channel.

In respect to this religious foundation, Tanner says, "Bega, an holy woman from Ireland is said to have founded, about the year 650, a small monastery in Copeland, where afterwards a church was built in memory of her. This religious house being destroyed by the Danes, was restored by William, brother to Ranulph de Meschines, Earl of Cumberland, in the time of King Henry I., and made a cell for a prior and six Benedictine monks, to the Abbey of St. Mary, York."

The earliest documents connected with this place call it *Kirkby-Begogh*, the market town of St. Bega; and *St. Bee*, or *St. Bees*, the Saint's house or houses, names given to it *after* the Irish Saint resided there.

St. Bega is said to have been the daughter of an Irish king, "who was a Christian, and an earnest man, to boot." He wished to marry his daughter to a Norwegian prince; but she, having determined to be a nun, ran away from her father's house, and joining some strange sailors, took ship, and sailed to the coast of Cumberland.

The accounts given of the first foundation of the nunnery of St. Bees are very contradictory, the common version being the traditionary account in Mr. Sandford's MS., namely, that the extent of the territories was originally designated by a preternatural fall of snow, through the prayers of the Saint, on the eve of St. John's or Midsummer day. From this MS. it would appear that a ship, containing a lady abbess and her sisters, being "driven in by stormy weather at Whitehaven," the abbess applied for relief to the lady of Egremont, who, taking compassion on her destitution, obtained of her lord a dwelling place for them, "at the now St. Bees;" where they "sewed and spinned, and wrought carpets and other work and lived very godly lives, as got them much love." It goes on to say that the lady of Egremont, at the request of the abbess, spoke to her lord to give them some land "to lay up treasure in heaven," and that "he laughed and said he would give them as much as snow fell upon the next morning, being Midsummer day ; and on the morrow as he looked out of his castle window, all was white with snow for three miles together. And thereupon builded this St. Bees Abbie, and gave all those lands was snowen unto it, and the town and haven of Whitehaven, &c."

The "Life of Sancta Bega," however, a latin chronicle of the Middle Ages, in which are recorded the acts of the Saint, gives the Snow Miracle somewhat differently, and places it many years after the death of the mild recluse, in the time of Ranulph de Meschines. The monkish historian relates that certain persons had instilled into the ears of that nobleman, that the monks had unduly extended their possessions. A dispute arose on this subject, for the settlement of which, by the prayers of the religious, "invoking most earnestly the intercession of their advocate the blessed Bega," the whole land became white with snow, except the territories of the church which stood forth dry.

It is certain that the name of *Sancta Bega* is inseparably connected with the Snow Miracle ; but the anachronism which refers the former of the accounts just given to the period of William de Meschines would seem to show that the narrator has mixed up the circumstances attending its foundation in the middle of the seventh century with its restoration in the twelfth ; for, says Denton, "the said Lord William de Meschines seated himself at Egremont, where he built a castle upon a sharp topped hill, and thereupon called the same *Egremont.*" This writer elsewhere says, "The bounders of William Meschines aforesaid, which he gave the priory are in these words : ' Totam terram et vis totum feodum inter has divisas, viz. a pede de Whit of Haven ad Kekel, et per Kekel donec cadit in Eyre et per Eyre quousque in mare.' Kekel runneth off from Whillymore by Cleator and Egremont, and so into Eyne ; at Egremont Eyre is the foot of Eyne, which falleth out of Eynerdale."

The monkish version of the legend, therefore, refers to William de Meschines, as the Lord of Egremont, and to the lands which were given by him at the restoration of the Priory in the twelfth century : whilst that related by Sandford alludes to some other powerful chief, who, in the life time of the Saint in the seventh century had his seat at Egremont, which, as has been stated elsewhere, "was probably a place of

strength during the Heptarchy, and in the time of the Danes."
It might almost seem as if some such legend as that of the
Snow Miracle were necessary to account for the singular form
of this extensive and populous parish : which includes the
large and opulent town of Whitehaven ; the five chapelries of
Hensingham, Ennerdale, Eskdale, Wastdale-Head, and Ne-
ther-Wastdale ; and the townships of St. Bees, Ennerdale,
Ennerdale High End, Eskdale and Wastdale, Hensingham,
Kinneyside, Lowside-Quarter, Nether-Wastdale, Preston-
Quarter, Rottington, Sandwith, Weddicar, and Whitehaven.
It extends ten miles along the coast, and reaches far inland,
so that some of its chapelries are ten and fourteen miles from
the mother-church.

In the monkish chronicle of the Life and Miracles of Sancta
Bega occurs the following passage :—

" A certain celebration had come round by annual revolu-
tion which the men of that land use to solemnise by a most holy
Sabbath on the eve of Pentecost, on account of certain tokens
of the sanctity of the holy virgin then found there, which they
commemorate, and they honor her church by visiting it with
offerings of prayers and oblations."*

In allusion to which, Mr. Tomlinson the editor and trans-
lator of the MS. observes that "this is another of those marks
of dependence of the surrounding chapelries which formerly
existed ; a mark the more interesting because to this day some
traces of it remain. Communicants still annually resort to
the church of St. Bees at the festival of Easter from consider-
able distances ; and the village presents an unusual appear-
ance from their influx ; and at the church the eucharist is
administered as early as eight in the morning, in addition to
the celebration of it at the usual time. There can be no doubt
but that Whitsuntide, and perhaps Christmas, as well as Easter,
were formerly seasons when the church of St. Bees was re-
sorted to by numbers who appeared within it at no other
time, save perhaps at the burial of their friends. The great
festivals of the church appear in the middle ages to have been
considered by the English as peculiarly auspicious for the
solemnization of marriages. At these seasons then, from con-
curring causes, the long-drawn solemn processions of priests

---

* Advenerat annua revolutione quædam celebritas quam sacro sancto
sabbato in vigilia pentecosten homines illius terræ ob quædam insignia
sanctitatis sanctæ virginis tunc illio inventa, et signa ibidem perpetrata
solent solempnizare ; et ecclesiam illius visitando orationum et obla-
tionum hostiis honorare.

Vita S. Begæ, et de Miraculis Ejusdem, p. 73.

and people would be chiefly seen, and then also, the accustomed oblations of the latter to the mother church of St. Bees would be discharged."

As to the "town and haven of Whitehaven" included in the gift to "St. Bees Abbie," its eligibility as a fishing ground, when the tides ran nearer the meadows than at present, would doubtless attract the attention of the monks of St. Bees ; and the fact of its being denominated *Whittoft-haven, Quitofthaven, Wythoven, Whyttothaven, Whitten,* &c., in the register of St. Bees and other ancient records, evidently shows that it is a place of greater antiquity than has generally been ascribed to it ; and some fragments of tradition, still extant, seem to countenance this opinion.

Denton (MS.) speaking of Whitehaven or White-Toft Haven, says "It was belonging to St. Beghs of antient time, for the Abbot of York, in Edward I.'s time was impleaded for wreck, and his liberties there, by the King, which he claimed from the foundation, to be confirmed by Richard Lucy, in King John's time, to his predecessors."

That Whitehaven was anciently a place of resort for shipping appears from some particulars respecting it mentioned in those remarkable Irish documents, called the *Annals of the Four Masters*, much of which was written at the Abbey of Monesterboice, in the county of Louth—nearly opposite, on the Irish shore. In the account of the domestic habits and manufactures of the Irish, it is stated that their *coracles*, or *Wicker Boats*, their Noggins, and other domestic utensils, were made of wood called *Wythe* or *Withey*, brought from the opposite shore of *Baruch* (i.e. rocky coast) and that a small colony was placed there for the purpose of collecting this wood. That Barach mouth, or Barrow mouth, and Barrow mouth wood is the same as that alluded to by the Four Masters, is evident from the legend of St. Bega, which places it in the same locality ; and that the colony of Celts . resided in the neighbourhood of the now *Celts*, or *Kell's Pit*, in the same locality also, is manifest from the name. About the year 930, it appears that one of the Irish princes or chiefs, accompanied an expedition to this place for wood (for that a great portion of the site of the present town and the neighbouring heights were formerly covered with forest trees there can be no doubt) and that the inhabitants who were met at *Whitten*, or *Wittenagemote*, fell upon and took the chief and several of the accompanying expedition prisoners from a jealousy of their sanctuary being invaded. Many of the Irish utensils were imported hither, particularly the *noggin*, or small 'water pail, which was made of closely woven wicker work, and covered inside with skin, having a projecting handle for the purpose of dipping into a river or well. The same article, in its primitive shape, though made of a different material, called a *geggin*, is still used by some of the farmers in that neighbourhood. When *Adam de Harris* gave lands at Bransty Beck to the church of Holm Cultram, he also gave privilege to the monks to cut wood for making geggins or noggins.

From an old history of the county of Durham, Whitehaven appears to have been a resort for shipping in the tenth century ; and when the Nevills of Raby were called upon to furnish their quota of men to accompany Henry in his expedition to Ireland in 1172, they were brought to *Wythop-haven*, or *Witten-haven*, and transported thence in ships to the Irish coast. When Edward was advancing against Scotland, in the fourteenth century, he found a ship belonging to this place, in which he sent a cargo of oats, to be ground by the monks of St. Bees.

In nearly all histories of Cumberland, the name of Whitehaven has been attributed either to some imaginary whiteness of the rocks on the east side of the harbour, or to the cognomen of an old fisherman who resided there about the year 1566, at which time the town is said to have had only six houses. In 1633 it consisted of only nine thatched cottages. Sir Christopher Lowther, second son of Sir John Lowther, purchased Whitehaven and the lands lying in its neighbourhood, and built a mansion on the west end of the haven at the foot of a rock. He died in 1644, and was succeeded by his son, Sir John Lowther, who erected a new mansion on the site of the present castle, described by Mr. Denton, in 1688, as a "stately new pile of building, called the Flatt," and having conceived the project of working the coal mines, and improving the harbour, he obtained from Charles the Second, about the year 1666, a grant of all the "derelict land at this place," which yet remained in the crown ; and in 1678, all the lands for two miles northward, between high and low water mark, the latter grant containing about 150 acres. Sir John having thus laid the foundation of the future importance of Whitehaven, commenced his great work, and lived to see a small obscure village grow up into a thriving and populous town.

There is a traditionary account of the existence of an ancient ruin where the castle stands (probably Druidical ; or, where at a later period, the Whitten, or Wittenagemote, was held) the remains of which were broken up about the year 1628. Respecting these real or imaginary stones it has been related, that the inhabitants believed them to be enchanted warriors, and gave them the appellation of "*Dread Ring,* or *Circle,*" and occasionally "*Corpse Circle*"—corrupted into the word *Corkickle,* the name which the locality now bears.

A reminiscence of the old mansion of the Lowthers is preserved by the road which skirts the precincts of the castle. This is still called, by the older townspeople, the Flatt Walk.

CREWL-WORK.

Krull, or *Crewel,* is a word evidently derived from the old Norse *Krulla,* signifying to blend, to mix, and also to curl; in fact, "crewel" work is embroidery, the Berlin wool work of modern days; but the word is generally applied, in this locality, to the covering of a hand ball with worsted work of various colours and devices, the tribute of mothers and sisters in our boyhood.

HART'S-HORN TREE.

When wild deer ranged the forest free,
Mid Whinfell oaks stood Hart's-Horn Tree ;
Which, for three hundred years and more,
Upon its stem the antlers bore
Of that thrice-famous Hart-of-Grease
That ran the race with Hercules.

The King of Scots, to hunt the game
With brave de Clifford southward came :
Pendragon, Appleby, and Brough'm,
Gave all his bold retainers room ;
And all came gathering to the chase
Which ended in that matchless race.

Beneath a mighty oak at morn
The stag was roused with bugle horn ;
Unleashed, de Clifford's noblest Hound
Rushed to the chase with strenuous bound;
And stretching forth, the Hart-of-Grease
Led off with famous Hercules.

They ran, and northward held their way ;
They ran till dusk, from dawning grey ;
O'er Cumbrian waste, and Border moor,
Till England's line was speeded o'er ;
And Red-kirk on the Scottish ground
Mark'd of their chase the farthest bound.

Then turned they southward, stretching on,
They ran till day was almost gone ;
Till Eamont came again in view ;
Till Whinfell oaks again they knew ;
They ran, and reached at eve the place
Where first began their desperate race.

They panted on, till almost broke
Each beast's strong heart with its own stroke !
They panted on, both well nigh blind,
The Hart before, the Hound behind !
And now will strength the Hart sustain
To take him o'er the pale again ?

He sprang his best ; that leap has won
His triumph, but his chase is done !
He lies stone dead beyond the bound;
And stretched on this side lies the Hound !
His last bold spring to clear the wall
Was vain ; and life closed with his fall.

The steeds had fail'd, squires', knights', and king's,
Long ere the chase reached Solway's springs !
But on the morrow news came in
To Brough'm, amidst the festive din,
How held the chase, how far, how wide
It swerved and swept, and where they died.

Ah ! gallant pair ! such chase before
Was never seen, nor shall be more :   ·
And Scotland's King and England's Knight
Looked, mutely wondering, on the sight,
Where with that wall of stone between
Lay Hart and Hound stretched on the green.

Then spoke the King—" For equal praise
This hand their monument shall raise !
These antlers from this Oak shall spread ;
And evermore shall here be said,
That Hercules killed Hart-of-Grease,
And Hart-of-Grease killed Hercules.

" From Whinfell woods to Red-kirk plain,
And back to Whinfell Oaks again,
Not fourscore English miles would tell !
But"—said the King—" they spann'd it well.
And by my kingdom, I will say
They ran a noble race that day ! "—

Then said de Clifford to the King—
" Through many an age this feat shall ring !
But of your Majesty I crave
That Hercules may have his grave
In ground beneath these branches free,
From this day forth called Hart's-Horn Tree."

And there where both were 'reft of life,
And both were victors in the strife,
Survives this saying on that chase,
In memory of their famous race—
" Here Hercules killed Hart-of-Grease,
And Hart-of-Grease killed Hercules."

85

NOTES TO "HART'S-HORN TREE."

I.—The memorable Westmorland Forest, or Park of Whin-fell, anciently written Qwynnefel, was a grant to Robert de Veteripont from King John.· This grant restrained him from committing waste in the woods, and from suffering his servants to hunt there in his absence during the king's life. Till the beginning of last century it was famous for its prodigious oaks ; a trio of them, called The Three Brothers, were the giants of the forest ; and a part of the skeleton of one of them, called *The Three Brothers' Tree*, which was thirteen yards in girth, at a considerable distance from the root, was remaining until within a very recent period.

On the east side of this park is Julian's Bower, famous for its being the residence of Gillian, or Julian, the peerless mistress of Roger de Clifford, about the beginning of the reign of Edward III. The Pembroke memoirs call it "a little house hard by Whinfell-park, the lower foundations of which standeth still, though all the wall be down long since." This record also mentions the Three Brother Tree and Julian's Bower, as curiosities visited by strangers in the Countess of Pembroke's time, prior to which a shooting seat had been erected near these ruins, for she tells us, that her grandson, Mr. John Tufton, and others at one time, "alighted on their way over *Whinfield* park at Julian's Bower, to see all the rooms and places about it." Its hall was spacious, wainscotted, and hung round with prodigious stags' horns, and other trophies of the field. One of the rooms was hung with very elegant tapestry ; but since it was converted into a farm-house all these relics of ancient times have been destroyed.

A large portion of the park was divided into farms in 1767 ; and the remainder in 1801, when its deer were finally destroyed. It was thus stripped of its giant trees, and consigned to its present unsheltered condition.

II.—A fine oak formerly stood by the way side, near Hornby Hall, about four miles from Penrith on the road to Appleby, which, from a pair of stag's horns being hung up in it, bore the name of Hart's-Horn Tree. It grew within the district which to this day is called Whinfell Forest. Concerning this tree there is a tradition, confirmed by Anne, Countess of Pembroke in her memoirs, that a hart was run by a single greyhound (as the ancient deer hound was called) from this place to Red-Kirk in Scotland, and back again. When they came near this tree the hart leaped the park paling, but, being worn out with fatigue, instantly died ; and the dog, equally exhausted, in attempting to clear it, fell backwards and expired. In this situation they were found by the hunters, the dog dead on one side of the paling, and the deer on the other. In memory of this remarkable chase, the hart's horns were nailed upon the tree, whence it obtained its name. And as all extraordinary events were in those days recorded in rhymes, we find the following popular one on this occasion, from which we learn the name of the dog likewise :—

Hercules killed Hart-o-Grease,
And Hart-o-Grease killed Hercules.

This story appears to have been literally true, as the Scots preserve it without any variation, and add that it happened in the year 1333 or 1334, when Edward Baliol King of Scotland came to hunt with Robert de Clifford in his domains at Appleby and Brougham, and stayed some time with him at his castles in Westmorland. In course of time, it is stated, the horns of the deer became grafted, as it were, upon the tree, by reason of its bark growing over their root, and there they remained more than three centuries, till, in the year 1648, one of the branches was broken off by some of the army, and ten years afterwards the remainder was secretly taken down by some mischievous people in the night. "So now," says Lady Anne Clifford in her Diary, "there is no part thereof remaining, the tree itself being so decayed, and the bark so peeled off, that it cannot last long ; whereby we may see time brings to forgetfulness many memorable things in this world, be they ever so carefully preserved—for this tree, with the hart's horn in it, was a thing of much note in these parts."

The tree itself has now disappeared ; but Mr. Wordsworth, "well remembered its imposing appearance as it stood, in a decayed state by the side of the high road leading from Penrith to Appleby."

This remarkable chase must have been upwards of eighty miles, even supposing the deer to have taken the direct road.

Nicolson and Burn remark, when they tell the story, "So say the Countess of Pembroke's Memoirs, and other historical anecdotes. But from the improbable length of the course, we would rather suppose, that they ran to Nine Kirks, that is the Church of Ninian the Scottish Saint, and back again, which from some parts of the park might be far enough for a greyhound to run." These writers have overlooked the circumstance, that the animal which in those days was called a greyhound was the ancient deerhound, a large species of dog having the form of the modern greyhound, but with shaggy hair and a more powerful frame. The breed is not yet extinct : Sir Walter Scott's Maida was of the species.

Dr. Burn deals another blow at the tradition ; for he goes on to say, "And *before* this time there was a place in the park denominated from the *Hart's horns ;* which seem therefore to have been put up on some former occasion, perhaps for their remarkable largeness. For one of the bounder marks of the partition aforesaid between the two daughters of the last Robert de Veteripont is called *Hart-horn sike.*

III.—Dr. Percy, referring to the expression *hart-o-greece* in a verse given below from the old ballad of "Adam Bell," explains it to mean a fat hart, from the French word *graisse.*

"Then went they down into a lawnde,
    These noble archarrs thre ;
Eche of them slew a hart of greece,
    The best that they cold se."

Clarke, in an appendix to his "Survey of the Lakes," speaking of the Red Deer which is bred upon the tops of the mountains in Martindale, gives *Hart of Grease* as the proper name of the male in the eighth year.

In Black's "Picturesque Guide to the English Lakes," it is stated in a note upon this subject, that there is an ancient broadside proclamation of a Lord Mayor of London, preserved in the Archiepiscopal Library at Lambeth, in which, after denouncing "the excessyve and unreasonable pryses of all kyndes of vytayles," it is ordered that "no citizen or freman of the saide citie shall sell or cause to be solde," amongst other things, "Capons of grece above xxd. or Hennes of grece above viid."

BEKAN'S GHYLL.

Dim shadows tread with elfin pace
   The nightshade-skirted road,
Where once the sons of Odin's race
   In Bekan's vale abode ;
Where, long ere rose Saint Mary's pile,
   The vanquish'd horsemen laid
Their idol Wodin, stained and vile,
   Beneath the forest's shade.

There hid—while clash of clubs and swords
   Resounded in the dell,
To save it from the Briton's hordes
   When Odin's warriors fell—
It lay with Bekan's mightiest charms
   Of magic on its breast ;
While Sorcery, with its hundred arms,
   Had sealed the vale in rest.

It woke when fell with sturdy stroke
   The Norman axe around,
And builders' hands in fragments broke
   The Idol from the ground ;

And hewed therefrom that corner stone
  Which yet yon tower sustains,
Where Wodin's Moth sits, grim and lone,
  And holds the dell in chains.

There youth at love's sweet call oft glides
  By cloister, aisle, and nave,
To stop above the stone that hides
  The beauteous Fleming's grave :—
Fair flower of Aldingham—the child
  Of old Sir William's days,—
Low where the Bekan straggling wild
  Its deadly arms displays.

There in the quiet more profound
  Than sleep, than death more drear,
Her shadow walks the silent ground
  When leaves are green or sere ;
When autumn with its cheerless sky
  Or winter with its pall,
Puts all the year's fair promise by
  With fruits that fade and fall.

And where the Bekan by the rill
  So bitter once, now sweet,
Its lurid purples ripens still
  While ages onward fleet,
She tastes the deadly flower by night,—
  If yet its juices flow
Sweet as of yore ; for then to light
  And rest her soul shall go.

7

Ah, blessed forth from far beyond
　　The Jordan once he came,—
Her Red-cross Knight,—the marriage bond
　　To twine with love and fame :
His meed of valour, Beauty's charms,
　　Pledged with one silvery word,
Beneath the forest's branching arms
　　And by the breezes stirred.

Another week ! and she would stand
　　In Urswick's halls a bride :
Another week ! the marriage band
　　Had round her life been tied :
When wild with joyfulness of heart
　　That beat not with a care,
She carolled forth alone, to start
　　The grim Moth from its lair.

She bounded from his heart elate !
　　But Urswick's halls of light,
And Aldingham's embattled gate
　　No more shall meet her sight.
For her no happy bridal crowd
　　Press out into the road,
But Furness monks with dirges loud
　　Bend round her last abode.

To chase the moth that guards the flower
　　That makes the dell its own,
Flew forth the maid from hall and tower
　　Through wood and glen alone.

Where Odin's men had left their god
  In earth, long overgrown
With tangled bushes rude, she trod
  Enchanted ground unknown.

The abbey walls before her gaze
  At distance rising fair,
While deep within the magic maze
  She wandered unaware :
She loitered with the song untired
  Upon her lips, nor thought
What foes against her peace conspired,
  While love his lost one sought !

They found her with close-lidded eyes,
  Watched by that Moth unblest,
Perched high between her and the skies,
  And nightshade on her breast.
There lay she with her lips apart
  In peace ; by Wodin's power
Stilled into death her truest heart
  With Bekan's lurid flower.

Woe was it when Sir William's hall
  Received the mournful train :
No more her voice with sweetest call
  His morns to wake again !
No more her merry step to cheer
  The days when clouds were wild !
No more her form on palfrey near
  When sport his noons beguiled !

Worse woe when Furness monks with dole—
    While gentle hands conveyed
Her body—for a parted soul
    The solemn ritual said ;   .
And laid her where the waving leaves
    Breathed low amidst the calm,
When loud upon the fading eves
    Rolled organ-chant and psalm.

With Urswick's hand in fondest grasp
    Said Fleming—" Vainly rise
My days for me : my heart must clasp
    Her image, or it dies !
Through mass and prayer I hear her voice ;
   . I know the fiends have power—
That chant and dole and choral noise
    Can purge not—o'er that flower ! "

They wandered where Engaddi's palms
    And Sharon's roses wave ;
Where Hebrew virgins chant their psalms
    By many a mountain cave :
Mid rock-hewn chambers by the Nile,
    Where Magian fathers lay ;—
The secret of the spell-struck pile
    To drag to realms of day.

In vain !   His gallant heart sleeps well,
    Beneath the Lybian air ;
And still the enchantment holds the dell,
    And her so sweet and fair.

Still on yon loop hole stretched by night,
The tyrant-moth is laid :
While circling in their ceaseless flight
The ages rise and fade.

There sometimes as in nights of yore,
Heard faint and sweet, a sound
Peals from yon tower, while o'er and o'e·
The vale repeats it round.
And down the glen the muffled tone
Floats slowly, long upborne ;
Answered as if far off were blown
A warrior's bugle-horn.

Yet one day, with unconscious art,
May some rude hand unfold
Great Wodin's breast, and rend apart
The fragment from its hold.
Then, while the deadly nightshade's veins
In bitter streams shall pour
Their juices, his usurped domains
Shall own the Moth no more.

Then him a milk white swallow's power
Shall timely overthrow.
And fair, as from a beauteous bower,
In raiment like the snow,
The Flower of Aldingham—the child
Of old Sir William's days—
Shall break the bondage round her piled ;
But not to meet his gaze.

Nor forth beneath the dewy dawn,
   All radiant like the morn,
Shall Urswick's Knight lead up the lawn
   Beside the scented thorn,
His bride into the blighted halls
   Whence once she wildly strayed
In ages past, by Furness walls,
   And with the Bekan played.

The sea-snake through the chambers roves
   Of old Sir William's home—
Fair Aldingham, its bowers, and groves,
   And fields she loved to roam :
And where the gallant Urswick graced
   His own ancestral board,
Now ferns and wild weeds crowd the waste,
   The creeping fox is lord.

But gracious spirits of the light
   Shall call a welcome down
On her, the beauteous lady bright,
   And lead her to her own.
Not to that home o'er which the tide
   Unceasing heaves and rolls ;
But through that porch which opens wide
   Into the land of souls.

NOTES TO "BEKAN'S GHYLL."

In the Chartulary of Furness Abbey, some rude Latin verses, written by John Stell a monk, refer to a plant called *Bekan*, which at some remote period grew in the valley in great abundance, whence the name of Bekansghyll was anciently derived. The etymology is thus metrically rendered :

"Hæc vallis, tenuit olim sibi nomen ab herba
Bekan, qua viruit ; dulcis nunc tunc sed acerba,
Inde domus nomen Bekanes-gill claruit ante."

This plant "whose juice is now sweet, but was then bitter," is assumed to be one of the species of Nightshade which are indigenous in the dell and flourish there in great luxuriance ; probably the Solanum Dulcamara, the bitter-sweet or woody nightshade, although the Atropa Belladonna, the deadly nightshade, also grows among the ruins of the Abbey. This "lurid offspring of Flora," as Mr. Beck calls it, the emblem of sorcery and witchcraft, might well give the name of Nightshade to that enchanting spot. But what authority the monks may have had for their derivation it is now impossible to ascertain. Various glossaries and lexicons are said to have been consulted for *bekan*, as signifying the deadly nightshade but without effect ; "and after all," says Mr. Beck, "I am inclined to believe that Beckansgill is a creation of the monastic fancy."

Bekan is Scandinavian, and a proper name : and has probably been localised in this district by the Northmen from the period of its colonisation. It is said to have been quite in accordance with the practice of these rovers to give the name of their chiefs not only to the mounds in which they were buried, but also in many cases to the valley or plain in which these were situated, or in which was their place of residence ; or to those ghylls or small ravines, which, with the rivers or brooks, were most frequently the boundaries of property.

Bekan's gill may be associated in some way with one of the northern settlers whose name has thus far outlived his memory in the district.

An interesting passage in Mr. Ferguson's "Northmen in Cumberland and Westmorland" bears upon this subject. It refers to the opening of an ancient barrow at a place called Beacon Hill, near Aspatria in Cumberland, in 1790, by its proprietor. Speaking of the barrow, Mr. Ferguson says :— " From its name and its commanding situation has arisen the very natural belief that this hill must have been the site of a beacon. But there is no other evidence of this fact, and as Bekan is a Scandinavian proper name found also in other instances in the district, and as this was evidently a Scandinavian grave, while the commanding nature of the situation would be a point equally desired in the one case as the other, there can hardly be a doubt that the place takes its name from the mighty chief whose grave it was. On levelling the artificial mound, which was about 90 feet in circumference at the base, the workmen removed six feet of earth before they came to the natural soil, three feet below which they found a vault formed with two large round stones at each side, and one at each end. In this lay the skeleton of a man measuring seven feet from the head to the ankle bone—the feet having decayed away. By his side lay a straight two-edged sword corresponding with the gigantic proportions of its owner, being about five feet in length, and having a guard elegantly ornamented with inlaid silver flowers. The tomb also contained a dagger, the hilt of which appeared to have been studded with silver, a two-edged Danish battle-axe, part of a gold brooch of semi-circular form, an ornament apparently of a belt, part of a spur, and a bit shaped like a modern snaffle. Fragments of a shield were also picked up, but in a state too much decayed to admit of its shape being made out. Upon the stones composing the sides of the vault were carved some curious figures, which were probably magical runes. This gigantic Northman, who must have stood about eight feet high, was evidently, from his accoutrements, a person of considerable importance."

The situation of Furness Abbey, in Bekan's Ghyll, justifies the choice of its first settlers. The approach from the north is such that the ruins are concealed by the windings of the glen, and the groves of forest trees which cover the banks and knolls with their varied foliage : but unluckily it has been thought necessary to disturb the solitude of the place by driving a railway through it, within a few feet of the ruins, and erecting a station upon the very site of the Abbot's Lodge. A commodious road from Dalton enters this vale, and crossing a small stream which glides along the side of a fine meadow, branches into a shaded lane which leads directly to the ruins of the sacred pile. The trees which shade the bottom of the lane on one side, spread their bending branches over an ancient Gothic arch, adorned with picturesque appendages of ivy. This is the principal entrance into the spacious enclosure which contains the Monastery. The building appertaining to it took up the whole breadth of the vale ; and the rock from whence the stones were taken, in some parts made place for and overtopped the edifice. Hence it was so secreted, by the high grounds and eminences which surround it, as not to be discovered at any distance. The Western Tower must have originally been carried to a very considerable height, if we judge from its remains, which present a ponderous mass of walls, eleven feet in thickness, and sixty feet in elevation. These walls have been additionally strengthened with six staged buttresses, eight feet broad, and projecting nine feet and a half from the face of the wall ; each stage of which has probably been ornamented like the lower one now remaining, with a canopied niche and pedestal. The interior of the tower, which measures twenty-four feet by nineteen feet, has been lighted by a fine graceful window of about thirty feet in height, by eleven and a half in width ; the arch of which must have been beautifully proportioned. A series of grotesque heads, alternating with flowers, is introduced in the hollow of the jambs, and the label terminates in heads. On the right side of the window is a loophole, admitting light to a winding staircase in the south-west angle of the tower, by which its upper stories might be ascended, the entrance to the stairs being by a door, having a Tudor arch, placed in an angle of the interior. The stairs are yet passable, and the view from the top is worth the trouble of an ascent.

The workmen employed by the late Lord G. Cavendish, state that the rubbish in this tower, accumulated by the fall of the superstructure, which filled up the interior to the window sill, was rendered so compact by its fall, so tenacious by the rains, and was composed of such strongly cemented materials, as to require blasting with gunpowder into manageable pieces for its removal. Prior to its clearance, it was the scene of some marvellous tales disseminated and credited by many, who alleged that this heap covered a vault to which the staircase led, containing the bells and treasure of the abbey, with the usual accompaniments of the White Lady, at whose appearance the lights were extinguished, the impenetrable iron-grated door, and the grim guardian genius. Though many essayed, none were known to have succeeded in the discovery of this concealed treasure house, much less of its contents. The inhabitants of the manor house, on one occasion, were roused from their slumbers by a noise proceeding from the ruins, and on hastening to the spot, discovered that it was made by some scholars from the neighbouring town of Dalton, digging among the ruins at midnight, in quest of the buried spoils.

Within the inner enclosure, on the north side of the Church at St. Mary's Abbey in Furness, a few tombstones lie scattered about in what has formerly been a part of the cemetery. One of these bears the inscription, partly defaced,

   IIIC JACET ANA F.. ... .TI FLANDREN...,

and commemorates one of the ancient family of Le Fleming.

Michael Le Fleming, the first of the name, called also Flemengar, and in some old writings Flandrensis, was kinsman to Baldwin, Earl of Flanders, father-in-law to the Conqueror; by whom he was sent with some forces to assist William in his enterprise against England.

After the Conquest was completed, and William was seated on the throne of England, the valiant Sir Michael, for his fidelity, and good services against the Saxons and Scots, received from his master many noble estates in Lancashire ; Gleaston, and the manor of Aldingham, with other lands in Furness. William de Meschines also granted him Beckermet Castle, vulgarly at that time called Caernarvon Castle, with the several contiguous manors of Frizington, Rottington, Weddaker, and Arloghden, all in Cumberland.

Sir Michael and his heirs first settled at Aldingham. By a singular accident, the time of which cannot now be ascertained, the sea swallowed up their seat at this place, with the village, leaving only the church at the east end of the town, and the mote at the west end, which serve to show what the extent of Aldingham has been. About the same time, it is supposed, the villages of Crimilton and Ross, which the first Sir Michael exchanged with the monks for Bardsea and Urswick, were also swallowed up. After this, they fixed their residence at Gleaston Castle ; and it has been conjectured, from the nature of the building, that the castle was built on the occasion, and in such haste, as obliged them to substitute mud mortar instead of lime, in a site that abounds with limestone. Sir Michael, is said, to have also resided at Beckermet.

The little knowledge that we are now able to gather of the first Le Fleming exhibits him in a very favourable light. He was undoubtedly a valiant man ; and was acknowledged as such by his renowned master, when, with other Norman chiefs, he was dispatched into the north to oppose the Scots, and awe the partisans of Edwin and Morcar, two powerful Saxons who opposed themselves to the Conqueror for some time after the nation had submitted itself to the Norman yoke, and whose power William dreaded the most. His regard for the memory of his sovereign he expressed in the name conferred upon his son and heir, William. We have glimpses too that in his household there was harmony and kindness between him and his children. To the Abbey of Furness he was a great benefactor. There is an affecting earnestness in the language with which in the evening of his long life he declares in one of his charters—"In the name of the Father, &c. Be it known to all men present and to come, That I, Michael Le Fleming, consulting with God, and providing for the safety of my soul, and the souls of my father and mother, wife and children, in the year of our Lord 1153, give and grant to St. Mary of Furness, to the abbot of that place, and to all the convent there serving God, Fordeboc, with all its appurtenances, in perpetual alms ; which alms I give free from all claims of any one, with quiet and free possession, as an oblation offered to God"—*saltim vespertinum*, he pathetically adds, in allusion to his great age— "at least an evening one." He adds, "signed by me with consent of William my son and heir, and with the consent of all my children. Signed by William my son, Gregory my grandson, and Hugh." Few gifts of this kind show greater domestic harmony. That Michael lived to a very advanced age is evident from this charter signed eighty-seven years after the Conquest ; supposing him to be the same Michael Le Fleming who came over with the Conqueror. He was buried with his two sons within the walls of the Abbey Church. His arms, a fret, strongly expressed in stone over the second chapel in the northern aisle indicate the spot where he found a resting place ; not the least worthy among the many of the nobility and gentry who in those days were interred within the sacred precincts of St. Mary's Abbey in Furness.

The lands in Furness, belonging to Sir Michael, were excepted in the foundation charter of Stephen to the Abbey. This exception, and the circumstance of his living in Furness, occasioned his lands to be called Michael's lands, to distinguish them from the Abbey lands ; and now they are called Much-lands, from a corruption of the word Michael. In like manner Urswick is called Much-Urswick for Michael's Urswick ; and what was originally called the manor of Aldingham, is now called the manor of Muchland.

From Baldwin's kinsman, the first Le Fleming, the founder of the family in England, two branches issued. William, the eldest son of Sir Michael, inherited Aldingham Castle and his Lancashire estates. His descendants, after carrying the name for a few generations, passed with their manors into the female line ; and their blood mingling first with the de Cancefields, and successively with the baronial families of Harrington, de Bonville, and Grey, spent itself on the steps of the throne in the person of Henry Grey, King Edward the Sixth's Duke of Suffolk, who was beheaded by Queen Mary on the 23rd of February 1554. This nobleman being father to Lady Jane Grey, his too near alliance with the blood royal gave the occasion, and his supposed ambition of being father to a Queen of England was the cause of his violent death. By his attainder the manors of Muchland, the possessions of the le Flemings in Furness, were forfeited to the Crown.

Richard le Fleming, second son of the first Sir Michael, having inherited the estates in Cumberland which William le Meschines had granted to his father for his military services, seated himself at Caernarvon Castle, Beckermet, in Cope-land. After two descents his posterity, having acquired by marriage with the de Urswicks the manor of Coniston and other considerable possessions in Furness, returned to reside in that district. The Castle of Caernarvon was abandoned, then erased, and Coniston Hall became the family seat for seven descents. About the tenth year of Henry IV. Sir Thomas le Fleming married Isabella, one of the four daughters and co-heiresses of Sir John de Lancaster, and acquired with her the lordship and manor of Rydal. The manor of Coniston was settled upon the issue of this marriage ; and for seven generations more Rydal and Coniston vied with each other which should hold the family seat, to fix it in Westmorland or Lancashire. Sir Daniel le Fleming came, and gave his decision against the latter, about the middle of the seventeenth century. Since that event, the hall of Coniston, pleasantly situated on the banks of the lake of that name, has been deserted.

Singularly enough, the inheritance of this long line also has been broken in its passage through the house of Suffolk. Sir Michael, the 23rd in succession from Richard, married, in the latter part of the last century, Diana only child of Thomas Howard, 14th Earl of Suffolk and Berkshire, by whom he had one daughter, afterwards married to her cousin Daniel le Fleming, who succeeded her father in the title. This marriage being without issue, on the demise of Lady le Fleming, the estates passed under her will to Andrew Huddleston of Hutton-John, Esq., and at his decease, which occurred shortly after, in succession to General Hughes, who assumed the name of Fleming ; both these gentlemen being near of kin to the family at Rydal. The title descended to the brother of Sir Daniel, the late Rev. Sir Richard le Fleming, Rector of Grasmere and Windermere ; and from him to his son, the present Sir Michael, the twenty-sixth in succession from Richard, the second son of Michael, Flandrensis, *the* Fleming, who came over with the Conqueror, and founded the family in England.

In this family there have been since the Conquest twelve knights and seven baronets.

The article *le* is sometimes omitted in the family writings before the time of Edward IV., and again assumed. Sir William Fleming, who died in 1756, restored the ancient orthography, and incorporated the article *le* with the family name at the baptism of his son and heir.

Rydal Hall suffered much from the parliamentary party : the le Flemings remaining Catholic to the reign of James II. For their adherence to the royal cause in the reign of Charles I., they were forced to submit to the most exorbitant demands of the Commissioners at Goldsmiths' Hall, in London (23 Car. 1) and pay a very great sum of money for their loyalty and allegiance. They were very obnoxious to Oliver Cromwell's sequestrators, and subjected to very high annual payments and compositions, for their attachment to regal government.

THE CHIMES OF KIRK-SUNKEN.

Twelve sunken ships in Selker's Bay
  Rose up ; and, righting soon,
With mast and sail stretched far away
  Beneath the midnight moon.

They sailed right out to Bethlehem ;
  And soon they reached the shore.
They steered right home from Bethlehem ;
  And these the freights they bore.

The first one bore the frankincense ;
  The second bore the myrrh ;
The third the gifts and tribute pence
  The Eastern Kings did bear.

The fourth ship bore a little palm
  Meet for an infant's hands ;
The fifth the spikenard and the balm ;
  The sixth the swathing bands.

The seventh ship bore without a speck,
A mantle fair and clean ;
The eighth the shepherds on her deck
With heavenward eyes serene.

One bore the announcing Angel's song ;
One Simeon's glad record ;
And one the bright seraphic throng
Whose tongues good tidings poured.

And midst them all, one, favoured more,
Whereon a couch was piled,
The blessed Hebrew infant bore,
On whom the Virgin smiled.

They sailed right into Selker's Bay :
And when the night was worn
To dawning grey, far down they lay,
Again that Christmas morn.

But through the brushwood low and clear
Came chimes and songs of glee,
That Christmas morning, to my ear
Beneath Kirk-sunken Tree.

Not from the frosty air above,
But from the ground below,
Sweet voices carolled songs of love,
And merry bells did go.

From out a City great and fair
  The joyous life up-flow'd,
Which once had breathed the living air,
  And on the earth abode.

A City far beneath my feet
  By passing ages laid ;
Or buried while the busy street
  Its round of life convey'd.

So to the ground I bent an ear,
  That heard, as from the grave,
The blessed Feast-time of the year
  Tell out the joy it gave ;

The gladness of the Christmas morn.
  O fair Kirk-Sunken Tree !
One day in every year's return
  Those sounds flow up by thee.

They chime up to the living earth
  The joy of them below,
At tidings of the Saviour's birth
  In Bethlehem long ago.

NOTES TO "CHIMES OF KIRK-SUNKEN."

In the parish of Bootle is a small inlet of the sea, called Selker's Bay, where the neighbouring people say, that in calm weather the sunken remains of several small vessels or galleys can be seen, which are traditionally stated to have been sunk and left there on some great invasion of the northern parts of this island, by the Romans, or the colonizing Northmen.

Various circles of standing stones, or what are generally called Druidical remains, lie scattered about the vicinity of Black Combe near the sea shore : several indicating by their name the popular tradition associated with them, to which the inhabitants around attach implicit credence, the spot beneath which lie the ruins of a church that sank on a sudden, with the minister and all the congregation within its walls. Hence, they say, the name Kirk-Sank-ton, Kirk-Sunken, Kirk-Sinking, and Sunken Kirks.

THE RAVEN ON KERNAL CRAG.

A Raven alighted on Kernal Rock
Amid thunder's roar and earthquake's shock.
O'er the tumbling crags he rolled his eye
Round valley and lake, and hills and sky.
'Twas a gloomy world.   He settled his head
Close into his shoulders and meekly said—
                    " Poor Raven ! "

The Raven on Kernal Crag grew old :
A human voice up the valley rolled.
Bel was worshipp'd on mountain brows :
Men made huts of the forest boughs :
And wrapt in skins in ambush lay
At the base of his crag, and seized their prey.
                    An old Raven.

The Raven sat in his purple cloke.
A Roman column the silence broke.
He had watched the eagles around him fly :
He saw them perched on spears go by.
The legions marched from hill to hill.
He settled his feathers ; and all was still—
     Still was the Raven.

The Raven was thinking, on Kernal Stone.
The hammers of Thor he heard them groan :
Regin, and Korni, and Lodinn, and Bor,
Clearing the forests from fell to shore ;
With Odin's bird on their banner upraised.
And he quietly said as he downward gazed—
     " A Raven ! "

The Raven on Kernal was musing still.
King Dunmail's hosts went up the hill,
In the narrow Pass, to their final fall.
With an iron gaze he followed them all ;
Till, piled the cairn of mighty stones,
Was heaped the Raise o'er Dunmail's bones.
     Ha ! hungry Raven !

The Raven on Kernal saw, in a trance,
Knights with gorgeous banner and lance,
Castles, and towers, and ladies fair.
Music floating high on the air
Reached his nest on Kernal's Steep,
And broke the spell of his solemn sleep.

A lonely Raven.

That Raven is sitting on Kernal Rock ;
Counting the lambs in a mountain flock.
Pleasant their bleat is, pleasant to hear,
Pleasant to think of ; but shepherds are near.
Cattle are calling below in the vale,
Maidens singing a true-love tale.

List to them, Raven.

That Raven will sit upon Kernal Rock
Till the mountains reel in the world's last shock.
Till the new things come to end like old,
He will roll his eye, and his wings unfold,
And settle again ; and his solemn brow
Draw close to his shoulders, and muse as now.

That Raven.

NOTES TO "THE RAVEN ON KERNAL CRAG."

Kernal Crag is a huge mass of solid rock, with a face of broken precipice, on the side of Coniston Old Man. In that unique and admirable Guide Book entitled "The Old Man; or Ravings and Ramblings round Conistone," it is said; "on this Crag, probably for ages, a pair of ravens have annually had their nest, and though their young have again and again been destroyed by the shepherds, they always return to this favourite spot; and frequently when one of the parents has been shot in the brooding season, the survivor has immediately been provided with another helpmate; and, what is still more extraordinary, and beautifully and literally illustrative of a certain impressive scripture passage—it happened a year or two since, that both the parent birds were shot, whilst the nest was full of unfledged young, and their duties were immediately undertaken by a couple of strange ravens, who attended assiduously to the wants of the orphan brood, until they were fit to forage for themselves."

LORD DERWENTWATER'S LIGHTS.

1716.

You yet in groves round Dilston Hall
May hear the chiding cushat's call ;
Its true-love burden for the mate
That lingers far and wanders late.

But who in Dilston Hall shall gaze
On all its twenty hearths ablaze ;
Its courteous hosts, its welcome free,
And all its hospitality ;

The grace from courtly splendour, won
By Royal Seine, that round it shone ;
Or feel again the pride or power
Of Radcliffe's name in hall and bower ;—

As when the cause of exiled James
Filled northern hearts with loyal flames,
And summers wore their sweetest smile
Round Dilston's Courts and Derwent's Isle ;

Ere Mar his standard wide unrolled,
And tower to tower the rising told,
And Southwards on the gathering came,
All kindling at the Prince's name ?—

The glory and the pomp are shorn ;
The banners rent, the charters torn ;
The loved, the loving, dust alone ;
Their honours, titles carved in stone.

———

On Witches' Peak the winds were laid :
Crept Glenderamakin mute in shade :
El-Velin's old mysterious reign
Hung stifling over field and plain.

Around on all the hills afar
Had died the sounds foreboding war.
Only a dull and sullen roar
Reached up the valley from Lodore.

Through all the arches of the sky
The Northern Lights streamed broad and high.
Wide o'er the realm their shields of light
Flung reddening tumults on the night.

Then dalesmen hoar and matrons old
Look'd out in fear from farm and fold :
Look'd out o'er Derwent, mere and isle,
On Skiddaw's mounds, Blencathra's pile.

They saw the vast ensanguined scroll
Across the stars the streamers roll :
The Derwent stain'd with crimson dyes :
And portents wandering through the skies.

And prophet-like the bodings came—
" The good Earl dies the death of fame ;
For him the Prince that came in vain,
A King, to enjoy his own again."—

The sightless crone cried from her bed—
" 'Tis blood that makes this midnight red.
I dreamed the young Earl heavenward rode ;
His armour flashed, his standard glow'd."

The fearful maiden trembling spoke—
" The good Earl blessed me, and I woke.
The white and red cockade he wore ;
He bade adieu for evermore."—

Far show'd huge Walla's craggy wall
The ' Lady's Kerchief' white and small,
Dropt when, pursued like doe from brake,
She scaled its rampart from the lake.

" I served my Lady when a bride :
I was her page :"—A stripling cried.
" I served her well on bended knee,
And many a smile she bent on me."—

—" Upon this breast, but twenty years
Are pass'd"—a matron spoke with tears—
" I nursed her ; and in all her ways,
She was my constant theme of praise."—

Like flaming swords, that round them threw
Their radiance on the star-lit blue,
Flash'd and re-flash'd with dazzling ray
The splendours of that fiery fray.

—" When spies and foes watch'd Dilston Hall,
To seize him ere the trumpet-call"—
A yeoman spake that loved him well—
" I brought him mid our huts to dwell.

" We shelter'd him in farm and bield,
Till all was ready for the field,
Till all the northern bands around
Were arm'd, and for the battle bound.

" Then came he forth, and if he stay'd
A few short hours, and still delay'd,
'Twas for those priceless treasures near,
My lady and her children dear.

" I heard reproaches at his side !
—' Or take this jewelled fan'—she cried,
With high-born scornful look and word—
And I will bear the warrior's sword !'

" He called, ' To horse !'—his dapple grey
He welcomed forth, and rode away.
The white and red unstained he wore :
His heart was stainless evermore !"—

And thus the night was filled with moan.
And was the good Earl slain and gone ?
For him the Prince that came in vain,
A King, to enjoy his own again.

From Derwent's Island-Castle gate,
In robe and coronet of state,
A phantom on the vapours borne,
Passed in the shadows of the morn.

Pale hollow forms in suits of woe
Appear'd like gleams to come and go.
And wreathed in mists was seen to rest
A 'scutcheon on Blencathra's breast.—

Full soon the speeding tidings came.
The Earl had died the death of fame,
By axe and block, on bended knee,
For true-love, faith, and loyalty.

And still, when o'er the Isles return
The Northern lights to blaze and burn ;
The vales and hills repeat the moan
For him the good Earl slain and gone.

NOTES TO "LORD DERWENTWATER'S LIGHTS."

Lord's Island, in Keswick Lake, is memorable as having been the home of James Radcliffe, third and last Earl of Derwentwater, whose life and great possessions were forfeited in 1716, in the attempt to restore the royal line of Stuart to the throne, and whose memory is affectionately cherished in the north of England. An eminence upon its shores, called Castle-Rigg, which overlooks the vale of Keswick, was formerly occupied by a Roman fort, and afterwards by the stronghold of the Norman lords, who were called, from the locality of this their chief residence, de Derwentwater. Their early history is wrapt in obscurity ; but their inheritance comprised the greater part of the parish of Crosthwaite, in addition to possessions in other parts of Cumberland, and in other counties. These became vested in the Radcliffe family in the reign of Henry the Fifth, by the marriage of Margaret daughter and heiress of Sir John de Derwentwater, with Sir Nicholas Radcliffe, of lineage not less ancient than that of his wife, he being of Saxon origin, and of a family which derived its name from a village near Bury in Lancashire. In later time the Norman tower on Castle-Rigg was abandoned, and its materials are said to have been employed in building the house upon that one of the three wooded islands in the lake, which is called Lord's Island, and upon which the Radcliffe family had a residence. This island was originally part of a peninsula ; but when the house was built, it was separated from the main land by a ditch or moat, over which there was a draw-bridge, and the approaches to this may still be seen. Of the house itself, little more than the moss-covered foundations remain. The stones, successively, of the Roman Castrum, of the Norman Tower, and of the lord's residence, are said to have been subsequently used in building the town-hall of Keswick.

The estate of the Derwentwater family seems to have
originally extended along the shores of the lake for nearly two
miles, and for a mile eastward of the shore. On one side of it lies
the present road from Keswick to Ambleside, on the other
its boundary approached Lodore, whilst the crest of Walla
Crag, divided it from the common. There, surrounded by a
combination of grandeur and beauty which is almost unrivalled
in this country, the Knightly ancestors of James Radcliffe, the
third and last Earl of Derwentwater, whose virtues and whose
fate have encircled his name with traditional veneration, had
their paternal seat.

This chivalrous and amiable young nobleman was closely
allied by blood to the Prince Edward, afterwards called "the
Pretender," in whose cause he fell a sacrifice ; his mother, the
Lady Mary Tudor, a natural daughter of King Charles II.
and Mrs. Davis, being first cousin to the Prince. He was
nearly the same age as the Prince, being one year younger :
and in his early childhood was taken to France to be educated,
when James the Second and his consort were living in exile
at St. Germain's, surrounded, however, by the noble English,
Scottish, and Irish emigrant royalists, who followed the for-
tunes of their dethroned monarch. The sympathies of his
parents having also led them thither, the youthful heir of
Derwentwater was brought up with the little Prince, at St.
Germain's, sharing his infantine pleasures and pastimes, and
occasionally joining his studies under his governess the
Countess of Powis. A friendship thus formed in youth,
nurtured by consanguinity, strengthened by ripening age, and
cemented by the extraordinary good qualities of the young
nobleman, and his power to win affection and esteem, culmi-
nated in that attachment and devotion to the cause of his
Prince and friend, which terminated only with his life.

The Earl appears to have visited Dilston, his ancestral home
in Northumberland, for the first time in 1710, when he was
in his twenty-first year ; and in the spring of the same year he
spent some time on the Isle of Derwent, where the ancient
mansion of the Radcliffes was then standing. During a con-
siderable portion of the two next succeeding years, his chief
residence appears to have been at Dilston, where he lived in
the constant exercise of hospitality, and in the practice of active
benevolence towards not only the peasantry on his wide
estates, but all who needed his assistance, whether known to
him or not, and whether Papist or Protestant. He seems to
have taken great delight in rural pursuits, and in the pleasures

of the chase, and in the charms of nature by which he was surrounded.

On the 10th of July 1712, when he had completed his 23rd year, he espoused Anna Maria, eldest daughter of Sir John Webb, of Canford, in the county of Dorset, Bart. His acquaintance with this charming young lady began in the early springtime of their lives, when both were receiving their education in the French capital. The lady had been placed in the convent of Ursuline Nuns in Paris for instruction : and they had frequent opportunities of seeing each other at the Chateau of St. Germain's, where the exiled monarch took pleasure in being surrounded by the scions of his noble English and Scottish adherents, who were then living at Paris.

On the rising of the adherents of the house of Stuart under the Earl of Mar in August 1715, it was very well known to the government, that the Earl's religion, his affections, and sympathies, were all on the side of the exiled heir of that family, and that his influence in the north of England was not less than his constancy and devotion. A warrant was issued for the apprehension of the Earl and his brother, the government hoping by thus, as it were, gaining the move in the game, to prevent the exercise of the Earl's influence against King George. A friendly warning of the attentions which were being paid to him at Whitehall reached the Earl in time ; and on hearing that the government messengers had arrived at Durham, on their way to arrest him and his brother, they withdrew from their home, and proceeded to the house of Sir Marmaduke Constable, where they stayed some days. The Earl afterwards took refuge in the home of a humble cottager near Newbiggin House, where he lay hidden some time. He remained in concealment through the latter part of August, and the whole of September. During this time of anxiety and surveillance, all the money, and even all the jewels of the Countess, are said by local tradition to have become exhausted : and to such straits was she reduced, that a silver medal of Pope Clement XI. struck in the 14th year of his Pontificate (1713), for want of money is said to have been given by her, when encompassed by the Earl's enemies, to a peasant girl, for selling poultry, or rendering some such trifling service.

Early in October it was represented to the Earl that the adherents of the exiled Prince were ready to appear in arms, and to be only waiting for him and his brother to join them. It would appear that at this critical moment, the Earl, influenced by many considerations, personal and domestic, as well as prudential, wavered in his resolution ; and tradition avers that, on stealthily revisiting Dilston Hall, his Countess reproached him for continuing to hide his head in hovels from the light of day, when the gentry were in arms, for their rightful sovereign ; and throwing down her fan before her lord, told him in cruel raillery to take it, and give his sword to her. Something of this feeling is attributed to her in the old ballad poem entitled "Lord Derwentwater's Farewell," wherein the following lines are put into his mouth :—

> "Farewell, farewell, my lady dear :
> Ill, ill thou counselled'st me :
> I never more may see the babe
> That smiles upon thy knee."

The popular notion that the Earl was driven into his fatal enterprise by the persuasions of his lady is evidently here referred to. But the amiable and gentle character of the Countess, that affectionate and devoted wife, whom the Earl in his latest moments declared to be all tenderness and virtue, and to have loved him constantly, is a sufficient refutation of the popular opinion, which does so much injustice to her memory. Nevertheless there is historical reason for believing that the Earl did suddenly decide on joining the Prince's friends, who were then in arms ; and his lady's persuasions may have contributed to that fatal precipitation. On the 6th of October, the little force of horse and men, consisting of his own domestic levy, was assembled in the courtyard of his castle ; arms were supplied to them ; the Earl, his brother, and the company, crossed the Devil's Water at Nunsburgh Ford ; and the fatal step was irrevocably taken. Old ladies of the last century used to tell of occurrences of evil omen which marked the departure of the devoted young nobleman from the home of his fathers, to which he was destined never to return ; how on quitting the courtyard, his favourite dog howled lamentably ; how his horse, the well-known white or dapple gray, associated with his figure in history and poetry, became restive, and could with difficulty be urged forward ; and how he soon afterwards found that he had lost from his finger a highly prized ring, the gift of his revered grandmother, which he constantly wore.

It is not necessary to dwell upon the details of this unfortunate and ill-conducted enterprise, in the course of which James III. was proclaimed in town and village, in Warkworth and Alnwick, in Penrith and Appleby, Kendal and Lancaster, to the final catastrophe of the little band at Preston.   There, hemmed in by the government troops, the brave and devoted friends of the royal exiles, who had been led into this premature effort contrary to their better judgments, and went forth with a determined loyalty which good or bad report could not subdue, saw reason to regret, when too late, their misplaced confidence in their leaders.   Already they saw themselves about to be sacrificed to the divided counsels of their comrades and the incapacity of Foster, their general.   Defensive means imperfectly planned, and hastily carried out, enabled them to hold the approaches to the town for three or four days against the Brunswickers, whom they gallantly repulsed, in a determined attack upon their barricades.   But overmatched by disciplined troops ; out-generalled, and out-numbered ; and finding resistance to be unavailing ; on the morning of Monday the 14th of October they surrendered at discretion to the forces sent to oppose them.   Being assembled in the market place to the number of 1700, they delivered up their arms, and became prisoners.   The young Earl was sent to London, which he reached on the 9th of December, and was conducted to the Tower on the capital charge of high treason.   Unavailing efforts were made by his wife and friends to save him. It appears that on the 20th of February his life was offered to him by two noblemen who came to him in the tower, in the name of the King, if he would acknowledge the title of George I. and conform to the Protestant religion : but these terms were refused by him.   The offer of his life and fortune was repeated on the scaffold, but he answered that the terms "would be too dear a purchase."   The means proposed to him, he looked upon as "inconsistent with honour and conscience, and therefore I rejected them."   He went to the block with firmness and composure : and his behaviour was resolute and sedate.   In an address which he delivered on the scaffold, he said "If that Prince who now governs had given me my life, I should have thought myself obliged never more to have taken up arms against him."   And the axe closed, by a "violent and 'vengeful infliction," the brief career of the beloved, devoted, and generous Earl of Derwentwater.   He was twenty-seven years of age.

Lady Derwentwater, who had been unceasing in her efforts to save her husband, and solaced him in his confinement by her society and tender care, after his death succeeded eventually in having his last request in the Tower fulfilled.   She had his body borne to its last resting place in the peaceful chapel at Dilston to be interred with his ancestors. She made a short sojourn at Dilston before leaving it for ever ; and then repaired with her little son and daughter to Canford, under the roof of her parents.

Before leaving the North, the Countess visited the house and estates at Derwentwater ; and while there her life seems to have been in some danger ; for the rude peasantry of the neighbourhood, to whom her southern birth and foreign education, as well as the principles and attachments in which she was brought up, were doubtless uncongenial, blamed her, in the unreasoning vehemence of their grief, for the tragic fate of their beloved lord and benefactor. Accordingly, not far from the fall of Lodore, a hollow in the wild heights of Walla Crag is pointed out by the name of Lady's Rake,* in which the noble widow is said to have escaped from their vengeance. Her misfortunes needed not to be thus undeservedly augmented. A more pleasing version of the story of her flight is, that the Countess escaped through the Lady's Rake with the family jewels, when the officers of the crown took possession of the mansion on Lord's Island. No doubt this loving woman did her utmost for the release of her lord. And this steep and dangerous way has a human interest associated with it which has given a special hold upon the hearts of the Keswick people. In old times a large white stone in among the boulders used to be pointed out as the Lady's Pockethandkerchief, and that it still hung among the crags, where no one could get at it.

In June, 1716, the Countess was living at Kensington Gravel Pits, near London : whence she soon afterwards went to Hatherhope ; and subsequently made a brief sojourn under the roof of her parents at Canford Manor ; after which she took up her residence at Louvaine. Here she died on the 30th of August, 1723, at the early age of thirty ; having survived her noble husband little more than seven years ; and was interred there in the Church of the English regular Canonesses of St. Augustine.

The white or gray horse of the Earl is historical. Shortly

---

* This hollow, in the summit of Walla Crag, is visible from the road below. Rake, the term applied in this country to openings in the hills like this, is an old Norse word, signifying a journey or excursion. It is now commonly applied to the scene of an excursion as the Lady's Rake in Walla Crag, and the Scot's Rake at the head of Troutbeck, by which a band of Scottish marauders is said to have descended upon the vale.

before the rising, and when he was in danger of apprehension, the following short note was written by him :—

"Dilston, July 27th, 1715.

"Mr. Hunter,

"As I know nobody is more ready to serve a friend than yourself, I desire the favour you will keep my gray horse for me, till we see what will be done relating to horses. I believe they will be troublesome, for it is said the D. of Ormond is gone from his house. God send us peace and good neighbourhood,—unknown blessings since I was born. Pray ride my horse about the fields, or any where you think he will not be known, and you will oblige, Sir, your humble servant,

"DARWENTWATER."

"He is at grass."

In the first sentence the reference is made to the jealous penal regulation, which forbade a Roman Catholic to possess a noble animal of height and qualities suited to military equipment.

From tradition preserved in the family of Mr. Hunter of Medomsley, the person addressed, there is every reason to believe that the gray horse mentioned in the above letter, was the identical steed which was brought by the son of Mr. Hunter to Bywell, and taken thence by Lord Derwentwater's servant to Hexham for his lordship's use; and upon which the devoted Earl rode from Hexham, with the gallant champions of the Prince's right, on the 19th of October following.

A man named Cuthbert Swinburn, then 90 years of age, who was born at Upper Dilston, and whose family resided there for some generations, related to a correspondent of W. S. Gibson, Esq., the author of Memoirs of the Earl of Derwentwater, that he remembered the young Earl, and saw him pass their house riding on a white horse, and accompanied by several retainers, on the morning when he joined his neighbours in the Prince's cause.

In a ballad relating to that fatal expedition it is said—

"Lord Derwentwater rode away
Well mounted on his dapple gray."

And in the touching verses well known as "Derwentwater's Farewell," his "own gray steed" is one of the earthly objects of his regard to which he is supposed to bid adieu.

Of the house on Lord's Island, itself, only some low walls now remain. A few relics of the mansion are preserved in the neighbourhood. The ponderous lock and key of the outer door, the former weighing eleven pounds, are preserved in Crosthwaite's museum. The door itself, which was of oak studded with knobs and rivets, was sold to a person named Wilson, of Under Mozzer, a place thirteen miles from Keswick. A bell, probably the dinner bell of the mansion, is in the town hall of Keswick, and is of fine tone. A fine old carved chair is preserved in the Radcliffe Room at Corby Castle, and known as " My Lady's Chair." In Crosthwaite's museum is preserved another ancient one of oak, which came from Lord Derwentwater's house, and has the Radcliffe arms carved upon it. And a stately and most elaborately carved oak bedstead which belonged to Lord Derwentwater was purchased at the sale of the contents of his house on Lord's Island, by an ancestor of Mr. Wood, of Cockermouth, in whose family it has remained, highly valued, ever since 1716.

Many articles of furniture, some family portraits, and other property, that once belonged to Dilston Hall, still linger in the vicinity of that place, where they are greatly treasured.

The Northumbrian and Cumbrian peasantry believed that miraculous appearances marked the fatal day on which the Earl of Derwentwater was beheaded. It was affirmed that the "Divel's Water" acquired a crimson hue, as if his fair domains were sprinkled with the blood of their gallant possessor ; and that at night the sky glowed ominously with ensanguined streams. "The red streamers of the north" are recorded to have been seen for the first time in that part of England, on the night of the fatal 24th of February, 1716 ; and in the meteor's fiery hue, the astonished spectators beheld a dreadful omen of the vengeance of heaven. The phenomenon has ever since been known as "Lord Derwentwater's Lights." On the 18th of October, 1848, a magnificent and very remarkable display of aurora borealis was witnessed in the northern counties. The crimson streamers rose and spread from the horizon in the form of an expanded fan, and the peasantry in Cumberland and elsewhere said at the time, that nothing like that display had been seen since the appearance of "Lord Derwentwater's Lights," in February, 1716, which may therefore be presumed to have been of a crimson or rosy hue.

THE LAURELS ON LINGMOOR.

High over Langdale, vale and hill,
   The swans had winged their annual way ;
By Brathay pools and Dungeon-Ghyll
   The lambs as now were wild at play ;
The mighty monarchs of the vale,
   Twins in their grandeur, towered on high ;
And brawling brooks to many a tale
   Of lowly life and love went by.

There cheerful on the lonely wild
   One happy bower through shine and storm,
Amidst the mountains round it piled,
   Preserved its hearth-stone bright and warm ;
Where now a mother and her boy
   Stood parting in one fond embrace ;
The shadow of their faded joy,   .
   Between them, darkening either face.

" I'll think, when that great city's folds
   Enclose me like a restless sea,
Of all this northern valley holds
   In its warm cottage walls for me.

I'll think amidst its ceaseless roar,
  Within these little bounds how blest
Was here our life, and long the more
  For that far-off return and rest."—

Forth sped the youth : the valley closed
  Behind him : adamantine hills,
Like giants round the gates reposed
  Of his lost Eden, frowned ; the rills
With fainter murmurs far away
  Died in the distance ; and at length
He stood amidst the proud array
  Of London in his youth and strength.

He came when mid the moving life
  The Terror and the Plague went by.
He walked where Panic fled the strife
  Of Strength with Death the Shadow nigh.
The shaft that flew unseen by night,
  The deadly plague-breath, striking down
Thousands on thousands in its flight,
  Made soon the widow's boy its own.

Ah ! woe for her ! in that far vale
  The sorrow reached her ; for there came
Dread tidings and the mournful tale,
  Dear relics and the fatal Name.
All in the brightness of the noon
  She bent above those relics dear ;
And ere the glimmering of the moon
  The Shadow from his side was near.

And forth from out her home there stalked
  The Terror with the name so dread ;
It pass'd the dalesman as he walked ;
  It dogg'd the lonely shepherd's tread ;
It breathed into the farms ; it smote
  The homesteads on the loneliest moor ;
And shuddering Nature cowered remote ;
  All fled the plague-struck widow's door.

Alone, in all the vale profound :
  Alone, on Lingmoor's mosses wide :
Alone, with all the hills around
  From Langdale head to Loughrigg's side ;
Alone, beneath the cloud of night,
  The morning's mist, the evening's ray ;
The hearthstone cold, and quenched its light ;
  The Shadow wrestled with its prey.

And day by day, while went and came
  The sunlight in the cheerless vale,
Her hearth no more its wonted flame
  Renewed, the opening morns to hail :
Glow'd not, though beating blasts and rain
  Drove in beneath her mournful eaves,
Through Springs that brought the buds again,
  And Autumns strew'd with fading leaves.

No human foot its timorous falls
  Led near it, venturing to unfold
The scene within those mouldering walls,
  The mystery in that lonely hold.

Nor on that mountain side did morn
   Or noon show how, or where, for rest
That Earth to kindlier earth was borne—
   The kinless to the kindred breast.

Only the huntsman on the height,
   The herdsman on the mountain way,
Looked sometimes on the far-off site
   How desolate and lone it lay.
Till when the years had rolled, their eyes
   Saw wondering, where that home decay'd,
A little plot of green arise
   Contiguous to the ruined shade.

A little grove of half a score
   Of laurels, intertwining round
One nameless centre, blossomed o'er
   That homestead's desolated bound ;
And where their leaves hang green above—
   A lowly circling fence of stone
Sprang, reared by Powers that build to Love
   When man, too weak, forsakes his own.

And there where all lies wild and bare—
   Where mountains rise and waters flow,
From Langdale's summits high in air,
   To Brathay pools that sleep below—
A green that never fades, one grove
   Of brighest laurels rears its boughs ;
While o'er that home's foundations rove
   The wild cats, and the asses browse.

There, if the song birds come, their notes
    Are hushed, that nowhere else are still :
And when the winds pipe loud, and floats
    The mist-cloud down from Dungeon-Ghyll,
Again the cottage-eaves arise
    Within it, as of old, serene,—
Its lights shine forth, its smoke up flies,
    And fades the grove of laurels green.

But dimly falls the gleam of morn
    Around it ; on the ferns the shade
Of evening leaves a look forlorn
    That elsewhere Nature has not laid.
So, lonely on its height, so, drear,
    It stands, while seasons wax and fail,
Unchanged amid the changing year,
    The voiceless mystery of the vale.

NOTES TO "THE LAURELS ON LINGMOOR."

There seems to have been a long hereditary emulation among the inhabitants of these districts to raise their sons beyond the situation of their birth ; a laudable practice, but one which until recent times was clouded by a comparative neglect of their daughters, whose education at the best was very indifferent. Hence many of these youths have risen to be respectable merchants, whose early circumstances compelled them to toil for their daily bread, and to be educated in night schools taught during the winter by a village schoolmaster, a parish clerk, or some industrious mechanic. Dr. Todd states, that in his time it was reported that Sir Richard Whittington, knight, thrice Lord Mayor of London, was born of poor parents in the parish of Great Salkeld, in East Cumberland ; that he built the church and tower from the foundation ; and that he intended to present three large bells to the parish, which by some mischance stopped at Kirkby-Stephen on their way to Salkeld. And a similar tradition is yet current in the neighbourhood. Less apocryphal, perhaps, is the instance of Richard Bateman, a native of the township of Staveley, near Windermere ; who, being a clever lad, was sent by the inhabitants to London, and there by his diligence and industry raised himself from a very humble situation in his master's house to be a partner in his business, and amassed a considerable fortune. For some years he resided at Leghorn ; but his end was tragical. It is said, that in his voyage to England, the captain of the vessel in which he was sailing, poisoned him and seized the ship and cargo. The pretty little Chapel of Ings, in the vicinity where he was born, was erected at his expense, and the slabs of marble with which it is floored were sent by him from Leghorn. Hodgson states, that he gave twelve pounds a year to the Chapel, and a thousand pounds more to be applied in purchasing an estate, and building eight cottages in the Chapelry for the use of its poor.

In Westmorland and Cumberland, thanks to the piety and
local attachments of our ancestors, endowed, or, as they are
more commonly called, free, schools abound. Grammar
schools were established on the verge of, and even within, the
lake district, prior to the dissolution of monasteries. From
these institutions a host of learned and valuable men were
distributed over England ; many of them rose to great
eminence in the literary world ; and contributed to the
establishment of Schools in the villages where they were born.
Before the conclusion of the 17th century, seminaries of this
kind were commenced in every parish, and in almost every
considerable village ; and education to learned professions,
especially to the pulpit, continued the favourite method of the
yeomanry of bringing up their younger sons, till about the year
1760, when commerce became the high road to wealth, and
Greek and Latin began reluctantly, and by slow gradation, to
give way to an education consisting chiefly in reading, writing,
and arithmetic. Many of this new species of scholars were
annually taken into the employment of merchants and bankers
in London, and several of them into the Excise. The clergy-
man generally found preferment at a distance from home,
where he settled and died ; but the merchant brought his
riches and new manners and habits among his kindred.

The predilection for ancient literature and the learned pro-
fessions seems to have been a kind of instinctive propensity
among the people of these secluded vales. In the grammar
schools the discipline was severe, and the instruction imparted
was respectable. In addition to the endowment, the master's
industry was usually rewarded at Shrovetide with a gift in
money or provisions, proportioned to his desert, and the cir-
cumstances of the donor. This present was called Cock-penny,
a name derived from the master being obliged by ancient usage
and the "barring-out" rules, to give the boys a prize to
fight cocks for ; which cock-fighting was held either at
Shrovetide or Easter. Indeed this custom seems to have
originated in the care which was taken to instil into youth a
martial and enterprising spirit. This appears from the
founders, in many of the schools, having made half of the
master's salary to depend on the cock-pennies ; and if the
master refused to give the customary prize, the scholars with-
held the present. The vacations were at Christmas and
Pentecost, for about a fortnight ; and all red-letter days were
half-holidays. But between the former seasons the Barring-
out occurred ; which consisted in the boys taking possession

of the schoolroom early in the morning, and refusing the master admittance until he had signed certain rules for the regulation of the holidays, and a general pardon for all past offences, demanding a bondsman to the instrument. Then followed a feast and a day of idleness.

The youths of a neighbourhood, rich and poor, were all educated together; a circumstance which diffused and kept alive a plain familiarity of intercourse among all ranks of people, which inspired the lowest with independence of sentiment, and infused no insolent or unreal consequence into the wealthy. Thus it was no unusual thing for the yeoman and the shepherd to enliven their employments or festivities with recitations from the bucolics of Virgil, the idyls of Theocrites, or the wars of Troy. A story is told of the late Mr. John Gunson, a worthy miller, who formerly kept the Plough Inn, a small public-house near the Church at Ulpha. Two or three young fellows from a neighbouring town, or, as some say, a party of students from St. Bees School, being out on a holiday excursion, called at John's, and after regaling themselves with his ale, and indulging in a good deal of quizzing and banter at the landlord's expense, demanded their bill. John in his homely country dialect, said, "Nay, we niver mak' any bills here, ye hev so much to pay"—mentioning the sum. "O," replied one of the wags, "you cannot write : that is the cause of your excuse." John, who had quietly suffered them to proceed in their remarks, retired, and in a short time brought them in a bill written out in the Hebrew language, which it need scarcely be said quite puzzled them. He then sent them one in Greek, and afterwards in Latin, neither of which they could make out. They then begged that he would tell them in plain English what they had to pay. John laughed heartily at their ignorance, which on this occasion shone as conspicuous as their impertinence to their learned and unassuming host.

If such was the level upon which the yeomanry stood in an educational sense, their favourite plan of bringing up their younger sons to the learned professions, and especially the pulpit, may account for a saying which is almost proverbial in Cumberland, " Owt 'll mak' a parson !" meaning thereby that if one of their sons proved more stupid than another, the church was the proper destination for him.

In the more secluded valleys the scholars were taught in the church ; the curate, who was also schoolmaster, sitting within the communion rails, and using the table as a desk, while the children occupied the pews or the open space beside him.

In the parish register of the last named chapelry is a notice, that a youth who had quitted the valley, and died in one of the towns on the coast of Cumberland, had requested that his body should be brought and interred at the foot of the pillar by which he had been accustomed to sit while a school-boy.

Teachers of writing and arithmetic also wandered from village to village, being remunerated by a whittle gate. The churches and chapels have mostly a little school-house adjoining. In some places the school-house was a sort of antichapel to the place of worship, being under the same roof, an arrangement which was abandoned as irreverent. It continues however to this day in Borrowdale and some other chapelries.

Superstitious fears were sometimes entertained lest a boy should *learn too far.* It was usual to consider all school-masters as *wise men* or conjurors. Wise men were such as had spent their lives in the pursuit of science, and had *learned too much.* For conjuration was supposed to be a science which as naturally followed other parts of learning as compound addition followed simple addition. The wise man possessed wonderful power. He could recover stolen goods, either by fetching back the articles, showing the thief in a black mirror, or making him walk round the cross on a market day, with the stolen goods on his shoulders. The last, however, he could not do, if the culprit wore a piece of *green sod* upon his head. When any person applied to the wise man for information, it was necessary for him to reach home before midnight, as a storm was the certain consequence of the application, and the applicant ran great risk of being tormented by the devil all the way home. The wise men were supposed to have made a compact with the devil, that he was to serve them for a certain number of years, and then have them, body and soul, after death. They were compelled to give the devil some living animal whenever he called upon them, as a pledge that they intended to give themselves at last. Instances are recorded of boys, in the master's absence, having got to his books, and raised the devil. The difficulty was to lay him again. He must be kept employed, or have one of the boys for the trouble given to him. The broken flag through which he rose is no doubt shown to this day. Such superstitions are not so completely exploded in the country, but that many equally improbable tales are told and believed.

The old register-book of the parish of Penrith, which appears to have been commenced about the year 1599, contains some entries of an earlier date, which have been either copied from a former register, or inserted from memory. The following entries occur :—

"Liber Registerii de Penrith scriptus in anno dni 1599 anno regni regine Elizabethe 41.

Proper nots worth keeping as followethe.

Floden feild was in anno dni 15 . . .

Comotion in these north parts 1536.

St. George day dyd fall on good friday.

Queene Elizabethe begene her rainge 1558.

Plague was in Penrith and Kendal 1554.

Solloine Mose was in the yere . . . .

Rebellion in the North Partes by the two earls of Northumberland & Westmorland & leonard Dacres in the year of our lord god 1569 & the 9th day of November.

A sore plague was in London, notinghome Derbie & lincolne in the year 1593.

A sore plague in new castle, durrome & Dernton in the year of our lord god 1597.

A sore plague in Richmond Kendal Penrith Carliell Apulbie and other places in Westmorland and Cumberland in the year of our lord god 1598 of this plague there dyed at Kendal" —a few words more, now very indistinct, follow, and the remainder of the page is cut or torn off.

Several records of the ravages committed by the plague in Cumberland and Westmorland are preserved in the more populous parts. The following inscription on the wall in Penrith Church is singular :—

AD MDXCVIII

Ex gravi peste quæ regionibus hisce

incubuit, obierunt apud

Penrith 2260

Kendal 2500

Richmond 2200

Carlisle 1196

Posteri

Avertite vos et vivite

Ezek. 18th —— 32 ——

From the Register it appears that William Wallis was vicar at the time ; the following entries noting the beginning and end of the calamity are interesting :—

"1597. 22d of September, Andrew Hodgson, a foreigner, was buried."

"Here begonne the plague (God's punismet in Perith.)"

"All those that are noted with the ltre P. dyed of the infec-
tion ; and those noted with F. were buried on the Fell."

"December 13th, 1598, Here ended the visitation."

The fear of infection prevented the continuance of the usual
markets ; and places without the town were appointed for
purchasing the provisions brought by the country people.

The Church register in the neighbouring parish of Edenhall
takes notice of 42 persons dying in the same year, of the
plague, in that village.

Some centuries previous to this, in 1380, when the Scots
made an inroad into Cumberland, under the Earl of Douglas,
Penrith was suffering from a visitation of the same nature ;
they surprised the place at the time of a fair, and returned
with immense booty ; but they introduced into their country
the plague contracted in this town, which swept away one-
third of the inhabitants of Scotland.

It is not at all likely that these calamitous visitations were
confined to the towns and villages.   Although few traces may
be found of this frightful disease having invaded the more re-
mote and scattered population of the dales.   Records of
isolated cases might easily be lost in the course of ages ; and,
as mere memorials of domestic affliction, were not likely to be
preserved in families.   Yet tradition has its utterances where
purer history fails.   On the side of Lingmoor in Great Lang-
dale, a small stone-fenced enclosure, a few feet across, of green
and shining laurels, indicates a spot which the pestilence had
reached.   This bright circular patch of evergreens is very
conspicuous amid the ferns, from the heights on the opposite
side of the valley.   On a near approach, the foundations of
what appear to be the remains of an ancient dwelling may be
traced at a little distance from it.   Still more distant are the
ruins of one or two deserted cottages, where the sheep pasture
along the base of the mountain.   What has been gathered
from the dalespeople about the laurels, so singular in such a
spot, is, that in the time of the great plague in England a
woman and her son occupied a cottage near the place.   The
youth went from this remote district, in the spirit of enterprise,
to push his fortunes in London, was smitten by the pestilence,
and died.   After a time some clothes and other things belong-
ing to him were sent to his home among the hills, infected the
mother, and spread terror throughout the neighbourhood.
The woman having fallen a victim to the disease, so great was
the dread of the pestilence that the ordinary rites of burial
could not be obtained for her.   The body could not be borne

for interment in consecrated ground. It mouldered away, it is supposed, on the spot which to this day is marked by the little enclosure of evergreens, a memorial of the fearful visitation in the lonely dale.

One of the most pleasing characteristics of manners in secluded and thinly-peopled districts, is a sense of the degree in which human happiness and comfort are dependent on the contingency of neighbourhood. This is implied by a rhyming adage common here, "*Friends are far, when neighbours are nar*" (near). This mutual helpfulness is not confined to out-of-doors work; but is ready upon all occasions. Formerly, if a person became sick, especially the mistress of a family, it was usual for those of the neighbours who were more particularly connected with the party by amicable offices, to visit the house, carrying a present; this practice, which is by no means obsolete, is called *owning* the family, and is regarded as a pledge of a disposition to be otherwise serviceable in a time of disability and distress.

THE VALE OF SAINT JOHN.

The morn was fresh ; and ere we won
The famous Valley of Saint John,
For many a rood our thoughts had plann'd
The scenery of that magic land.
We pictured bowers where ladies fair
Had breathed of old enchanted air ;
Groves where Sir Knights had uttered vows
To Genii through the silvery boughs ;
Piles of the pride of ages gone
Cleft between night and morning's sun,
Or veiled by mighty Merlin's power ;
And her, too, Britain's peerless flower—
Her, chained in slumbering beauty fast
While generations rose and pass'd,
Gyneth 'mid the Wizard's dens,
King Arthur's child and Guendolen's !
So, led by many a wandering gleam
From youth and poetry's sweet dream,
We climbed the old created hills,
And cross'd the everlasting rills,
Which lay between us and the unwon
But glorious Valley of Saint John.

The morn was fresh, and bright the sun
Burst o'er the drowsy mountains dun.
·A moment's pause for strength renewed,
And we our pleasant march pursued.
Blythely we scaled the steep, surpass'd
By steeps each loftier than the last ;
O'er rocks and heaths and wilds we follow
The vapoury path from height to hollow ;
And through the winding vale below,
Where yellowing fields with plenty glow ;
And, scattered wide and far between,
Lay white-walled farms and orchards green ;
The hedge-rows with their verdure crowned
Hemming the little plots of ground ;
The happy kine for pastures lowing ;
The rivulets through the meadows flowing ;
The sunshine glittering on the slopes ;
The white lambs on the mountain tops ;
No vision and no gleam to call
Enchantment from her airy hall ;
But beauty through all seasons won '
From Nature and her parent sun,
There brightening as through ages gone,
Lay round us as our hearts sped on
To reach the Valley of Saint John.

The noon was past ; the sun's bright ray
Sloped slowly down his westering way
With mellower light ; the sobering gleams
Touched Glenderamakin's farthest streams ;

Flung all the richness of their charms
Round lonely Threlkeld's wastes and farms :
And high beyond fired with their glow
Blencathra's steep and lofty brow ;
When suddenly—as if by power
Of Magic wrought in that bright hour—
Shone out, with all the circumstance
And splendour of restored Romance,
Southwards afar behind us spread,
With its grey fortress at its head,
The Valley, spell-bound as of old,
In all its mingling green and gold ;
In all the glory of the time
When Uther's son was in his prime,
And chivalry ranged every clime ;
And peaceful as when Gyneth, kept
In Merlin's halls, beneath it slept.
There had we roamed the live-long day
Saint John's fair fields and winding way,
With hearts unconsciously beguiled
By witcheries and enchantment wild !
And not till steps that toiled no more
It's utmost bound had vanish'd o'er,
Knew youth's wild thought our hearts had won,
And thrid the Valley of Saint John.

NOTES TO "THE VALE OF SAINT JOHN."

Near the village of Threlkeld, the road from Keswick to Penrith, branching off on the right, discloses obliquely to the view, the Vale of St. John. The well known description of this beautiful dell by Mr. Hutchinson, who visited it in the year 1773, conferred upon it a reputation which was greatly increased when the genius of Scott made it the scene of his tale of enchantment "'The Bridal of Triermain." The interest which it derives from its traditional connection with the wiles of Merlin, whose magic fortress continues to attract and elude the gaze of the traveller, is well given in the words of the former writer.

" We now gained a view of the Vale of St. John's, a very narrow dell, hemmed in by mountains, through which a small brook makes many meanderings, washing little enclosures of grass ground, which stretch up the risings of the hills. In the widest part of the dale you are struck with the appearance of an ancient ruined castle, which seems to stand upon the summit of a little mount, the mountains around forming an amphitheatre. This massive bulwark shews a front of various towers, and makes an awful, rude, and Gothic appearance, with its lofty turrets and rugged battlements : we traced the galleries, the bending arches, the buttresses. The greatest antiquity stands characterized in its architecture ; the inhabitants near it assert it is an antidiluvian structure.

"'The traveller's curiosity is roused, and he prepares to make a nearer approach, when that curiosity is put upon the rack, by his being assured that, if he advances, certain genii, who govern the place, by virtue of their supernatural arts and necromancy will strip it of all its beauties, and by enchantment transform the magic walls. The vale seems adapted for the habitation of such beings ; its gloomy recesses and retirements look like the haunts of evil spirits. There was no delusion in the report ; we were soon convinced of its truth ; for this piece of antiquity, so venerable and noble in its aspect, as we drew near, changed its figure, and proved no other than a shaken massive pile of rocks, which stand in the midst of this little vale, disunited from the adjoining mountains, and have so much the real form and resemblance of a castle, that they bear the name of *The Castle Rocks of St. John's*."

The more familiar appellation of this rocky pile among the dalesmen is *Green Crag*. The approach into the valley from Threlkeld displays it in the most poetical point of view, and under some states of atmosphere it requires no stretch of the imagination to transform its grey perpendicular masses into an impregnable castle, whose walls and turrets waving with ivy and other parasitical plants, form the prison of the immortal Merlin.

Other atmospheric effects, which occasionally occur in this District, have been alluded to elsewhere in these notes ; as the aerial armies seen on Souter Fell, and the Helm Cloud and Bar, with their accompanying wind, generated upon Cross Fell.

Phenomena of a singular character, which may be ascribed to reflections from pure and still water in the lakes, have also attracted observation. Mr. Wordsworth has described two of which he was an eye-witness. "Walking by the side of Ulswater," says he, "upon a calm September morning, I saw deep within the bosom of the lake, a magnificent Castle, with towers and battlements ; nothing could be more distinct than the whole edifice ;—after gazing with delight upon it for some time, as upon a work of enchantment, I could not but regret that my previous knowledge of the place enabled me to account for the appearance. It was in fact the reflection of a pleasure house called Lyulph's Tower—the towers and battlements magnified and so much changed in shape as not to be immediately recognised. In the meanwhile, the pleasure house itself was altogether hidden from my view by a body of vapour stretching over it and along the hill-side on which it extends, but not so as to have intercepted its communication with the lake ; and hence this novel and most impressive object, which, if I had been a stranger to the spot, would, from its being inexplicable, have long detained the mind in a state of pleasing astonishment. Appearances of this kind, acting upon the credulity of early ages, may have given birth to, and favoured the belief in, stories of sub-aqueous palaces, gardens, and pleasure-grounds—the brilliant ornaments of Romance.

"With this inverted scene," he continues, "I will couple a

much more extra-ordinary phenomenon, which will shew how other elegant fancies may have had their origin, less in in-vention than in the actual process of nature.

"About eleven o'clock on the forenoon of a winter's day, coming suddenly, in company of a friend, into view of the Lake of Grasmere, we were alarmed by the sight of a newly created Island ; the transitory thought of the moment was, that it had been produced by an earthquake or some con-vulsion of nature. Recovering from the alarm, which was greater than the reader can possibly sympathize with, but which was shared to its full extent by my companion, we proceeded to examine the object before us. The elevation of this new island exceeded considerably that of the old one, its neighbour ; it was likewise larger in circumference, com-prehending a space of about five acres ; its surface rocky, speckled with snow, and sprinkled over with birch trees ; it was divided towards the south from the other island by a firth, and in like manner from the northern shore of the lake ; on the east and west it was separated from the shore by a much larger space of smooth water.

"Marvellous was the illusion ! comparing the new with the old Island, the surface of which is soft, green, and unvaried, I do not scruple to say that, as an object of sight, it was much the more distinct. ' How little faith,' we exclaimed, ' is due to one sense, unless its evidence be confirmed by some of its fellows ! What stranger could possibly be persuaded that this, which we know to be an unsubstantial mockery, is *really* so ; and that there exists only a single Island on this beautiful Lake?' At length the appearance underwent a gradual transmutation ; it lost its prominence and passed into a glimmering and dim *inversion*, and then totally disappeared ;— leaving behind it a clear open area of ice of the same dimen-sions. We now perceived that this bed of ice, which was thinly suffused with water, had produced the illusion, by reflecting and refracting (as persons skilled in optics would no doubt easily explain,) a rocky and woody section of the opposite mountain named Silver-how."

Southey describes a scene that he had witnessed on Derwent Lake, as "a sight more dreamy and wonderful than any scenery that fancy ever yet devised for Faery-land. We had walked down," he writes, "to the lake side, it was a delightful day, the sun shining, and a few white clouds hanging motion-less in the sky. The opposite shore of Derwentwater consists of one long mountain, which suddenly terminates in an arch,

thus ⌐, and through that opening you see a long valley
between mountains, and bounded by mountain beyond moun-
tain ; to the right of the arch the heights are more varied and
of greater elevation.   Now, as there was not a breath of air
stirring, the surface of the lake was so perfectly still, that it
became one great mirror, and all its waters disappeared ; the
whole line of shore was represented as vividly and steadily as
it existed in its actual being—the arch, the vale within, the
single houses far within the vale, the smoke from the chimneys,
the farthest hills, and the shadow and substance joined at their
bases so indivisibly, that you could make no separation even
in your judgment.   As I stood on the shore, heaven and the
clouds seemed lying under me ; I was looking down into the
sky, and the whole range of mountains, having the line of
summits under my feet, and another above me, seemed to be
suspended between the firmaments.   Shut your eyes and dream
of a scene so unnatural and so beautiful.   What I have said is
most strictly and scrupulously true ; but it was one of those
happy moments that can seldom occur, for the least breath
stirring would have shaken the whole vision, and at once
unrealised it.   I have before seen a partial appearance, but
never before did, and perhaps never again may, lose sight of
the lake entirely ; for it literally seemed like an abyss of sky
before me, not fog and clouds from a mountain, but the blue
heaven spotted with a few fleecy pillows of cloud, that looked
placed there for angels to rest upon them."

THE LUCK OF EDENHALL.

The martial Musgraves sheathed the sword,
    And held in peace sweet Edenhall.
For never that house or that house's lord
    May evil luck or mischance befal,
While their crystal chalice can soundly ring,
Or sparkle brim-full at St. Cuthbert's spring.

Rude warlike men were the race of old :
    And seldom with priest of holy rood
Or penance discoursed their knights so bold,
    Who won them the Forest of Inglewood.
For better lov'd they to grasp the spear,
Than beads to count or masses to hear.

There came a bright Lady from over the sea,
    Once to look on their youthful heir.
Saintly and like a spirit was she ;
    And sweetest words did her tongue declare ;
When filling a beautiful glass to the brim
At St. Cuthbert's Well, she gave it to him.

Radiant and rare—from her garment's hem
  To her shining forehead, all dazzling o'er,
As of crystal and gold and enamel the gem
  Of sparkling light from the fount she bore—
Her snow-white fingers unringed she spread
On the gallant young Musgrave's lordly head.

With his ruby lips he touch'd the glass,
  And quaff'd off the crystal draught within.
" From thee and from thine if ever shall pass
  The pledge of this hour, shall their doom begin.
Whenever that cup shall break or fall,   '
Farewell the luck of Edenhall ! "

While marvelling much at so fair a sight,
  And wooing a vision so sweet to stay,
Like a vanishing dream of the closing night
  Within the dark Forest she pass'd away ;
And left him musing, with senses dim,
On the gifts the bright chalice had brought to him.

He clasped it close, and he turn'd it o'er ;
  Within and without its form survey'd ;
Till the deeds and thoughts of his sires of yore
  Seem'd to him like rust on a goodly blade.
And the more the glass in his hands he turned,
The more for a nobler life he yearned.

And there on the verge of the Forest, where stood
  The Hall for ages, he vow'd to be
The servant of Him who died on the Rood,
  And lay in the Tomb of Arimathee ;
And to drink of that cup at the Holy Well.
So wrought within him the Lady's spell.

And down the twilight came on his thought ;
  And sleep fell on him beneath the trees ;
When an errand for water the butler brought
  To the spot, where around the slumberer's knees
The envious fairies, a glittering band,
Were loosing the cup from his slackening hand.

He scared them forth : and in fierce despite
  They mocked, and mowed, and sang in his ear,—
"See you yon horsemen along the height ?
  They had harried the Hall had'st thou not come
    near.
Whenever that cup shall break or fall,
Farewell the luck of Edenhall."

And the martial lords of Edenhall
  They kept their cup with enamel and gold
Where never the goblet could break or fall,
  Or fail its measure of luck to hold ;
That birth or bridal, beneath its sway,
Might never befal on an evil day ;

And land and lordship stretching wide,
  And honour and worship might still be theirs ;
As long as that cup, preserved with pride, ·
  Should be honoured and prized by Musgrave's
    heirs :
The goblet the Lady from over the wave
To their sire in the Forest of Inglewood gave.

It has sparkled high o'er the cradled babe :
  It has pledged the bride on her nuptial day :   ,
It has bless'd their lips at life's last ebb,
  With its sacred juice to cleanse the clay.
For the touch the bright Lady left on its brim
Can give light to the soul when all else is dim.

Long prosper the luck of that noble line.
  May never the Musgrave's name decay.
And to crown their board, when the goblets shine,
  May the crystal chalice be found alway !
For Whenever that cup shall break or fall,
Farewell the luck of Edenhall !

The curious ancient drinking glass, called the Luck of Edenhall, on the preservation of which, according to popular superstition, the prosperity of the Musgrave family depends, is well known from the humourous parody on the old ballad of Chevy Chase, commonly attributed to the Duke of Wharton, but in reality composed by Lloyd, one of his jovial companions, which begins,

" God prosper long from being broke
The Luck of Edenhall."

The Duke, after taking a draught, had nearly terminated "the Luck of Edenhall;" but fortunately the butler caught the cup in a napkin as it dropped from his grace's hands. It is understood that it is no longer subjected to such risks. It is now generally shown with a damask cloth securely held by the four corners beneath it, which for this purpose is deposited along with the vessel in a safe place where important family documents are preserved.

Not without good reason do the Musgraves look with superstitious regard to its careful preservation amongst them. The present generation could, it is said, tell of disasters following swift and sure upon its fall, in fulfilment of the omen embodied in the legend attached to it.

The vessel is of a green coloured glass of Venice manufacture of the 10th century, ornamented with foliage of different colours in enamel and gold ; it is about seven inches in height and about two in diameter at the base, from which it increases in width and terminates in a gradual curve at the brim where it measures about four inches. It is carefully preserved in a stamped leather case, ornamented with scrolls of vine leaves, and having on the top, in old English characters, the letters I. H. C. ; from which it seems probable that this vessel was originally designed for sacred uses. The covering is said to be of the time of Henry VI. or Edward IV. The glass is probably one of the oldest in England.

The tradition respecting this vessel is connected with the still current belief, that he who has courage to rush upon a fairy festival, and snatch from them their drinking cup or horn, shall find it prove to him a cornucopia of good fortune or plenty, if he can bear it safely across a running stream. The goblet still carefully preserved in Edenhall is supposed to have been seized at a banquet of the elves, by one of the ancient family of Musgrave ; or, as others say, the butler, going to fetch water from St. Cuthbert's Well, which is near the hall, surprised a company of fairies who were dancing on the green, near the spring, where they had left this vessel, which the butler seized, and on his refusal to restore it, they uttered the ominous words,—

" Whenever this cup shall break or fall,
Farewell the luck of Edenhall."

The name of the goblet was taken from the prophecy. There is no writing to shew how it came into the family, nor any record concerning it. Its history rests solely on the tradition. Dr. Todd supposes it to have been a chalice, when it was unsafe to have those sacred vessels made of costlier metals, on account of the predatory habits which prevailed on the borders. He also says, that the bishops of this diocese permitted not only the parochial or secular, but also the monastic or regular clergy, to celebrate the eucharist in chalices of that clear and transparent metal. The following was one of the canons made in the reign of king Athelstan :—*Sacer calix fusilis sit, non ligneus*—*Let the holy chalice be fusile, and not of wood, which might imbibe the consecrated wine.*

William of Newbridge relates how one of these drinking-vessels, called elfin goblets, came into the possession of King Henry the First. A country-man belonging to a village near his own birthplace, returning home late at night, and tipsy, from a visit to a friend in a neighbouring village, heard a sound of merriment and singing within a hill ; and peeping through an open door in the side of the hill, he saw a numerous company of both sexes feasting in a large and finely lighted hall. A cup being handed to him by one of the attendants, he took it, threw out the contents, and made off with his booty, pursued by the whole party of revellers, from whom he escaped by the speed of his mare, and reached his home in safety. The cup, which was of unknown material and of unusual form and colour was presented to the king.

At Muncaster Castle there is preserved an ancient glass

vessel of the basin form, about seven inches in diameter, ornamented with some white enamelled mouldings ; which, according to family tradition, was presented by King Henry VI. to Sir John Pennington, Knight, who was steadily attached to that unfortunate monarch, and whom he had the honour of entertaining at Muncaster Castle, in his flight from the Yorkists. In acknowledgment of the protection he had received, the King is said to have presented his host with this curious glass cup with a prayer that the family should ever prosper, and never want a male heir, so long as they preserved it unbroken : hence the cup was called "the luck of Muncaster." The Hall contains, among other family pictures, one representing "King Henry VI. giving to Sir John Pennington, on his leaving the Castle 1461, the luck of Muncaster."

It is probable that the king was here on two occasions ; the first being after the battle of Towton, in 1461, when accompanied by his queen and their young son, with the dukes of Exeter and Somerset, he fled with great precipitation into Scotland : the second, after the battle of Hexham, which was fought on the 15th of May, 1463. On his defeat at Hexham, some friends of the fugitive king took him under their protection, and conveyed him into Lancashire. During the period that he remained in concealment, which was about twelve months, the king visited Muncaster. On this occasion the royal visit appears to have been attended with very little of regal pomp or ceremony. Henry, having made his way into Cumberland, with only one companion arrived at Irton Hall soon after midnight ; but his quality being unknown, or the inmates afraid to receive him, he was denied admittance. He then passed over the mountains towards Muncaster, where he was accidentally met by some shepherds at three o'clock in the morning, and was conducted by them to Muncaster Castle. The spot where the meeting took place is still indicated by a tall steeple-like monument on an eminence at some distance from the castle.

The "luck of Burrell Green," at the house of Mr. Lamb, yeoman, in Great Salkeld, Cumberland, is less fragile in structure, is not less venerated for its traditional alliance with the fortunes of its possessors than the lordly cups of the Penningtons and Musgraves. It is an *ancient* brass dish resembling a shield, with an inscription round it, now nearly effaced. Like the celebrated glass of Edenhall, this too has its legend and couplet, the latter of which runs thus :—

" If this dish be sold or gi'en,
Farewell the luck of Burrell Green."

When Ranulph de Meschines had received the grant of Cumberland from William the Conqueror, he made a survey of the whole county, and gave to his followers all the frontiers bordering on Scotland and Northumberland, retaining to himself the central part between the east and west mountains, "a goodly great forest, full of woods, red deer and fallow, wild swine, and all manner of wild beasts." This Forest of Inglewood comprehends all that large and now fertile tract of country, extending westward from Carlisle to Westward, thence in a direct line through Castle Sowerby and Penrith to the confluence of the Eamont and the Eden, which latter river then forms its eastern boundary all the way northward to Carlisle, forming a sort of triangle, each side of which is more than twenty miles in length. The Duke of Devonshire, as lord of the Honour of Penrith, has now paramount authority over the manors of Inglewood Forest.

The Forest, or Swainmote, court, for the seigniory, is held yearly, on the feast of St. Barnabas the apostle (June 11.) in the parish of Hesket-in-the-Forest, in the open air, on the great north road to Carlisle; and the place is marked by a stone placed before an ancient thorn, called *Court-Thorn.* The tenants of more than twenty mesne manors attend here, from whom a jury for the whole district is empanelled and sworn; and Dr. Todd says, that the chamberlain of Carlisle was anciently foreman. Here are paid the annual dues to the lord of the forest, compositions for improvements, purprestures, agistments, and puture of the foresters.

Until the year 1823, there was an old oak on Wragmire Moss, well known as *the last tree of Inglewood Forest,* which had survived the blasts of 700 or 800 winters. This "time-honored" oak was remarkable, not only for the beauty of the wood, which was marked in a similar manner to satin-wood, but as being a boundary mark between the manors of the Duke of Devonshire and the Dean and Chapter of Carlisle, as also between the parishes of Hesket and St. Cuthbert's, Carlisle; and was noticed as such for upwards of 600 years. This oak, which had weathered so many hundred stormy winters was become considerably decayed in its trunk. It fell not, however, by the tempest or the axe, but from sheer old age on the 13th of June, 1823. It was an object of great interest, being the veritable last tree of Inglewood Forest: under whose spreading branches may have reposed victorious

Edward I., who is said to have killed 200 bucks in this ancient forest ; and, perhaps at a later period, "John de Corbrig, the poor hermit of Wragmire," has counted his beads beneath its shade.

On the same day on which this tree fell, Mr. Robert Bowman, who was born at Hayton, in 1705, died at Irthington, at the extraordinary age of 117 years and 8 months, retaining his faculties till about three months before his death. He lived very abstemiously, was never intoxicated but once in his life, and at the age of 111, used occasionally to assist his family at their harvest work. The last forty years of his life were spent at Irthington, and in his 109th year he walked to and from Carlisle, being 14 miles, in one day.

The most remarkable instance of longevity in a native of Cumberland is that of John Taylor, born at Garragill in the parish of Aldston moor. He went underground to work in the lead mines at eleven years of age. He was fourteen or fifteen at the time of the great solar eclipse, called in the North *mirk Monday*, which happened 29th of March, 1652. From that time till 1752, except for two years, during which he was employed in the mint at Edinburgh, he wrought in the mines at Aldston, at Blackhall in the Bishoprick of Durham, and in various parts of Scotland. His death happened sometime in the year 1772, in the neighbourhood of Moffat, near the Lead-hills mines, in which he had been employed several years. He worked in the mines till he was about 115. At the time of his decease he must have been 135 years of age.

The Rev George Braithwaite, who died, curate of St. Mary's Carlisle, in 1753, at the age of 110, is said to have been a member of the Cathedral, upwards of one hundred years, having first become connected with the establishment as a chorister.

In Cumberland the prevalence of longevity seems to be confined to no particular district : the parishes which border on the fells on the east side of the county, are rather more remarkable for longevity than those on the Western coast : but there is little difference except in the large-towns.

A list of remarkable instances of longevity, chiefly taken from the registers of burials in the several parishes in Cumberland, is given in Lyson's Magna Britannia. It embraces the period between 1664 and 1814 inclusive, and gives the date, name, parish, and age of each individual. In that space of 150 years, the list comprises 144 individuals ranging from 100 to 113 years of age. Seventy were males, seventy-four were females.

The number of persons in Cumberland who have reached from 90 to 99 years inclusive, since the ages have been noted in the parish registers is above 1120: of these about one fourth have attained or exceeded the age of 95 years.

HOB-THROSS.

Millom's bold lords and knights of old
Quaff'd their mead from cups of gold.
A lordly life was theirs, and free,
With revel and joust and minstrelsy.
Their fields were full, and their waters flow'd ;
On a hundred steeds their warriors rode :
And glorious still as their line began,
It broaden'd out as it onward ran.

Millom's proud courts had page and groom,
To serve in hall, to wait in room ;
Maid and squire in fair array :
But better than these, at close of day—
Better than groom or page in hall,
Than maid and squire, that came at a call,
Was the Goblin Fiend, that shunn'd their sight,
And wrought for the lords of Millom by night.

When sleepy maidens left their fires,
Hob-Thross forth from barns and byres
Came tumbling in, and stretching his form
Out over the hearthstone bright and warm,

11

He folded his stunted thumbs, to dream
For an idle hour ere he sipp'd his cream ;
Or smoothed his wrinkled visage to gaze
On his hairy length at the kindly blaze.

His snipp'd brown bowl of creamy store
Set nightly—nothing Hob wanted more.
He scoured, and delved, and groom'd, and churned ;
But favour or hire he scorned and spurned.
Leave him alone to will and to do,
Never were hand and heart so true.
Tempt him with gift, or lay out his hire—
Farewell Hob to farm and fire.

Blest the manor, and blest the lord,
That had Hob to work by field and board !
Blest the field, and blest the farm,
That Hob would keep from waste and harm !
Or ever a wish was fairly thought,
Hob was ready, and all was wrought ;
Was grain to be cut, or housed the corn,
All was finish'd 'twixt night and morn.

Millom's great lords rode round their land
With courteous speech and bounteous hand.
Hob-Thross too went forth to roam ;
Made every hearth in Millom his home.
He thresh'd the oats, he churn'd the cream,
He comb'd the manes of the stabled team,
And fodder'd them well with corn and hay,
When the lads were laggards at peep of day.

Millom's good lord said—" Nights are cool ;
Weave Hob a coat of the finest wool.
Service long he has tender'd free :
Of the finest wool his hood shall be."—
For his service good, in that ancient hold,
To them and to theirs for ages told,
They wove him a coat of the finest wool,
And a hood to wrap him when nights were cool.

It broke his peace, and he could not stay.
Hob took the clothes and went his way.
He wrapp'd him round and he felt him warm :
But his life at Millom lost all its charm.
Night and day there was heard a wail
In his ancient haunts, through wind and hail,—
" Hob has got a new coat and new hood,
And Hob no more will do any good."

Blight and change pass'd over the place.
Came to end that ancient race.
Millom's great lords were found alone
Stretch'd in chancels, carved in stone.
Gone to dust was all their power ;
Spiders wove in my lady's bower.
While Hob in his coat and hood of green
Went wooing by night the Elfin Queen.

Call him to field, or wish him in stall,
Hob-Thross answers no one's call.
The snipp'd brown bowls of cream in vain
On the hearths he loved are placed again.

The old and glorious days are flown.
Hob is too proud or lazy grown ;
Or he goes in his coat and his hood of green
By night a-wooing the Elfin Queen.

NOTES TO "HOB-THROSS."

The lords of Millom are connected with an ancient legend
of Egremont Castle, which is given elsewhere, and which
especially alludes to the horn and hatterell which they bore on
their helmets.   This crest is said to have been assumed in the
time of Henry I., on the occasion of the grant of this seignory
by the Lord of Egremont to Godard de Boyvill or Boisville,
whose descendants retained possession of the greater part of it
for about one hundred years when it became vested by marriage
in Sir John Hudleston, whose pedigree is alleged to be trace-
able for five generations before the Conquest.   In this family
it remained for about five hundred years, when, for failure of
male issue it was sold to Sir James Lowther, nearly a century
ago.   The names of the first possessors are now almost
forgotten in their own lands.   The castle is of great antiquity.
It is uncertain at what date it was originally built ; but it was
fortified and embattled by Sir John Hudleston, in 1335.   In
ancient times it was surrounded by a fine park, of which there
are some scanty remains on a ridge to the north.   The great
square tower is still habitable, though its old battlements are
gone.   The castle was invested during the parliamentary war,
and the old vicarage house was pulled down at the same time,
"lest the rebels should take refuge there."   There are traces
of the ancient moat still visible.   Between the broken pillars
of an old gateway, an avenue leads to the front of the ruin,
which, though not of great extent, presents a fine specimen of
the decayed pomp of early times.   The walls of the court yard
are all weather-stained and worn ; and, here and there, deli-
cate beds of moss have crept over them, year after year, so
long, that the moist old stones are now matted with hues of
great beauty.   The front of the castle is roofless, and some
parts of the massive walls are thickly clothed with ivy.   A
fine flight of worn steps leads up through the archway, to the
great tower, in the inner court.   Above the archway a stone
shield bears the decayed heraldries of the Hudleston family ;

and these arms appear, also, on a slab in the garden wall, and in other parts of the buildings.   The front entrance of the great tower, from the inner court, when open, shews within a fine old carved staircase, which leads one to suppose that the interior may retain many of its ancient characteristics.

The church is a venerable building, with its quaint little turret, containing two bells.   The edifice consists of a nave and chancel, a south aisle, and a modern porch on the same side.   The aisle was the burial place of the Hudlestons.   Here is an altar-tomb, ornamented with Gothic tracery and figures bearing shields of arms, on which recline the figures of a knight and his lady, in alabaster, very much mutilated.   The knight is in plate armour, his head resting on a helmet, and having a collar of S. S. ; the lady is dressed in a long gown and mantle, with a veil.   They appear to have originally been painted and gilt, but the greater part of the colouring has been rubbed off.   Near the altar-tomb are the very mutilated remains of a knight, carved in wood, apparently of the fourteenth century.   A few years ago there was a lion at his feet.   A mural marble tablet to the memory of the Hudleston family is on the wall of the aisle.

The lordship of Millom is the largest seignory within the barony of Egremont ; its ancient boundaries being described as the river Duddon on the east, the islands of Walney and Piel de Foudray on the south, the Irish Sea on the west, and the river Esk and the mountains Hardknot and Wrynose on the north.   It anciently enjoyed great privileges : it was a special jurisdiction into which the sheriff of the county could not enter : its lords had the power of life and death, and en-joyed *jura regalia* in the six parishes forming their seignory, namely, Millom, Bootle, Whicham, Whitbeck, Corney, and Waberthwaite.   Mr. Denton, writing in 1688, says that the gallows stood on a hill near the Castle, on which criminals had been executed within the memory of persons then living.   To commemorate the power anciently possessed by the lords of this seignory, a stone has recently been erected with this inscription—"Here the Lords of Millom exercised Jura Regalia."

This lordship still retains its own coroner.

.A small nunnery of Benedictines formerly existed within this seignory, at Lekely in Seaton, which lies westward from Bootle, near the sea.   The precise date of its foundation can-not be ascertained : but it appears to have taken place on or before the time of Henry Boyvill, the fourth lord of Millom,

who lived about the commencement of the thirteenth century ;
and who "gave lands in Leakly, now called Seaton, to the
nuns ;" and who in the deed of feofment of the manor of
Leakley made by the said Henry to Goynhild, his daughter,
on her marriage with Henry Fitz-William, excepts "the land
in Leakley which I gave to the holy nuns serving God and
Saint Mary in Leakley."

The nunnery was dedicated to St. Leonard ; and was so
poor that it could not sufficiently maintain the prioress and
nuns. Wherefore the Duke of Lancaster, afterwards Henry
IV., by his charter, in 1357, granted to them in aid the hos-
pital of St. Leonard, at Lancaster, with power to appoint the
chantry priest to officiate in the said hospital. At the dissolu-
tion the possessions of the priory were only of the annual value
of £12 12s. 6d. according to Dugdale, or £13 17s. 4d. by
Speed's valuation.

When at the suppression of Abbeys it came to the crown,
Henry VIII. gave the site and lands at Seaton to his servant
Sir Hugh Askew, and his heirs. This Knight was descended
from Thurston de Bosco, who lived in the days of King John
at a place then called the Aikskeugh, or Oakwood, near Mil-
lom, and afterwards at Graymains, near Muncaster ; and from
a poor estate was raised to great honour and preferment, by
his service to King Henry VIII. in his house and in the field.
Anne Askew, whose name stands so eminent in the annals of
martyrology, was one of his descendants.

There are few remains of the convent now left : some part
of the priory-chapel is still standing, particularly a fine window
with lancets, in the style of the thirteenth century. Seton-
Hall, formerly a part of the conventual buildings, and subse-
quently the residence of Sir Hugh Askew, is now occupied as
a farm house.

Of Seton and Sir Hugh Askew, we have the following
quaint story in Sandford's M.S. account of Cumberland :—

"Ffour miles southward stands Seaton, an estate of £500
per annum, sometimes a religious house, got by one Sir Hugo
Askew, yeoman of the sellar to Queen Catherine in Henry
Eight's time, and born in this contry. And when that Queen
was divorced from her husband, this yeoman was destitute.
And he applied for help to (the) Lo. Chamberlain for some
place or other in the King's service. The Lord Steward knew
him well, because he had helpt to a cup (of) wine ther before,
but told him he had no place for him but a charcoal carrier.
'Well' quoth this monsir Askew, 'help me in with one foot,

and let me gett in the other as I can.' And upon a great
holiday, the king looking out at some sports, Askew got a
courtier, a friend of his, to stand before the king ; and Askew
gott on his velvet cassock and his gold chine, and basket of
chercole on his back, and marched in the king's sight with it.
' O,' saith the king, ' now I like yonder fellow well, that dis-
dains not to do his dirty office in his dainty clothes : what is
he ?' Says his friend that stood by on purpose, ' It is Mr
Askew, that was yeoman of the sellar to the late Queen's
M^{tie}, and now glad of this poor place to keep him in your
ma$^{tie's}$ service, which he will not forsake for all the world.'
The king says, ' I had the best wine when he was i'th cellar.
He is a gallant wine-taster : let him have his place againe ;'
and after knighted him ; and he sold his place, and married
the daughter of Sir John Hudleston ; (and purchased* this
religious place of Seaton, nye wher he was borne, of an ancient
freehold family,) and settled this Seaton upon her, and she
afterwards married monsir Penengton, Lo : of Muncaster, and
had Mr. Joseph and a younger son with Penington, and gave
him this Seaton."

A brass plate on the south wall of the chancel of Bootle
Church, bears the effigies of a knight in armour, with the fol-
lowing inscription in old English characters, indicating his
tomb. " Here lieth Sir Hughe Askew, knyght. late of the
seller to Kynge Edward the VI. which Sir Hughe was made
knyght, at Musselborough felde, in ye yeare of our Lord,
1547, and died the second day of Marche, in the yere of our
Lord God, 1562."

Among the local spirits of Cumberland, whose existence is
believed in by the vulgar, is one named Hob-Thross, whom
the old gossips report to have been frequently seen in the
shape of a "Body aw ower rough," lying by the fire side at
midnight. He was one of the class of creatures called Brownies,
and according to popular superstition, had especially attached
himself to the family at Millom Castle. He was a solitary
being, meagre, flat-nosed, shaggy and wild in his appearance,
and resembled the " lubbar fiend," so admirably described
by Milton in L'Allegro. Gervase of Tilbury speaks of him
as one of the " dæmones, senile vultu, facie corrugata, statura
pusilli, dimidium pollicis non habentes." In the day time he
lurked in remote recesses of the old houses which he delighted
to haunt,; and, in the night, sedulously employed himself in
discharging any laborious task which he thought might be

* Qu. Had a graut of?

acceptable to the family, to whose service he had devoted himself. He loved to stretch himself by the kitchen fire when the menials had taken their departure. Before the glimpse of morn he would execute more work than could be done by a man in ten days. He did not drudge from the hope of recompense : on the contrary, so delicate was his attachment, that the offer of reward, but particularly of food, infallibly would occasion his disappearance for ever. He would receive, however, if placed for him in a *snipped pot*, a quart of cream, or a mess of milk-porridge. He had his regular range of farm houses ; and seems to have been a kind spirit, and willing to do any thing he was required to do. The servant girls would frequently put the cream in the churn, and say, "I wish Hob would churn that," and they always found it done. Hob's readiness to fulfil the wishes of his friends was sometimes productive of ludicrous incidents. One evening there was every prospect of rain next day, and a farmer had all his grain out. "I wish," said he, "I had that grain housed." Next morning Hob had housed every sheaf, but a fine stag which had helped him was lying dead at the barn door. The day however became extremely fine, and the farmer thought his grain would have been better in the field : "I wish," said he, "that Hob-Thross was in the mill-dam ;" next morning all the farmer's grain was in the mill-dam. Such were the tales which were constantly told of the Millom Brownie, and as constantly believed. He left the country at last, through the mistaken kindness of some one, who made him a coat and hood to keep him warm during the winter. He was heard at night singing at his favourite haunts for a while about his apparel, and "occupation gone," and at length left the country.

The Cumberland tradition affirms that those persons who on Fasting's-Even, as Shrove Tuesday is vulgarly called in the North of England, do not eat heartily, are crammed with barley chaff by Hob-Thross : and so careful are the villagers to set the goblin at defiance, that scarcely a single hind retires to rest without previously partaking of a hot supper.

Sir Walter Scott tells us that the last Brownie known in Ettrick Forest, resided in Bodsbeck, a wild and solitary spot, near the head of Moffat Water, where he exercised his functions undisturbed, till the scrupulous devotion of an old lady induced her *to hire him away*, as it was termed, by placing in his haunt a porringer of milk and a piece of money. After receiving this hint to depart, he was heard the whole night to howl and cry, "Farewell to bonnie Bodsbeck !" which he was compelled to abandon for ever.

THE ABBOT OF CALDER.

The Abbot of Calder rode out from his gate
To the town, saying, "Sorrow lies, early and late,
In this wretched wide world upon every degree;
And each child of the Church must have comfort
    from me!
So on palfrey I wend to Lord Lucy's strong hold:
For this life must press hard on these barons so
    bold."

The Abbot was welcome to Lucy's proud hall.
And he sat down with knights, and with ladies, and
    all,
High at feast, joyous-hearted, light, gallant, and fair:
Where to speak upon woe were but jesting with care.
So his palfrey re-mounting at evening, he troll'd,
" The world goes not ill with these barons so bold."

Ambling on by the forge, he drew up by the flame,
"Well, my son ! how is all with the children and
    dame ?
Toiling on !"—"Yes ! but, father, not badly we
    speed ;
We have health ; and for wealth, we lack nought
    that we need."
Then at least, thought the Monk, here no text I
    need urge,
For the world passes well with my friend at the forge !

Turning off by the stream at the foot of the hill,
All were busy, as bees in a hive, at the mill.
" Benedicite !" cried he to women and wives,
Where they sang at their labour as if for their lives,
All so fat, fair, and fruitful.   The Abbot jogg'd on,
Humming, "Sweet, too, is rest when the labour is
    done."

As he pass'd by the lane that leads up to the stile,
Pretty Lillie came down with her curtsey and smile,—
"Well, my daughter !" the Abbot said, chucking
    her chin ;
" How is Robin ?—or Reuben ? which—which is to
    win ?"
" —Thank you !—Robin," she said, as she blushed
    in her sleeve ;
While the Monk, spurring on, laughed a joyous
    "good eve !"

On the verge of the chase rode the falconer by :
With a song on his lip and a laugh in his eye,
All the day o'er the moors he had gallop'd, and now
He was off to the quintain-match over the brow ;
Then to crown with good cheer all the sports of the
  day.
And the Abbot sighed, " Springtime, and beautiful
  May ! "

And at length in the hollow he came, as he rode,
To the forester Robin's trim cottage abode.
And there stood the youth, ruddy, stalwart, and
  curled :—
"—Ha, Robin ! this looks not like strife with the
  world ! "—
" No !·and please you, good father, *she's* coming to-
  morrow ! "
"—Well ! a blessing on both of you !—keep you
  from sorrow."

So he reached his fair Abbey by Calder's sweet
  stream,
Well believing all troubles in life are a dream ;
Looked around on his park and his fertile domain,
With a thought to his cellars, a glance at his grain ;
While the stream through his meadow-lands rippled
  and purled ;
And exclaimed, " What a place is a sorrowful
  world ! "

And the Abbot of Calder that night o'er his bowl
Felt a peace passing speech in the depths of his soul.
And he dreamt mid the noise and the merry uproar
Of the brethren beneath—all his fasting was o'er ;
That earth's many woes had to darkness been driven ;
And the sweet woods of Calder were gardens in
    Heaven.

NOTES TO "THE ABBOT OF CALDER."

On the northern bank of the river Calder, in a deeply secluded vale, sheltered by majestic forest trees, which rise from the skirts of level and luxuriant meadows to the tops of the surrounding hills, stands the ruined Abbey and home of that little colony of Monks, who, with their Abbot Gerold at their head, were detached from the mother Abbey of Furness in 1134 to begin their fortunes under the auspices of Ranulph de Meschines (the second of the name) their powerful neighbour and founder. Here they contrived to live "in some discomfort and great poverty for four years, when an army of Scots under King David despoiled the lately begun Abbey and carried away all its possessions. Finding they could get no help elsewhere, the hapless thirteen resolved to return to the maternal monastery" for refuge. This happened about the third year of King Stephen.

The Abbot of Furness refused to receive Gerold and his companions, reproaching them with cowardice for abandoning their monastery, and alleging that it was rather the love of that ease and plenty which they expected in Furness, than the devastation of the Scottish army, that forced them from Calder. Some writers say that the Abbot of Furness insisted that Gerold should divest himself of his authority, and absolve the monks from their obedience to him, as a condition of their receiving any relief. This, Gerold and his companions refused to do, and turning their faces from Furness, they, with the remains of their broken fortune, which consisted of little more than some clothes and a few books, with one cart and eight oxen, taking providence for their guide, went in quest of better hospitality.

The result of the next day's resolution was to address themselves to Thurstan, Archbishop of York, and beg his advice and relief. The reception they met with from him, answered their wishes; the Archbishop graciously received them, and charitably entertained them for some time, then recommended them to Gundrede de Aubigny, who sent them to Robert de Alneto, her brother, a hermit, at Hode, in the East Riding of Yorkshire, where for a period she supplied them with necessaries. They afterwards obtained a monastery of their own called Byland, when they voluntarily made themselves dependant upon Savigny, in order that Furness should exercise no right of paternity over them.

In the same year, 1142, the Abbot of Furness understanding that Gerold had obtained a settlement, sent another colony, with Hardred, a Furness monk, for their Abbot, to take possession of ravaged Calder, which the Lord of Egremont, William Fitz-Duncan, nephew of David, King of Scots, had refounded. Their endowments and revenues were chiefly from the founder's munificence, and were small, being valued, at the suppression, at about sixty pounds per annum.

The ruins of this Abbey are approached from Calder-Bridge by a pleasant walk for about a mile on the banks of the river, presenting several glimpses of the tower rising out of the foliage of the forest trees by which it is surrounded.

The Abbey Church was in the form of a cross, and small, the width of the chancel being only twenty five feet, and that of the transepts twenty two. Of the western front little more than the Norman doorway remains. The five pointed arches of the north side of the nave, dividing it from the aisle ; the choir ; the transepts, with a side chapel on the south ; the square tower supported by four lofty pointed arches ; the walls and windows of a small cloister running south ; with the remains of upper chambers, showing a range of eight windows to the west and seven to the east, beautiful specimens of early English Architecture, terminated by a modern mansion, occupying the site of the conventual buildings, but built in a style altogether unsuited to the locality ; these, with the porter's lodge at a short distance from the west end, and a large oven by the side of a rapid stream in the meadow on the east, all so changed since the times of Gerold and Hardred, constitute in our days the Abbey of Calder.

Against the walls of the Abbey are fragments of various sepulchral figures, which from the mutilated sculptures and devices on the shields, would seem to have belonged to the tombs of eminent persons. One of them is represented in a coat of mail, with his hand upon his sword ; another bears a shield reversed, as a mark of disgrace for cowardice or treachery ; "but," says Hutchinson, "the virtues of the one, and the errors of the other, are alike given to oblivion by the hand of time and by the scourging angel Dissolution."

Sir John le Fleming, of Beckermet, ancestor of the Flemings of Rydal Hall, Westmorland, gave lands in Great Beckermet to this abbey, in the 26th year of Henry III, A. D. 1242. He died during that long reign, and was buried in the abbey. One of the effigies above alluded to, with the shield charged fretty, is probably that mentioned by Sir Daniel Fleming, who says that in his time (in the seventeenth century) here was "a very ancient statue of a man in armour, with a frett (of six pieces) upon his shield, lying upon his back, with his sword by his side, his hands elevated in a posture of prayer, and legs across ; being so placed probably from his taking upon him the cross, and being engaged in the holy war. Which statue was placed there most probably in memory of this Sir John le Fleming."

Among some ancient charters and documents in the possession of William John Charlton, of Hesleyside, Esq., (1830) and which came into his family, in 1680, by the marriage of his great-great-grandfather, with Mary, daughter of Francis Salkeld, in the parish of All-Hallows, in Cumberland, Esq., is one that is very curious. It is an assignment made in A. D. 1291, by John, son of John de Hudleston, of William, son of Richard de Loftscales, formerly his native, with all his retinue and chattels, to the Abbot and Monks of Caldra. The deed is witnessed by "Willmo. Wailburthuait. Willmo. Thuaites. Johe de Mordling. Johe Corbet. Johe de Halle et aliis :" and is alluded to in the following passages quoted by Mr. Jefferson from *Archælogia Æliana.* "It is, in fact, that species of grant of freedom to a slave, which is called manumission implied, in which the lord yields up all obligation to bondage, on condition of the native agreeing to an annual payment of money on a certain day. The clause, 'so that from this time they may be free, and exempt from all servitude and reproach of villainage from me and my heirs,' is very curious, especially to persons of our times, on which there has been so much said about the pomp of Eastern lords, and the reproachful slavery in which their dependents are still kept. Here the Monks of Caldra redeemed a man, his family, and property from slavery, on condition of his paying them the small sum of two pence a-year. The Hudleston family were seated at Millum, in the time of Henry the Third, when they acquired that estate, by the marriage of John de Hudleston with the Lady Joan, the heiress of the Boisville family."

"Slavery continued to thrive on the soil of Northumberland long after the time of Edward the First ; for in 1470, Sir Roger

Widdrington manumitted his native, William Atkinson, for the purpose of making him his bailiff of Woodhorn."

The inmates of Calder were probably neither better nor worse than other cowled fraternities. A certain Brother Beesley, a Benedictine Monk, of Pershore, in Worcestershire, speaks very boldly of certain shortcomings, in his own experience of "relygyus men." The following passage occurs in a petition addressed by him to the Vicar-General Cromwell, at the time of the visitation of the Monasteries :—

"Now y wyll ynstrux your grace sumwatt of relygyus men ——. Monckes drynke an bowll after collatyon tyll ten or twelve of the clok, and cum to matyns as dronck as myss (mice)—and sum at cardys, sum at dyes, and at tabulles ; sum cum to mattyns begenying at the mydes, and sum wen yt ys almost dun, and wold not cum there so only for boddly punyshment, nothyng for Goddes sayck."

THE ARMBOTH BANQUET.

To Calgarth Hall in the midnight cold
Two headless skeletons cross'd the fold,
Undid the bars, unlatched the door, .
And over the step pass'd down the floor
    Where the jolly round porter sat sleeping.

With a patter their feet on the pavement fall ;
And they traverse the stairs to that window'd wall,
Where out of a niche, at the witch-hour dark,
Each lifts a skull all grinning and stark,
    And fits it on with a creaking.

Then forth they go with a ghostly march ;
And bending low at the portal arch,
Through Calgarth woods, o'er Rydal braes,
And over the Pass by Dunmail-Raise
    The Two their course are keeping.

Now Wytheburn's lowly pile in sight
Gleams faintly beneath the new-moon's light;
And farther along dim forms appear,
All hurrying down to the darksome Mere,
  The drunken ferry-man seeking.

From old Helvellyn's domain they come,
A spectral band demure and dumb;
By twos, and threes, and fours, and more,
They beckon the man to ferry them o'er,
  To where yon lights are breaking.

And thither the twain are wending fast;
For there from many a casement cast,
The festal blaze is burning high
In Armboth Hall; the hills thereby
  In uttermost darkness sleeping.

In Wytheburn City there wakes not one
To see those dim forms hastening on;
But at Wytheburn Ferry may travellers wait,
For busy with guests for Armboth gate,
  The boatman's sinews are aching.

They've reached the shore, they've cross'd the sward
To where the old portal stands unbarr'd.
With courteous steps and bearing high
They pass the hollow-eyed porter by,
  With his torch high over him sweeping.

Then might the owls that move by night
Have seen thin shadows flit through the light,
Where the windows glared along the wall
In every chamber of Armboth Hall,
  And the guests high revel were keeping.

Then too from cold and weary ways
A traveller's eyes had caught the rays :
And wandering on to the silent door
He knocked aloud—he knew no more;
  But the lights went out like winking.

A wreath of mist rushed over the Mere,
And reached Helvellyn as dawn grew near ;
And two thin streaks went down the wind
O'er Dunmail-raise with a storm behind,
  The leaves in Grasmere raking.

On Rydal isles the herons awoke ;
A pattering cloud by Wansfell broke ;
And the grey cock stretched his neck to crow
In Calgarth roost, that ghosts might know
  It was time for maids to be waking.

The skeletons two rushed through the yard,
They pushed the door they left unbarr'd,
Laid by their skulls in the niched wall,
And flew like wind from Calgarth Hall
  Where still the round porter sat sleeping.

As out they rattled, the wind rushed in ·
And slamm'd the doors with a terrible din;
The grey cock crew; the dogs were raised;
And the old porter rubb'd his eyes amazed
 At the dawn so coldly breaking.

And lying at morn by Armboth gate
Was found the form that knocked so late;
A traveller footworn, mired, and grey,
Who, led by marsh lights lost his way,
 And coldly in death was sleeping.

NOTES TO "THE ARMBOTH BANQUET."

The Old Hall of Calgarth, whose history, it has been said, belongs to the world of shadows, but whose remains still form an object of interest from their picturesqueness and antiquity, - is situated within a short distance of the water, upon the narrowest part of a small and pleasant plain on the eastern shore of Windermere. The house has been so much injured and curtailed of its original proportions, that it is impossible to make out what has been its precise form : many parts having gone entirely to decay, and others being much out of repair ; the materials having been used in the erection of offices and out-buildings, for the accommodation of farmers, in whose occupation it has been for a long period. Its original character has been quite lost in the additions and alterations of later days. It is however said to have been constructed much after the style of those venerable Westmorland mansions, the Halls of Sizergh and Levens. But there are few traces of the "fair old building," which even so late as the year 1774, Dr. Burn described it to be ; and the destruction of this ancient home of the Philipsons has well nigh been complete. What is now called the kitchen, and the room over it, are the only portions of the interior remaining, from which a judgment may be formed of the care and finish that have been applied to its internal decoration. In the former, which appears to have been one of the principal apartments, though now divided, and appropriated to humble uses, the armorial achievements of the Philipsons, crested with the five ostrich plumes of their house, and surmounted by their motto, "Fide non fraude," together with the bearings of Wyvill impaling Carus, into which families the owners of Calgarth intermarried, are coarsely represented in stucco over the hearth, and still serve to connect their name with the house. The large old open fireplace has been filled up by an insignificant modern invention. The window still retains some fragments of its former display of heraldic honours; the arms of the early owners, impaling those of Wyvill, and the device of Briggs, another Westmorland family, with whom the Philipsons were also matrimonially connected, yet appear in their proper blazon. And in the same window, underneath the emblazonry, is this legend, likewise in painted glass :—

> Robart. Phillison.
> and. Jennet. Laibor
> ne. his. wife. he. die
> d. in. anno. 1539
> the. ZZ. Dece
> mbar 1579

The old dining table of black oak, reduced in its dimensions, occupies one side of this apartment. The room over the kitchen, to which a steep stair rises from the threshold of the porch, and which looks over the lake, has been nobly ornamented after the fashion of the day, by cunning artists, and it still retains in its dilapidated oak work, and richly adorned ceiling, choice, though rude remnants of its former splendour. It has a dark polished oak floor, and is wainscotted on three sides, with the same tough wood, which, bleached with age, is elaborately carved in regular intersecting panels, inlaid with scroll-work and tracery, enriched by pilasters, and surmounted by an embattled cornice. In this wainscot two or three doors indicate the entrances to other rooms, whose approaches are walled up, the rooms themselves having been long since destroyed. The ceiling is flat, and formed into compartments by heavy square intersecting moulded ribs, the intermediate spaces of which are excessively adorned with cumbrous ornamental work of the most grotesque figures and designs imaginable, amidst which festoons of flowers, fruits, and other products of the earth, mingled with heraldic achievements, moulded in stucco, yet exist, to tell how many times the fruitage and the leaves outside have come and gone, have ripened and decayed, whilst they endure unchanged.

In the window of the staircase leading to this chamber tradition has localized the famous legend of the skulls of Old Calgarth. The dilapidated, and somewhat melancholy appearance of the dwelling, in concurrence with the superstitious notions which have ever been common in country places, have probably given rise to a report, which has long prevailed, that the house is haunted. Many stories are current of the frightful visions and mischievous deeds, which the goblins of the place are said to have performed, to terrify and distress the harmless neighbourhood ; and these fables are not yet entirely disbelieved. Spectres yet are occasionally to be seen within its precincts. And the two human skulls, whose history and reputed properties are too singular not to have contributed greatly to the story of the house being haunted, are, although out of sight, still within it, and as indestructible as ever.

These were wont to occupy a niche beneath the window of the staircase : and in 1775, when Mr. West visited the Hall, they still remained in the place where they had lain from time immemorial. All attempts, it is said, to dispossess them of the station they had chosen to occupy, have invariably proved fruitless. As the report goes, they have been buried, burnt, reduced to powder and dispersed in the wind, sunk in the well, and thrown into the lake, several times, to no purpose as to their permanent removal or destruction. Till at length, so persistent was found to be their attachment to the niche which they had selected for their abiding place, they are said to have been, as a last resource to keep them out of sight, walled up within it ; and there they remain. Of course, many persons now living in the neighbourhood can bear testimony to the fact that the skulls did really occupy the place assigned to them by tradition.

A popular tale of immemorial standing relates that the skulls were those of an aged man and his wife, who lived on their own property adjoining the lands of the Philipsons, whose head regarded it with a covetous eye, and had long desired to number it among his extensive domains. ˙ The owners however not being willing to part with it, he determined in evil hour to have it at any cost.

The old people, as the story runs, were in the habit of going frequently to the Hall, to share in the viands which fell from the lord's table, for he was a bounteous man to the poor ; and it happened once that a pie was given to them, into which had been put some articles of plate. After their return home, the valuables were missed, and the cottage being searched, the things were found therein. The result was as the author of the mischief had plotted. They were accused of theft, tried, convicted, and sentenced to be executed, and their persecutor ultimately got their inheritance. When brought up for execution, the condemned persons requested the chaplain in attendance to read the 109th psalm ; for under their circumstances, there was an awful significance in the imprecatory verses, which denounced the conduct of evil doers like Philipson ;

and in the solemn malison prophesied against the cruel, they pronounced a curse upon the owners of Calgarth, which the gossips of the neighbourhood say has ever since cast its blight upon the proprietorship of the estate ; and that, notwithstanding whatever authentic records may prove to the contrary, the traditionary malediction has been regularly fulfilled down to the present time.   After the death of his victims, the oppressor was greatly tormented ; for, as if to perpetuate the memory of such injustice, and as a memento of their innocence, their skulls came and took up a position in the window of one of the rooms in the Hall, from whence they could not by any means be effectually removed, the common belief being that they were for that end indestructible, and it was stoutly asserted that to whatever place they were taken, or however used, they invariably reappeared in their old station by the window.

The property of Calgarth came by purchase into the possession of the late Dr. Watson, Lord Bishop of Llandaff, who built a mansion upon the estate, where he passed much of the later period of his life : and who lies buried in the neighbouring churchyard of Bowness.   The Bishop's grandson, Richard Luther Watson, Esquire, is the present possessor.

It is believed that anciently a burial ground was attached to the buildings of Old Calgarth ; as when the ground has been trenched thereabouts, quantities of human bones have frequently been turned over and re-buried.   There are now in the dairy of the Old Hall two flat tombstones, with the name of Phillipson inscribed upon them, which not very many years ago were dug up in the garden near the house ; their present use being a desecration quite in accordance with the associations which hang around the place.   This circumstance may afford a clue to the re-appearance of the skulls so frequently, after every art of destruction had been tried upon them, in the mysterious chambers of Old Calgarth Hall.

The old house at Armboth, on Thirlmere, has also the reputation of being occasionally at midnight supernaturally lighted up for the reception of spectres, which cross the lake from Helvellyn for some mysterious purpose within its walls. The long low white edifice lying close under the fells which rise abruptly behind it, with the black waters of the lake in front, has something very gloomy and weird-like about its aspect, which does not ill accord with those superstitious ideas with which it is sometimes associated.   As Miss Martineau has said, "there is really something remarkable, and like witchery, about the house.   On a bright moonlight night, the spectator who looks towards it from a distance of two or three miles, sees the light reflected from its windows into the lake ; and when a slight fog gives a reddish hue to the light, the whole might easily be taken for an illumination of a great mansion.   And this mansion seems to vanish as you approach,—being no mansion, but a small house lying in a nook, and overshadowed by a hill."

The City of Wytheburn is the name given to a few houses, some of them graced by native trees, and others by grotesquely cut yew trees, distant about half a mile from the head of Thirlmere.

BRITTA IN THE TEMPLE OF DRUIDS.

(THE LAST HUMAN SACRIFICE.)

Blencathra from his loftiest peak
Had often heard the victims' shriek,
    When lapp'd by wreathing fire,
Their limbs in wicker bondage caged,
Dying, the draught and plague assuaged,
    And calmed the Immortals' ire.

There came a Rumour,* strayed from far.
Helvellyn's bale-fire paled its star :
    Hoarse Glenderaterra moaned.
The dark destroying angel fled :
And from Blencathra's topmost head
    Old demons shrunk dethroned.

* Birth of Christ.

He saw beneath his rugged brow
The temple on the plain below,
     · By sacred Druids trod :
Mountains on mountains piled around ;
Forests of oak with acorns crowned :
     And distant, man's abode.

Where men had hewn by stream and dell
An opening in the woods to dwell,
     The pestilence by night
Had fallen amidst their little throng ;
Had changed, and stricken down the strong ;
     And put the weak to flight.

· Who may the angry god appease ?—
The oracle that all things sees,
     And knows all laws divine,
Spake from the awful forest bower—
"A maiden in her virgin flower
     "Must her young life resign."—

Fallen is the lot on thee, so late
Betrothed to love, and now to fate,
     Sweet Britta !—Forth she fares,
Led by the Druids to her doom,
Within that circle's ample room,
     · For which the rite prepares.

Fire cleanses : she must cleanse by fire.
With oaken garland, white attire,
 Bearing the mistletoe,
Beside the wicker hut her feet
Pause—till her eyes her lover greet,
 And cheer him as they go.

These two had heard of what had been
In Judah—of the Nazarene—
 And talked of new things born
To them, that in their fathers' place
They might not speak of to their race,
 But thought on eve and morn.

Now when the sound is given to pile
The branches each one—friends-erewhile,
 Strangers, yea sisters, sire,
And brethren—all from far and near,—
Must furnish for the victim's bier ;
 His they in vain require.

No might of Druid, lord, or king,
Could move that hand one leaf to bring—
 No, though they throng to slay.
Calmly beyond the crowd he stood,
Holding on high two staves of wood
 Cross'd—till she turned away.

Then hoary Chief, Arch Druid, came
Thy hands to minister the flame,
    Wrought from the quick-rubb'd pine.
It touch'd : it leapt : the branches blazed !
When to the hills they looked amazed,
    And owned the wrath divine.

Bellowed the mountains, and cast forth
Their waters, east, south, west, and north.
    Rivers and mighty streams
Down from their raging sides out-poured
Their cataracts, and in thunders roared
    Along earth's opening seams.

They rolled o'er all the temple's bound,
Quenching the angry fire around
    The hut unscathed by flame :
Then backward to their source retired.
While like a seraph's form inspired
    The white-robed maiden came.

Upon her fair head garlanded
No brightest leaflet withered—
    No berry from her hand
Dropt, of the branching mistletoe—
With crossing palms and paces slow
    She mov'd across the land.

Then loud the hoary Druid cried,
"The god we serve is satisfied !
    His are the unbidden powers.
A human sacrifice no more
He needs, our dwellings to restore,
    And devastated bowers.

For thee, a maiden fair and pure,
Thou hast a treasure made secure
    In heaven : depart in peace.
Earth's voices witness of a faith
In thee serene and sure, that saith
    Here we too soon must cease."

'

NOTES TO "BRITTA IN THE TEMPLE OF THE DRUIDS."

Traces of the Celts are clearly distinguishable in the names of some of the more prominent mountains within a few miles of Keswick, Skiddaw, Blencathra, Glaramara, Cat-Bells, Helvellyn. The first is derived from the name of the solar god, Ska-da, one of the appellations of the chief deity of Celtic Britain, to whom Skiddaw was consecrated. The second has been supposed to be a corruption of blen-y-cathern, the "peak of witches." ; the fourth to signify "the groves of Baal"; and the last El-Velin, "the hill of Baal or Veli." The worship of the Assyrian deity was celebrated amongst the Celtic inhabitants of our island with the greatest importance and solemnity. The stone circles are still remaining in many places where the bloody sacrifices to his honour were performed : and one of the most important of these is near Keswick. In the immediate vicinity is also a gloomy valley, Glenderaterra, the name of which is sufficiently indicative of the purpose for which, like Tophet of old, it was ordained ; Glyn-dera taran signifying in Celtic, "the valley of the angel or demon of execution."

It is a curious fact that till the last few years, a trace also of the ancient worship still lingered around two temples in this county, where it was once habitually performed. Both at Keswick, and at Cumwhitton where there is a similar druidical circle, the festival of the Beltein, or the fire of Baal, was till very recently celebrated on the first of May. As the Jews had by their "prophets of the groves," made their children "pass through the fire to Baal"; so the Britons, taught by their Druids, were accustomed once a year to drive their flocks and herds through the fire, to preserve them from evil during the remainder of the year. Indeed the custom still prevails. If the cows are distempered, it is actually a practice in many of the dales to light "the Need-fire"; notice being given throughout the neighbouring valleys, that the charm may be sent for if wanted. "Need-fire" is said to mean cattle-fire, and to be derived from the Danish *nod*, whence also is the northern word nolt or nowte. The Need-fire is produced by rubbing two sticks together. A great pile of combustible stuff is prepared, to give as much smoke as possible. When lighted, the neighbours snatch some of the fire, hurry home with it, and light their respective piles; and the cattle, diseased and sound, are then driven through the flame. Mr. Gibson says, that in 1841, when the cattle-murrain prevailed in Cumberland, he had many opportunities of witnessing the application of this charm to animals both diseased and sound. And he tells us, that to ensure its efficacy it was necessary to observe certain conditions. The fire had to be produced at first by friction, the domestic fires in the neighbourhood being all previously extinguished; then it had to be brought spontaneously to each farm by some neighbour unsolicited : and neither the fire so brought, nor any part of the fuel used, must ever have been under a roof. These conditions being observed, a great fire was made, and the cattle driven to and fro in the smoke. ·One honest farmer who had an ailing wife and delicate ·children passed *them* through this ordeal, as was averred with most beneficial effect. Another inadvertently carried the fire just brought to him into his house to save it from extinction by a sudden shower : and it was declared that in his case the need-fire would be inoperative. "It is interesting," says Mr. Ferguson, "to see how men cling to the performance of ancient religious rites, when the significance of the ceremony has long been forgotten ; and what a hold must that worship have held over the minds of men, which Thor and Odin have not supplanted, nor the christianity of a thousand years."

The tribe of ancient Britons who occupied Cumberland previous to the Roman conquest, the Brigantes, who were as wild and uncultivated as their native hills, subsisting principally by hunting and the spontaneous fruits of the earth; wearing for their clothing the skins of animals, and dwelling in habitations formed by the pillars of the forest rooted in the earth, and enclosed by interwoven branches, or in caves ; have left one undoubted specimen of their race behind them. In the parish of Scaleby, in Cumberland, the land on the north end is barren, and large quantities of peat are cut and sent to Carlisle and other places for sale. At the depth of nine feet

13

in this peat moss, has been found the skeleton of an ancient Briton, enclosed in the skin of some wild animal, and carefully bound up with thongs of tanned leather. It is conjectured that the body must have lain in the moss since the invasion of Julius Cæsar, and from the position in which the skeleton was found, grasping a stick about three feet long and twelve inches in circumference, it is supposed he must have perished accidentally on the spot. The remains were not long ago in the possession of the rector and Dr. Graham of Netherhouse.

In this part of the island the Britons were not in the worst state of mental darkness ; these were not ignorant of a Deity, and they were not idolators. Their druids and bards possessed all the learning of the age. And it is believed that some of the Chief Druids had their station in Cumberland, where many of their monuments still remain, and of these one of the most noble and extensive of any in the island is the circle near Keswick. It stands on an eminence, about a mile and a half on the old road to Penrith, in a field on the right hand. The spot is the most commanding which could be chosen in that part of the country, without climbing a mountain. Derwentwater and the vale of Keswick are not seen from it, only the mountains that enclose them on the south and west. Latrigg and the huge side of Skiddaw are on the north : to the east is the open country towards Penrith, with Mell fell in the distance, where it rises alone like a huge tumulus on the right, and Blencathra on the left, rent into deep ravines. On the south east is the range of Helvellyn, from its termination at Wanthwaite Craggs to its loftiest summits, and to Dunmail Raise. The lower range of Nathdale Fells lies nearer in a line parallel with Helvellyn. The heights above Leathes Water, with the Borrowdale mountains complete the panorama.

This circle is formed of stones of various forms, natural and unhewn, of a species of granite ; of a kind, according to Clarke, not to be found within many miles of this place. The largest is nearly eight feet high, and fifteen feet in circumference ; most of them are still erect, but some are fallen. They are set in a form not exactly circular ; the diameter being thirty paces from east to west, and thirty-two from north to south. At the eastern end a small enclosure is formed within the circle by ten stones, making an oblong square in conjunction with the stones on that side of the circle, seven paces in length, and three in width within. At the opposite side a single square stone is placed at the distance of three paces from the circle.

Concerning this, like all similar monuments in great Britain, the popular superstition prevails, that no two persons can number the stones alike, and that no person will ever find a second count confirm the first. This notion is curiously illustrated by the various writers who have described it. According to Gough, Stukely states the number to be forty; Gray says they are fifty; Hutchinson makes them fifty; Clarke made them out to be fifty-two; others, more correctly, forty-eight. Southey says, the number of stones which compose the circle is thirty-eight, and besides these there are ten which form three sides of a little square within, on the eastern side, three stones of the circle itself forming the fourth; this being evidently the place where the Druids who presided had their station; or where the more sacred and important part of the rites and ceremonies (whatever they may have been) were performed.

The singularity noticed in this monument, and what distinguishes it from all other druidical remains of this nature, is the recess on the eastern side of the area. Mr. Pennant supposes it to have been allotted for the Druids, the priests of the place, as a peculiar sanctuary, a sort of holy of holies, where they met, separated from the vulgar, to perform their rites, their divinations, or to sit in council to determine on controversies, to compromise all differences about limits of land, or about inheritances, or for the trial of greater criminals. The cause that this recess was on the east side, seems to arise from the respect paid by the ancient Britons to Baal or the Sun; not originally an idolatrous respect, but merely as a symbol of the Creator.

The rude workmanship, or rather arrangement, of these structures, for it cannot be called architecture, indicates the great barbarity of the times of the Druids; and furnishes strong proof of the savage nature of these heathen priests. Within this magical circle we may conceive any incantations to have been performed, and any rites of superstition to have been celebrated; their human executions, their imposing sacrifices; and their inhuman method of offering up their victims, by enclosing them in a gigantic figure of Hercules (the emblem of human virtue) made of wicker work, and burning them alive in sacrifice to the divine attribute of Justice.

This impressive monument of former times (the Keswick circle) is carefully preserved : the soil within the enclosure is not broken ; a path from the road is left, and a stepping style has been placed, to accommodate visitors with an easy access

to it. The old legend about the last human sacrifice of the
Druids belongs to this monument. Gilpin says, "a romantic
place seldom wants a romantic story to adorn it." And here
certainly, amidst unmistakeable evidences of the worship of
Baal : within sight of the vale (St. John's) which reveals the
isolated rock, once the enchanted fortress of the powerful Mer-
lin : within sound of the Greta, "the mourner," "the loud
lamenter," in whose torrents are heard voices complaining
among the stones : within range of Souter Fell with its
shadowy armies and spectres marching in military array, why
and whence and whither we know not ; here, if anywhere, the
very realm of mystery and superstition is made manifest to us,
with almost awful significance ; overlying the fairest scenes of
nature, and investing them with all the charms of a region of
romance.

The neighbourhood of this temple, too, is not without a
certain notoriety on account of the violent floods with which it
has been visited even in modern times. Hutchinson speaks of
a remarkable one caused by impetuous rains, which happened
on the twenty-second of August, 1749, in the vale of St.
John's. "The clouds discharged their torrents like a water-
spout; the streams from the mountains uniting, at length
became so powerful a body, as to rend up the soil, gravel, and
stones to a prodigious depth, and bear with them mighty frag-
ments of rocks ; several cottages were swept away from the
declivities where they had stood in safety for a century ; the
vale was deluged, and many of the inhabitants with their cattle
were lost. A singular providence protected many lives, a
little school, where all the youths of the neighbourhood were
educated, at the instant crowded with its flock, stood in the
very line of one of these torrents, but the hand of God, in a
miraculous manner, stayed a rolling rock, in the midst of its
dreadful course, which would have crushed the whole tenement
with its innocents ; and by its stand, the floods divided, and
passed on this hand and on that, insulating the school-house,
and leaving the pupils with their master, trembling at once for
the dangers escaped and as spectators of the horrid havock in
the valley, and the tremendous floods which encompassed
them on every side." He received this account from one of
the people then at school : and also gives the following des-
cription of that inundation, which he had met with. "It
began with most terrible thunder and incessant lightning, the
·preceding day having been extremely hot and sultry ; the in-
habitants for two hours before the breaking of the cloud, heard ·

a strange noise, like the wind blowing in the tops of high trees. It is thought to have been a spout or a large body of water, by which the lightning incessantly rarifying the air, broke at once on the tops of the mountains, and descended upon the valley below, which is about three miles long, half a mile broad, and lies nearly east and west, being closed on the south and north sides with prodigious high, steep, and rocky mountains. Legbert Fells on the north side, received almost the whole cataract, for the spout did not extend above a mile in length ; it chiefly swelled four small brooks, but to so amazing a degree, that the largest of them, called Catchertz Ghyll, swept away a mill and other edifices in five minutes, leaving the place where they stood covered with fragments of rocks and rubbish three or four yards deep, insomuch that one of the mill stones could not be found. During the violence of the storm, the fragments of rock which rolled down the mountain, choked up the old course of this brook ; but the water forcing its way through a shivery rock, formed a chasm four yards wide and about eight or nine deep. The brooks lodged such quantities of gravel and sand on the meadows, that they were irrecoverably lost. Many large pieces of rocks were carried a considerable way into the fields ; some larger than a team of ten horses could move, and one of them measuring nineteen yards about." Clarke says, " Many falsehoods are related of this inundation : for instance, the insulation of the school-house with its assembled master and scholars, which, though commonly told and believed, is not supported by any tradition of the kind preserved in the neighbourhood. No doubt, the circumstances are exaggerated : but even his own narrative shows it to have been one of the most dreadful and destructive inundations ever remembered in this country. He relates that "all the evening of that 22nd day of August, horrid, tumultuous noises were heard in the air ; sometimes a puff of wind would blow with great violence, then in a moment all was calm again. The inhabitants, used to bosom-winds, whirlwinds, and the howling of distant tempests among the rocks, went to bed as usual, and from the fatigues of the day were in a sound sleep when the inundation awoke them. About one in the morning the rain began to fall, and before four such a quantity fell as covered the whole face of the country below with a sheet of water many feet deep ; several houses were filled with sand to the first story, many more driven down ; and among the rest Legberthwaite mill, of which not one stone was left upon another ; even the heavy millstones were washed away ; one was found at a considerable distance, but the other was never discovered. Several persons were obliged to climb to the tops of the houses, to escape instantaneous death ; and there many were obliged to remain, in a situation of the most dreadful suspense, till the waters abated. Mr. Mounsey of Wallthwaite says, that when he came down stairs in the morning, the first sight he saw was a gander belonging to one of his neighbours, and several planks and kitchen utensils, which were floating about his lower apartments, the violence of the waters having forced open the doors on both sides of the house. The most dreadful vestiges of this inundation, or water spout, are at a place called Lob-wath, a little above Wallthwaite ; here thousands of prodigious stones are piled upon each other, to the height of eleven yards ; many of these stones are upwards of twenty tons weight each, and are thrown together in such a manner as to be at once the object of curiosity and horror.

"The quantity of water which had fallen here is truly astonishing ; more particularly considering the small space it had to collect in. The distance from Lob-Wath to Wolf-Crag, is not more than a mile and a' half, and there could none collect much above Wolf-Crag ; nor did the rain extend more than eight miles in any direction. At Melfell only three miles distant, the farmers were leading corn all night (as is customary when they fear ill weather,) and no rain fell there ; yet such was the fury of the descending torrent, that the fields at Fornside exhibited nothing but devastation. Here a large tree broken in two, there one torn up by the root, and the ground everywhere covered with sand and stones." The rivulet called Mosedale Beck, which has its source between the mountains Dodd and Wolf-Crag, was by its sudden and continuous overflow the chief contributory of the inundation.

THE LADY OF WORKINGTON HALL.

In her neat country kirtle and kerchief array'd,
A wild little maiden tripp'd through the green shade ;
With her pitcher, just filled from the rill, at her side,
And a song on her lip of the Solway's rude tide ;
When a rider came by, gallant, youthful, and gay—
" Pretty Maid, let me drink ! and good luck to
    your lay ! "

As he glanced o'er the brim, arch and sweet was
    her smile ;
Then "Adieu ! " passing on, he sang gaily the
    while—
"Who knows what may happen, or what may befall ?
I may be ——" something she could not recall :
For the tramp of his steed mingled in with the tone,
And the burden ceased, broken—the singer was
    gone.

There are words, notes, and whisperings, broken
    and few,
That from depths in the soul will oft start up anew,
Like a dream voice, unconsciously, early or late,
Mid all changes of circumstance, fortune, and fate,
Unappealed to, unsought for, unreck'd of, and
    brought
From afar to the tongue without effort or thought.

And 'twas thus the few notes which she caught of
    that strain
Often stirr'd on the lips of the Maiden again.
When a child at the school or a maid at the Hall—
" Who knows what may happen, or what may befall' ?
I may be—" lilted she low, as she sate
At her finger-work meekly, or stroll'd by the gate.

So it chanced as she robed on one morning her
    bloom
With a mantle of state, in her lost Lady's room ;
While the mirror gave back to her sight all her
    charms ;
Came that strain to her lip as she folded her
    arms—
" Who knows what may happen, or what may befall ?
I may be—Lady of Workington Hall !"

Thus the wild-hearted Maid ended gaily the song.
Like a flash from the mirror it glanced from her
    tongue,
Void of meaning or thought of the future ; but lo !
There's a witness beside her the glass does not
    show.
From a distance unseen are displayed to the eyes
Of her Lord all her pranks in that courtly disguise.

He charged the proud Butler, that evening to call
To high feast all the maidens and grooms of the
    Hall ;
To send round the bowl, and when mirth flowing
    high
Brought the heart to the lip, the bright soul to the
    eye,
At the sound of his footstep to crown their good
    cheer
With a round to the toast he has breathed in his
    ear.

Bold and stern, on that evening arose mid the
    crowd
The bold Butler, and called for a bumper aloud :
Look'd around on the bevy of maidens and men :
Glanced his eye past the Beauty, and spoke out
    again—
" Who knows what may happen, or what may befall ?
Let us drink to the Lady of Workington Hall."

How they stared at each other, how glanced at their
    Lord,
As he entered that moment and stood by the board,
How they trembled to witness his eye's flashing
    ray,
Was a sight to be seen that no art can portray.
But the one conscious Maid who could read it
    alone,
With a shriek, like a vanishing spirit was gone.

But in vain ! What the fates have determined will
    come !
And in time, tired of clangour of trumpet, and
    drum,
Came the Heir to the Hall of his ancestry old ;
Met the Maid of the pitcher once more as he
    stroll'd ;
Woo'd and won her, in spite of whate'er might
    befall ;
And made her the Lady of Workington Hall.

195

NOTES TO "THE LADY OF WORKINGTON HALL." '

The ancient family of the Curwens of Workington can trace their descent to Ivo de Tailbois and Elgiva daughter of Ethelred, King of England. Ivo came to England with the Conqueror, was the first lord of the barony of Kendal, and brother of Fulk, Earl of Anjou and King of Jerusalem. Ketel, the grandson of Ivo, had two sons ;—Gilbert, the father of William de Lancaster, from whom descended, in a direct line, the barons of Kendal ; and Orme, from whom descended the Curwens. These took their surname by agreement from Culwen, a family of Galloway, whose heir they married. It is said, that Culwen, which is on the sea-coast of Galloway, had its name from a neighbouring rock, which was thought to resemble a white monk ; that being the meaning of the word in the Irish language. It is also said, that the family name was changed to Curwen, by a corruption, which first appeared in the public records in the reign of King Henry VI. Orme having espoused Gunilda, sister of Waldieve, first lord of Allerdale, received in marriage with her the manor of Seaton below Derwent, and took up his abode there. Their son, Gospatrick, received the manors of Workington and Lamplugh from William de Lancaster in exchange for Middleton, in Westmorland. He was succeeded by his son Thomas, who became lord of·Culwen in Galloway, and died in 1152, and was buried in the Abbey of Shap, to which he had been a benefactor ; his estates descending to his second son, Patric de Culwen, who removed his residence from Seaton to Workington, where his descendants have since remained.

Sir Thomas Curwen, the seventh in descent from Patric, died in the thirty fourth year of Henry VIII. In reference to this member of the family, Sandford in his M.S. History of Cumberland relates an instance of the pleasant manner in which conventual property at the dissolution was dealt with, and disposed of, among that monarch's favourites and friends. It is thus given :—"Sir Tho. Curwen Knight in Henry the Eight's time, an excellent archer at twelve score merks : And went up with his men to shoote with that reknowned King at the dissolution of abbeis : And the King says to him, Curwen, why doth thee begg none of thes Abbeis : I wold gratifie the some way : Quoth the other, thank yow, and afterward said he wold desire of him the Abbie of ffurness (nye unto him) for 20 ty one years : Sayes the King, take it for ever : Quoth the other, its long enough, for youle set them up againe in that time : But they not likely to be set up againe, this Sir Tho. Curwen sent Mr· Preston who had married his daughter to renew the lease for him ; and he even renneued in his owne name ; which when his father in law questioned, quoth Mr. Preston, yow shall have it as long as " yow live : and I thinke I may as well have it with your daughter as another."*

There is probably some truth in the anecdote, related by Sandford. For it is said by West, that not long after the dissolution of Monasteries, Thomas Preston, of Preston-Patrick and Levens, purchased the site and immediate grounds of Furness Abbey from the trustees of the crown, with other considerable estates to the value of £3000 a year : after which he removed from Preston-Patrick, and resided at the Abbey, in a manor house built on the spot where the Abbot's apartments stood. Of his two sons, John the elder married the daughter of Curwen. His descendants were called Prestons of the Abbey, and of the Manor ; and continued for four generations, when the two great grandsons of the purchaser died without issue. The family of Christopher, his second son, were known as the Prestons of Holker. Of these, Catharine, the fifth in the direct line from Christopher, was the mother of Sir Thomas Lowther, Baronet, of Yorkshire, to whom on the failure of the elder branch, the property of the Prestons in Furness was granted by George the First. This gentleman, by his marriage with the Lady Elizabeth Cavendish, daughter of the Duke of Devonshire, had an only son and heir, Sir William Lowther, Baronet, the last descendant of the Prestons of Preston-Patrick, who died unmarried in 1756, bequeathing all his estates in Furness and Cartmel to

---

* "John Preston of the Manor in Furness, Esquire, married Margaret daughter of Sir Thos. Curwen, of Workington, and had issue, tempore Henry VIII."

his cousin Lord George Augustus Cavendish, through whom they passed by inheritance to the present Duke of Devonshire. In a report to the government of Queen Elizabeth, of the date of 1588, inserted among the Burghley Papers, the son and heir of this sharp-handed son-in-law of Curwen is mentioned in somewhat detractory terms, in a passage which describes "the Pylle of Folder," or Pile of Fouldrey. " The same Pylle is an old decayed castell of ' the dowchie of Lancaster, in Furness Felles, where one Thomas Preestone (a Papyshe Atheiste) is depute steward, and comaunders the menrede and lands ther, which were sometime members appertayninge to the Abbeye of Furnes.' "

Workington Hall, the seat of the Curwens, is a large quadrangular building, with battlemented parapets, situated on a woody acclivity over looking the river Derwent, at the east end of the town. It has been almost entirely rebuilt within the present century. The old mansion was castellated pursuant to the royal license granted by Richard II., in 1379, to Sir Gilbert de Culwen. It is remarkable for having been the first prison-house of the unfortunate Mary of Scotland, after she had landed within the dominions of her rival. Having left the Scottish shore in a small fishing boat, she landed with about twenty attendants near the Hall on Sunday, May 16th, 1568 ; and was received by Sir Henry Curwen as became her rank and misfortunes, and hospitably entertained by him, till she removed to Cockermouth, on her route to Carlisle. The apartment in which the Queen had slept was long preserved, out of respect to her memory, as she had left it. But some recent alterations of the mansion having become necessary, it was found that these could not be effected without the destruction of that portion which had been so long distinguished as the Queen's Chamber.

Mr. Denton, who wrote about the year 1676, says, " I do not know any seat in all Britain so commodiously situated for beauty, plenty, and pleasure as this is." And Mr. Sandford, who wrote about the same time, has the following rapturous description, " And a very fair mansion-house and pallace-like ; a court of above 60 yards long and 40 yards broad, built round about ; garretted turret-wise, and toors in the corner ; a gate house, and most wainscot and gallery roomes ; and the brave prospect of seas and ships almost to the house, the tides flowing up. Brave orchards, gardens, dovecoats, and woods and grounds in the bank about, and brave corn fields and meadows below, as like as Chelsay fields. And now the habitation of a brave young Sq. his father Monsir Edward Curwen, and his mother the grandchild of Sir Michael Wharton o' th' Wolds in Yorkshire."

Even Mr Gilpin, a century later, was struck with "its hanging woods and sloping lawns," and speaks of its situation as "one of the grandest and most beautiful in the country."

The anecdote upon which the poem is founded was related by a person who about fifty years ago was much acquainted with what was current in some of the principal families in the West of Cumberland. She stated that it was commonly repeated among the servants of the different houses, and was quite credited by them : and that she herself had not any doubt as to the truth of the story, but could not give the period to which the circumstances refer.

One of the domestics of the Hall was said to have been surprised by her master in the manner described, and to have been overheard by him, uttering the words,—

"Who knows what may happen, or what may befall ?
I may be Lady of Workington Hall !"

The butler was instructed to repeat the words publicly in the presence of the Maid, who fled from the mansion, overwhelmed with confusion. She subsequently formed a matrimonial alliance with a principal member of the family ; and thus in a manner her prediction was verified.

Such was the story, and such the narrator. It may be added, that the published notices of the family are devoid of anything to give confirmation to the story ; but as it was related in the neighbourhood in the spirit alluded to, a place has been given to it among the traditions of Cumberland.

THE ALTAR ON CROSS-FELL.

(FORMERLY FIENDS'-FELL.)

Come listen and hear of the Fiends'-Fell dread ;
And the helm of storm that shrouds its head,
When the imps and cubs of Evil that tread
 Its summit, their strifes are waging :
Who made their haunt on its topmost height,
And down the valleys came often by night,
To affright the Shepherds, the herds to blight,
 And set the strong winds raging.

Ah, dwellers in peaceful vales afar !
The cloudy Helm and the dismal Bar—
You know whose work on the Fell they are ;
 And you know whose wort they are brewing.
And you wish that the saintly Augustine
A warier man on his errand had been,
When the lizard crept into his chalice unseen,
 The power of his spells undoing.

For he came, by good men sought, they say,
To the Fiends'-Fell foot, a weary way,
To chase the fiends from the cloud that lay
    On its summit, as if to hide it.
At an hour unmarked, by paths unknown,
He climbed up the mountain side alone,
And built on the top an altar of stone,
    And reared the cross beside it.

And there within that mighty cloud,
Where wrathful spirits were raging loud,
The old good man, with mind unbow'd,
    But body so oft-times bending,
Moved to and fro on the haunted top,
And gathered the stones from off the slòpe,
Nor bated a jot of heart or hope
    While the Altar pile was ascending.

Then while the sun made bright below
And warmed the vales with its cheerful glow,
The mighty cloud began to blow,
    And deafening cries flew round him.
But still the altar on high begun
With heart and will, from his labours done
The crowning recompence now has won
    For him, to that end who bound him.

There stands the Altar the saint before.
The long laborious task is o'er.
The Cross which once the victim bore,
    It too spreads wide its arms.

The Chalice is there with the juice divine ;
The wafer that bares the sacred sign ;
And the tapers beside the Cross to shine ;
    To work out the counter-charms.

All ready beside the holy man
Stood—when for a moment his eyes began
To droop, and a feeling of slumber ran
    Through his veins oppress'd and weary.
For toil an old man's limbs will shake :
And toil an old man's frame will break :
But, that instant past, he stands awake
    Within that cloud so dreary.

It was enough : No counter-charm
Might work that day the fiend-cubs harm.
The Chalice he offers with outstretched arm
    Has a reptile form within it !
And neither the saint nor the wine has power
To banish one fiend from the Fell, that hour :
For a lizard the edge of the chalice crept o'er,
    While he slept but that tithe of a minute.

Then blew the fiends, as if they would blow
The mountain itself to the plain below.   ·
And when the saint turned round to go,
    Down tumbled the Altar behind him ;
And boiled and seethed the Helm and Bar,
And the winds rushed down on the valleys afar ;
While the Saint emerged, like a shining star,
    From the cloud where they could not bind him.

14

And he went his way ; and the fiends prevailed.
And still is the mountain by fiends assailed.
And the dismal Helm from afar is hailed
    As a tempest surely growing.
The herdsman shudders, and hies away
To his hut on the hills at close of day,
For he knows whose cubs are abroad at play
    And setting the Helm wind blowing.

His children mourn at the dolorous roar,
And rush to his arms from hearth and floor.
But the good man thinks of his stacks and store,
    His fields and his farmstead wasting.
The housewife prays that the rain may fall :
But the stars are shining high over all :
And the Bar extends like a pitchy wall
    In the West, where the storm is hasting.

The long loud roar, it deepens amain ;
And down from the Helm along valley and plain
Goes the wind with invisible hosts in its train,
    And they mount the black Bar-cloud appalling ;
And they heave it and row it, those mariners dread,
For days, till it anchors on Fiends'-Fell head :
Then the big drops pour from the skies o'er spread,
    And the torrents to torrents are calling.   •

NOTES TO "THE ALTAR ON CROSS-FELL."

The Editor of Camden (Bishop Gibson), speaking of huge stones found together on the top of steep and high mountains, thought they might possibly be the ruins of Churches or Chapels which had been built there. "For," says he, "it was thought an extraordinary piece of devotion, upon the planting of Christianity in these parts, to erect crosses, and build chapels on the most eminent places, as being both nearer heaven and more conspicuous : they were commonly dedicated to St. Michael. That large tract of mountains on the east side of the county (of Cumberland), called Cross-Fells, had the name given them upon that account ; for before, they were called Fiends'-Fell, or Devil's Fell ; and Dilston, a small town under them, is contracted from Devil's-town."

Among the several monuments on the pavement in the cross-aisle in Hexham Cathedral, is one ornamented with a crosier, and inscribed, " Hic Jacet Thomas de Devilston."

The mountain, Cross-Fell, which is remarkable for the phenomenon of the Helm-Cloud upon its summit, and the Helm-wind, as it is called, generated within it, which is sometimes productive of such destructive effects in the valleys below, is said to have been formerly designated Fiends'-Fell, from the common belief that evil spirits had their haunt upon it ; until St. Augustine, to whom and his forty followers, when travelling on their missionary labours in these parts, a legendary tradition ascribes the expulsion of the demons of the storms, erected a *Cross*, and built an altar on the summit, where he offered the holy eucharist, and thus was supposed to have counter-charmed the demons. Since that time it has borne the name of Cross-Fell ; and the people of the neighbourhood style a heap of stones lying there, the Altar upon Cross-Fell.

The common saying, "Its brewing a storm," or "A storm is brewing," is one of the many phrases in which we only repeat the thought of our primeval Scandinavian ancestors; amongst whom the beverage quaffed in the halls of Valhalla, the drink of the Gods, was conceived to be a product of the storm, and had more or less identity with the Cloud-Water. In Germany, the mists that gather about the mountain tops before a storm are said to be accounted for in like manner, as if they were steam from the brewing or boiling in which dwarfs, elves, or witches were engaged. Such modes of expression, according to the dictionary of the brothers Grimm, are of extreme antiquity.

Some such ideas seem to have been popularly associated with that enormous cloud, which is often seen, like a helmet, to cover the summit of Cross-Fell, and in which the Helm-Wind is generated.

In speaking of the Helm-Wind, it may be necessary to premise that Cross-Fell is one continued ridge, stretching without any branches, or even subject mountains, except two or three conical hills called Pikes, from the N.N.W. to the S.S.E., from the neighbourhood of Gilsland almost to Kirkby-Stephen, that is about forty miles. Its direction is nearly in a right line, and the height of its different parts not very unequal; but is in general such, that some of its more eminent parts are exceeded in altitude by few hills in Britain, being 2901 feet above the level of the sea. The slope to the summit from the east is gradual, and extends over perhaps fifty miles of country; whilst on the west it is abrupt, and has at five miles from its base the river Eden running parallel to the mountain.

Upon the upper part of this lofty ridge, there often rests, in dry and sunny weather, a prodigious wreath of clouds, extending from three or four to sixteen or eighteen miles each way, north and south, from the highest point; it is at times above the mountain, sometimes it rests upon its top, but most frequently descends a considerable way down its side. This mighty collection of vapour, from which so much commotion issues, exhibits an appearance uncommonly grand and solemn; and is named from a Saxon word, which in our language implies a covering, the Helm. The western front of this enormous cloud is clearly defined, and quite separated from any other cloud on that side. Opposite to this, and at a variable distance towards the west, and at the same elevation, is another cloud with its eastern edge as clearly defined as the Helm; this is called the Bar or Bur. It is said to have the appearance of being in continual motion, as if boiling, or at least agitated by a violent wind.

The distance between the Helm and the Bar varies as the Bar advances towards, or recedes from, the Helm; this is sometimes not more than half a mile, sometimes three or four miles, and occasionally the Bar seems to coincide with the western horizon ; or it disperses and there is no Bar, and then there is a general east wind extending over all the country westward.

The description of this remarkable phenomenon, the Helm-Wind, we will give from observations made by the Rev. John Watson, of Cumrew, and others. The places most subject to it are Milburn, Kirkland, Ousby, Melmerby, and Gamblesby. Sometimes when the atmosphere is quite settled, hardly a cloud to be seen, and not a breath of wind stirring, a small cloud appears on the summit of the mountain, and extends itself to the north and south ; the Helm is then said to be on, and in a few minutes the wind is blowing so violently as to break down trees, overthrow stacks, occasionally blow a person from his horse, or overturn a horse and cart. When the wind blows, the Helm seems violently agitated ; and on descending the fell and entering it, there is not much wind. Sometimes a helm forms and goes off without a wind ; and there are easterly winds without a Helm. The open space between the Helm and Bar varies from eight or ten to thirty or forty miles in length, and from half a mile to four or six miles in breadth ; it is of an elliptical form, as the Helm and Bar are united at the ends. A representation of the Helm, Bar, and space between, may be made by opening the forefinger and thumb of each hand, and placing their tips to each other ; the thumbs will then represent the Helm on the top of the fell, the forefingers the Bar, and the space between, the variable limits of the wind.

The open space is clear of clouds with the exception of small pieces breaking off now and then from the Helm, and either disappearing or being driven rapidly over the Bar ; but through this open space is often seen a high stratum of clouds quite at rest. Within the space described the wind blows continually ; it has been known to do so for nine days together, the Bar advancing or receding to different distances. When heard or felt for the first time it does not seem so very extraordinary ; but when heard or felt for days together, it gives a strong impression of sublimity. Its sound is peculiar, and when once known is easily distinguished from that of ordinary winds ; it cannot be heard more than three or four miles, but in the wind or near it, it is grand and awful, and has been compared to the noise made by the sea in a violent storm.

Its first effect on the spirits is exhilarating, and it gives a buoyancy to the body. The country subject to it is very healthy, but it does great injury to vegetation by beating grain, grass, and leaves of trees, till quite black.

It may further be remarked of this wind, that it is very irregular, rarely occurring in the summer months, and more frequent from the end of September to May. It generally blows from Cross-Fell longest in the spring, when the sun has somewhat warmed the earth beneath, and does not cease till it has effectually cooled it; thus it sometimes continues, according to Mr. Ritson, for a fortnight or three weeks, which he considers a peculiarity of the Helm wind of Cross-Fell. The wind itself is very chill, and is almost always terminated by a rain, which restores, or to which succeeds, a general warmth, and into which the Helm seems to resolve itself.

The best explanation of this very interesting and remarkable phenomenon is given in the following observations of Dr. T. Barnes of Carlisle.

The air or wind from the east ascends the gradual slope of the eastern side of the Penine chain or Cross-Fell range of mountains, to the summit of Cross-Fell, where it enters the Helm or cap, and is cooled to a low temperature; it then rushes forcibly down the abrupt declivity of the western side of the mountain into the valley beneath, in consequence of the valley being of a warmer temperature, and this constitutes the Helm wind.

The sudden and violent rushing of the wind down the ravines and crevices of the mountains occasions the loud noise that is heard.

At a varying distance from the base of the mountain the Helm wind is rarified by the warmth of the low ground, and meets with the wind from the west, which resists its further course. The higher temperature it has acquired in the valley, and the meeting of the contrary current, occasion it to rebound and ascend into the upper region of the atmosphere. When the air or wind has reached the height of the Helm, it is again cooled to the low temperature of this cold region, and is consequently unable to support the same quantity of vapour it had in the valley; the water or moisture contained in the air, is therefore condensed by the cold, and forms the cloud called the Helm-Bar.

The meeting of the opposing currents beneath,—where there are frequently strong gusts of wind from all quarters, and the sudden condensation of the air and moisture in the Bar-cloud, give rise to its agitation or commotion, as if "struggling with contrary blasts." The Bar is therefore not the cause of the limit of the Helm wind, but is the consequence of it. It is absurd to suppose that the Bar, which is a light cloud, can impede or resist the Helm wind ; but if it even possessed a sufficient resisting power, it could have no influence on the wind which is blowing near the surface of the earth, and which might pass under the Bar.

The variable distance of the Bar from the Helm is owing to the changing situation of the opposing and conflicting currents, and the difference of temperature of different parts of the low ground near the base of the mountain.

When there is a break or opening in the Bar, the wind is said to rush through with great violence, and to extend over the country. Here again, the effect is mistaken for the cause. In this case, the Helm-Wind, which blows always from the east, has, in some places underneath the observed opening, overcome the resistance of the air, or of the wind from the west, and of course does not rebound and ascend into the higher regions to form the Bar. The supply being cut off, a break or opening in that part of the Bar necessarily takes place.

When the temperature of the lower region has fallen and become nearly uniform with that of the mountain range, the Helm wind ceases ; the Bar and the Helm approach and join each other, and rain not unfrequently follows.

When the Helm-Wind has overcome all the resistance of the lower atmosphere, or of the opposing current from the west, and the temperature of the valley and of the mountain is more nearly equalized, there is no rebound or ascent of the wind, consequently the Bar ceases to be formed, the one already existing is dissipated, and a general east wind prevails.

There is little wind in the Helm-cloud, because the air is colder in it than in the valley, and the moisture which the air contains is more condensed and is deposited in the cloud upon the summit of the mountain.

There is rarely either a Helm, Helm-wind, or Bar, during the summer, on account of the higher temperature of the summit of the Cross-Fell range, and the upper regions of the atmosphere, at that season of the year.

The different situations of the Helm, on the side, on the summit, and above the mountain, will depend on the temperature of these places : when the summit is not cold enough to condense the vapour, the Helm is situated higher in a colder region, and will descend down the side of the mountains if the temperature be sufficiently low to produce that effect.

The sky is clear between the Helm and Bar, because the air below is warmer and can support a greater quantity of vapour rising from the surface of the earth, and this vapour is driven forward by the Helm-Wind, and ascends up in the rebound to the Bar.   In short, the Helm is merely a cloud or cap upon the mountain, the cold air descends from the Helm to the valley, and constitutes the Helm Wind, and when warmed and rarified in the valley, ascends and forms the Bar.

WILLIE O' SCALES.

Said Willie o' Scales, at break of day,
" The hunt's up ! I must busk and away !
Steed, good wife ? and saddle ? I trow,
Willie o' Scales is steed enow."

—Scotland's King is a hunting gone :
Willie o' Scales, he runs alone :
Knights and Nobles many a score :
Hounds full twenty tongues and more.

Through the covert the deer he sprang :
Over the heather the music rang.
Dogs and steeds well speeded they :
But Willie o' Scales, he show'd the way.

For speed of foot had Willie no peer.
He outstripp'd the horses, dogs, and deer.
He left the Nobles far behind.
He pass'd the King like a puff of wind.

At the close of day, with a greenwood bough,
Beside the deer he fann'd his brow.
And " There, my liege ! " to the Monarch he said,
" Is as gallant a stag as ever lay dead.

" I count him fleet, for a stag of ten ! "—
—" And I count thee chief of my Border men.
No gallanter heart, I dare be sworn,
Ever drew the shaft or wound the horn.

" No trustier hand than thine was found
When foes to Scotland hemm'd us round.
Now swifter of foot than our fleetest deer—
We'll try thy hold upon land and gear.

" For his speed in sport, for his might in fray, ˙
Write, 'GILL's broad lands' to 'Willie, THE RAE !'
And for ever a Willie the Rae be here,
When the King comes by to hunt the deer."—

Thus spoke King William, where he stood,
The Lion of Scotland, fierce of mood.
And musing turned, and look'd again
On his Border vassal ; and cross'd the plain.

Centuries long have rolled away :
The Monarch is dust, his Nobles clay :
Old lines are changed, are changing still :
But Willie the Rae is-lord of Gill.

NOTES TO "WILLIE O' SCALES."

The long and scattered hamlet of High and Low Scales, is on the west side of Crummock Beck, near Bromfield, and a few miles from Wigton in Cumberland. Skells or scales, from a Saxon or Gothic word signifying a cover, was the name given to those slight temporary huts made of turf or sods which in the mountainous district of this county and Scotland are called Bields. They were erected most commonly for the shelter of shepherds ; and during the later periods, in the border wars to protect the persons who were appointed to watch the cattle of the neighbourhood. Few estates in the kingdom have belonged to one family longer than this of THE GILL, which · was formerly, however, much more extensive, comprising most probably the neighbouring hamlet of Scales. Another somewhat uncommon circumstance belonging to it is, that, to the close of last century, and for anything we know to the contrary, to a much later date, the owner had always lived on and occupied it himself; it had never been in the hands of a farmer.

The Reays of Gill, however variously their name has been spelled and pronounced by different branches of the family, derived it from one on whom it was undoubtedly bestowed as being characteristical and descriptive of himself. The active hunter, the companion and the friend of William the Lion, was called in the commoner Saxon language of his time Ra, or Raa, a Roe, from his unparalleled swiftness. In Scotland and Germany a roe is still pronounced rae, as it was formerly in England.

> "When the deer and the rae
> Lightly bounding together,
> Sport the lang simmer day
> On the braes of Balquhither."

The tradition is that the head, or chief, of this family had a grant of the lands of Gill to him, and his heirs for ever, from William the Lion, King of Scotland, whose eventful reign lasted nearly half a century ; and who died in 1214. This grant is said to have been made, not only as a reward for his fidelity to his prince, but as a memorial of his extraordinary swiftness of foot in pursuing the deer, outstripping in fleetness most of the horses and dogs. The conditions of the grants were, that he should pay a pepper corn yearly, as an acknowledgment, and that the name of William should, if possible, be perpetuated in the family. "And this is certain," says a writer in the Gentleman's Magazine about the year 1794, "That ever since, till now, a "William Reay has been owner of the Gill. There is every reason to believe that the present John Reay is the first instance of a deviation." It is said that even in that instance the deviation was not made without deliberation ; William the father having first consulted an eminent lawyer, whether he might safely call his son John. It was replied that mere length of occupancy would quiet the possession and make the title good.

The great military tenure of lands in this district was by HOMAGE, FEALTY and CORNAGE. This last (cornage) drew after it *wardship, marriage*, and *relief.* And the service of this tenure was *knight's service.* HOMAGE was the most honourable service, and the most humble service of reverence, that a free tenant can do to his lord. For when he was to do homage to his lord, he was to appear ungirt, bareheaded, without his sword, and, kneeling on both knees, his hands held out and clasped between his lord's, was to say—"I become your man from this day forward of life, and limb, and earthly honour, and unto you will be true and faithful, and faith unto you will bear for the tenements that I claim to hold of you, saving the faith that I owe to our Sovereign Lord the King." And then the lord so sitting was to kiss him ; by which kiss he was bound to be his vassal for ever.

When a free tenant was to do FEALTY to his lord, he was to hold his right hand upon a book, and say thus—"Know ye this, my lord, that I will be faithful and true to you, and faith to you will bear for the tenements which I claim to hold of you, and that I will lawfully do to you the customs and services which I ought to do at the terms assigned ; so help me God and his Saints." But he was not to kneel, nor make such humble reverence as in homage ; and fealty might be done before the steward of the court, but homage could only be done to the lord himself.

CORNAGE, called also HORNGELD, and NOWTEGELD or (cow-tax) seems early to have been converted into a pecuniary fine, being a stipulated payment in the first instance for the finding of scouts or horners to procure intelligence. It was first paid in cattle. The tenants who held by cornage were bound to be always ready to serve the King and lord of the manor on horseback, or on foot, at their own charge; and when the King's army marched into Scotland, their post was in the vanguard as they advanced, and in the vanguard on their return. Because they best knew the passes and defiles, and the way and manner of the enemy's attacking and retreating. *Wardship* and *marriage* were included in this tenure. When the tenant died, and the heir male was within the age of twenty one years, the lord was to have the land holden of him until the heir should attain that age; because the heir by intendment of law was not able to do knight's service before his age of twenty-one years. And if such heir was not married at the time of the death of his ancestor, then the lord was to have the wardship and marriage of him. But if the tenant died leaving an heir female, which heir female was of the age of fourteen years or upwards, then the lord was not to have the wardship of the land, nor of the body; because a woman of that age might have a husband to do knight's service. But if such heir female was under the age of fourteen years, and unmarried at the time of the death of her ancestor, the lord was to have the wardship of the land holden of him until the age of such heir female of fourteen years; within which time the lord might tender unto her convenable marriage without disparagement; and if the lord did not tender such marriage within the said age, she might have entered into the lands, and ousted the lord.

Thus the consent of a superior lord was requisite for the marriage of a female vassal; and this power was distorted into the right of disposing of the ward in marriage. When the King or lord was in want of money it was by no means unusual to offer the wards, male or female, with their lands, in a sense to the highest bidder. If the ward refused to fulfil the marriage so made, then a sum was due from the estates equal to what they would have fetched.

Relief was a certain sum of money, that the heir, on coming of age, paid unto the lord, on taking possession of the inherit-ance of his ancestor.

A *Knight's fee* was estimated, not according to the quality but the quantity of the land, about 640 acres; and the relief was after the rate of one fourth part of the yearly value of the fee.

The *lord's rent* was called *white money*, or *white rent*, from its being paid in silver.

SCUTAGE or service of the shield, was another compensation in money, instead of personal service against the Scots.

The DRENGAGE tenure, which prevailed about Brougham and Clifton, was extremely servile.   The tenants seem to have been drudges to perform the most laborious and servile offices. Dr. Burn quotes authority to prove that Sir Hugh de Morville in Westmorland changed drengage into free service; and that Gilbert de Brougham gave one half of the village of Brougham to Robert de Veteripont to make the other half free of drengage.   One of the de Threlkelds also, who lived at Yanwath Hall, in the time of Edward I., relieved his tenants at Threlkeld of servile burdens at four pence a head. The services were half a draught for one day's ploughing; one day's mowing; one of shearing; one of clipping; one of salving sheep; one carriage load in two years, not to go above ten miles; to dig and load two loads of peat every year —the tenants to have their crowdy (a coarse mess of meal, dripping and hot water) while they worked; the cottagers the same, only they found a horse and harrow instead of the half plough, and a footman's load, not a carriage load.

Many of these have long been lost sight of; and now most of the lands, whether held on customary or arbitrary tenures, merely pay an almost nominal rent, besides certain fines, to the lord of the manor.   Nevertheless there is much truth in what Blackstone says : that "copy holders are only villeins improved."

Lands of arbitrary tenure pay, with certain deductions, fines of two years value on the death of lord or tenant, or of both, and on alienation.   Some pay dower to the widow; others do not.   Some pay a live heriot, which means the best animal in the tenant's possession; others, a dead heriot, that is, the most valuable implement, or piece of furniture. In Catholic times, the Church also, on some manors, claimed as heriot the second best animal the tenant might die possessed of, and on others the best.   In some instances a heriot is only payable when a widow remains in possession of the tenement, and in these cases the original object of the impost was to recompense the lord of the manor for the loss of a man's military service during the widow's occupancy.   In some joint manors where two, or perhaps three, lords have claims for heriots, very discreditable, and, to a dying tenant's family, very distressing scenes are enacted ; for, when it becomes known that the holder of a tenement so burdened is on his death-bed, the stewards of the several manors place watches round the premises, who ascertain what and where the best animal may be, and, as soon as the demise of the tenant is announced, a rush ensues, and an unseemly contest for possession.

In arbitrary lands some lords claim all the timber ; others only the oak ; others the oak and yew ; others oak and white thorn ; and so on. In some the tenant is bound to plant two trees of the same kind for every one he fells ; but tenants have a right to timber for repairs, rebuilding, or implements, though they must not cut down without license. Many lands are bound to carry their grain to the manorial mill to be ground and *multured* ; but this custom has fallen into disuse. Most lords retain the minerals and game if they enfranchise the soil, as many have done.

Many lands used to pay boons of various kinds ; and some of these services are still enforced. By these were demanded so many men or boys, horses, carts, &c., in peat cutting time, hay time, harvest, wood-cutting and carting, and so on. In Martindale Chace, near Ulswater, where Mr. Hasell has a herd of that now rare species, the Red Deer, the tenants are bound to attend the lord's hunt once a year, which is called on their court roll a *Boon Hunt.* On this occasion, they each held their district allotted on the boundaries of the Chace, where they are stationed, to prevent the stag flying beyond the liberty. In the east of Cumberland, the tenants were obliged to send horses and sacks to St. Bees, for salt for the lord's use ; some had to bring their own provisions when engaged in these services: some were entitled to a cake of a stated size for each man, and a smaller for a boy, on assembling in the morning at a fixed hour, under a certain tree, as was the custom at Irton Hall. Breach of punctuality forfeited this cake, but the work was always exacted. Certain farms in some manors were bound to maintain male animals for the use of all the tenants, subject to various conditions and regulations. Formerly many tenants paid a pound of pepper at the lord's court ; others only a pepper-corn ; and some lands are still held by this custom.

Many other peculiar customs connected with the tenure of land formerly existed.

Curious individual exemptions from certain burthens are to

be met with occasionally. In the parish of Renwick a copy-holder is released from payment of the prescription in lieu of tithe, paid by all his neighbours, because one of his ancestors slew "a cock-a-trice." This monster is alleged to have been nothing more than a bat of extraordinary size, which terrified the people in church one evening, so that all fled save the clerk, who valiantly giving battle, succeeded in striking it down with his staff. For this exploit, which is stated to have taken place about 260 years ago, he was rewarded with the exemption mentioned, which is still claimed by his successors.

In the parish of Castle-Sowerby, the ten principal estates were anciently called *Red Spears*, on account of the singular service by which the tenants held them, viz :—that of riding through the town of Penrith on Whit-Tuesday, brandishing their spears. Those who held by this tenure were of the order of Red Knights, mentioned in our law books ; a name derived from the Saxon, who held their lands by serving the lord on horseback. *Delient equitare cum domino suo de man-erio in manerium, vel cum domini uxore.* In times of peace, it is presumed they held the annual service above noted as a challenge to the enemies of their country, or those who might dispute the title of their lord, similar to the parade of the Champion of England at a coronation. The spears were about nine feet in length, and till within the last century, some of them remained in the proprietors' houses, where they were usually deposited ; and were sureties to the sheriff for the peaceable behaviour of the rest of the inhabitants.

The ancient owners of the Red Spears estates annually served as jurors at the forest court held near Hesket, on St. Barnabas Day, by which they were exempted from all parish offices.

ERMENGARDE.

It was the early summer time,
    When Maidens stint their praying
To wander forth at morning's prime,
    With happy hearts, a maying ;
To wash their rosy cheeks with dew,
    And roam the meadows over :
And ask the winds to tell them true
    Of some far distant lover.

Then little Ermengarde, the while
    To graver thoughts awaking,
Look'd sadly on St. Herbert's Isle
    As morn was brightly breaking.
Some tapestry for his altar wrought
    Beside her bed was lying ;
Her beads, and little scroll for thought,
    No conscious look descrying.

And now when might the gentle Saint
    Be at his service bending;
His earnest life, without a taint
    Of earth still heavenwards tending—
His silver voice, oft heard in prayer,
    Or in direction pleading—
His manhood's bright angelic air—
    Her thought too fond were feeding.

In little Ermengarde her love
    With God the Saint divided.
Unknown even to herself she wove
    The threads her passion guided.
And when she trembled on her knees
    Confessing faith before him—
Ah! can this be but Man she sees,
    So heart and soul adore him!

So little Ermengarde with pale
    And thoughtful cheek sat sighing,
When rode an Elf-man down the vale
    Her open lattice eyeing.
" Good morrow! May my Lady's thought,
    This happy May-day, blossom;
And tenfold blessedness be wrought
    Within that gentle bosom!"

" My tongue no thought or wish express'd"—
    —" Yet, trust me, fairest Lady!
" In Bowscale tarn, for thy behest,
    The undying twain are ready.

Ask from their breasts two tiny scales
    Of gold and pearly whiteness.
These on thy heart—fulfill'd prevails
    Thy wish in all its brightness !"—

The stranger pass'd. Away she hies,
    The mountain pathway keeping,
Where deep amid the silence lies
    The gloomy water sleeping.
" Come, faithful fishes ! give to me
    Two little scales"—she chanted—
That in my bosom peace may be,
    And all my wishes granted."—

They gave her from their pearly sides
    Two little scales.   She bore them
Down from the hill the Tarn that hides,
    And in her bosom wore them.
The simple Cross her mother gave
    Was on her neck, a token
Of that pure faith to which she clave ;
    But lo ! the link was broken !

Down Greta's side with wild delight
    The little Maiden wandered ;
And on the Saint before her sight,
    Her inmost sight, she pondered ;
Now thinking—O that wed with mine
    His holy heart were moving !
How shall we soar in thoughts divine,
    How walk in pathways loving !

It was a festal day, and bands
　Of youths and maids were trooping
With flowers and offerings in their hands,
　And round the altar grouping.
And hark the little bell ! it calls
　To every heart how sweetly !
But most on Ermengarde's it falls
　With joy that brings her fleetly.

But on the stony river's brim
　A moment's space delaying,
To gaze—before she look'd on him—
　On her own features playing
Within the mirror'd pool below—
　Its broken link dissevering,
Her little Cross fell sinking slow
　Beyond her vain endeavouring.

And from the stream two fin-like arms
　Leapt up and snatch'd her wailing,
And dragg'd her down with all her charms
　In anguish unavailing.
And down the rocks they bore her fast
　With struggles unrelenting :
And Greta's roar mix'd in the blast
　With Ermengarde's lamenting.

And far adown the rushing tide
　Was dragg'd and whirled the Maiden ;
And wildly mid the pools she cried
　In accents horror-laden.

The streams dash'd on with furious roar ;
　No aid the rude rocks lent her ;
Wild and more wild they gather'd o'er
　The loud and lost lamenter.

So she whom Magic's wiles had driven,
　And her own heart persuaded,
To tempt a Saint to turn from heaven,
　Feil, snatch'd from life unaided.
Yet, not for ever lost, she roves
　Amid the winding currents,
And utters to the hills and groves
　Her wail above the torrents.

For yet some bard shall wander by
　With harp and song so holy,
That they shall wrench the caves where lie
　Her limbs in anguish lowly.
And free her for the blessed light
　And air again to greet her
Awhile, before she takes her flight
　To where the Saint shall meet her.

Even I, for little Ermengarde,
　Would harp a life-long morrow,
But to reverse that doom so hard,
　And lead her back from sorrow ;
Mid happy thoughts again to beam,
　All joyousness partaking ;
But never more of Saints to dream
　When summer morns are breaking.

NOTES TO "ERMENGARDE."

I.—St. Herbert's Isle, placed nearly in the centre of Derwent Lake, derives its name from a hermit who lived there in the seventh century, and had his cell on this island.

It contains about four acres of ground, is planted with firs and other trees, and has a curious octagonal cottage built with unhewn stones, and artificially mossed over and thatched. This was erected many years ago by the late Sir Wilfred Lawson, to whose representative the island at present belongs. A few yards from its site are the ruins of the hermitage formerly occupied by the recluse. These vestiges, being of stone and mortar, give the appearance of its having consisted of two apartments ; an outer one, about twenty feet long and sixteen feet broad, which has probably been his chapel, and another, of narrower dimensions, his cell, with a little garden adjoining.

The scene around was well adapted to excite the most solemn emotions, and was in unison with the severity of his religious life. His plot of ground and the waters around him supplied his scanty fare ; while the rocks and mountains inspired his meditations with the most sublime ideas of the might and majesty of the Creator. It is no wonder that "St. Herbert, a priest and confessor, to avoid the intercourse of man, and that nothing might withdraw his attention from unceasing meditation and prayer, chose this island for his abode."

There is no history of St. Herbert's life and actions to be met with, or any tradition of his works of piety or miracles, preserved by the inhabitants of the country. His contemporary existence with St. Cuthbert, and his equo-temporary death with him obtained by the prayers of the saint, at the time and in the manner related below, according to the old legends, is all that is known of him.

Bede, in his History of the Church of England, writes thus

of the saint :—" There was a certain priest, revered for his uprightness and perfect life and manners, named Herberte, who had a long time been in union with the man of God (St. Cuthbert of Farn Isle) in the bond of spiritual love and friendship ; for living a solitary life in the isle of that great and extended lake from whence proceeds the river Derwent, he used to visit St. Cuthbert every year, to receive from his lips the doctrines of eternal life. When this holy priest heard of St. Cuthbert's coming to Luguballea (Carlisle), he came, after his usual manner, desiring to be comforted more and more with the hopes of everlasting bliss by his divine exhortations. As they sat together, and enjoyed the hopes of heaven, among other things the Bishop said, ' Remember, brother Herberte, that whatsoever ye have to say and ask of me, you do it now, for after we depart hence, we shall not meet again, and see one another corporeally in this world, for I know well the time of my dissolution is at hand, and the laying aside of this earthly tabernacle draweth on apace.' When Herberte heard this, he fell down at his feet, and, with many sighs and tears, beseeched him, for the love of the Lord, that he would not forsake him, but to remember his faithful brother and associate, and make intercession with the gracious God, that they might depart hence into heaven together, to behold his grace and glory whom they had in unity of spirit served on earth ; for you know I have ever studied and laboured to live according to your pious and virtuous instructions ; and· in whatsoever I offended through ignorance or frailty, I straightway used my earnest efforts to amend after your ghostly counsel, will, and judgment.'—At this earnest and affectionate request of Herberte's, the Bishop went to prayer, presently being certified in spirit that this petition to heaven would be granted—' Arise,' said he, ' my dear brother ; weep not, but let your rejoicing be with exceeding gladness, for the great mercy of God hath granted to us our prayer.'—The truth of which promise and prophecy was well proved in that which ensued ; for their separation was the last that befell them on earth ; on the same day, which was the 19th day of March, their souls departed from their bodies, and were straight in union in the beatific sight and vision—and were transported hence to the kingdom of heaven by the service and hands of angels."

It is probable that the hermit's little oratory, or chapel, might be kept in repair after his death, as a particular veneration seems to have been paid by the religious of after ages to this retreat, and the memory of the Saint.

There is some variation in the account given by authors of the day of the Saint's death ; Bede says the 19th day of March : other authors the 20th day of May, A.D., 687; and by a record given in Bishop Appleby's Register, it would appear that the 13th day of April was observed as the solemn anniversary.

But, however, in the year 1374, at the distance of almost seven centuries, we find this place resorted to in holy services and procession, and the hermit's memory celebrated in religious offices. The Vicar of Crosthwaite went to celebrate mass in his chapel on the island, on the day above mentioned, to the joint honour of St. Herbert and St. Cuthbert ; to every attendant at which forty days' indulgence was granted as a reward for his devotion. "What a happy holiday must that have been for all these vales," says Southey; "and how joyous on a fine spring day must the lake have appeared, with the boats and banners from every chapelry ; and how must the chapel have adorned that little isle, giving a human and religious character to the solitude !"

In the little church of St. John's in the Vale, which is one of the dependent chapelries of the church of Crosthwaite, is an old seat, with the date 1001 carved on the back of it, to which tradition assigns, that it was formerly in St. Herbert's Chapel, on the island in Derwent Lake.

These figures correspond with those on the bell in the Town Hall at Keswick, said to have been brought from Lord's Island.

II.—Bowscale Tarn is a small mountain lake, lying to the north-east of Blencathra. It is supposed by the country people in the neighbourhood, with whom it has long been a tradition, to contain two immortal fish ; the same which held familiar intercourse with, and long did the bidding of, the Shepherd Lord when he studied the stars upon these mountains, and gathered that more mysterious knowledge, which, matured in the solitude of Barden Tower, has till this day associated his name with something of supernatural interest in this district, where he so long resided.*

From some lines of Martial (lib. iv. 30) it appears that there were some fishes in a lake at Baiæ in Campania consecrated to Domitian, and like the undying ones of Bowscale Tarn, they knew their master :—

* Vide Notes to Sir Lancelot Threlkeld, for a notice of Lord Clifford the Shepherd.

"Sacris piscibus hæ natantur undæ,
Qui norunt dominum, manumque lambunt;
——————————— et ad magistri
Vocem quisquis sui venet citatus."

III.—It has been stated with reference to the river Greta, that its channel was formerly remarkable for the immense stones it contained; and that by their concussion in high floods were caused those loud and mournful noises which not inappropriately have gained for it the characteristic title of "Mourner." Mr. Southey has given the following description of it in his "Colloquies";—"Our Cumberland river Greta has a shorter course than even its Yorkshire namesake. St. John's Beck and the Glenderamakin take this name at their confluence, close by the bridge three miles east of Keswick on the Penrith road. The former issues from Leathes Water, in a beautiful sylvan spot, and proceeds by a not less beautiful course for some five miles through the vale from which it is called, to the place of junction. The latter receiving the stream from Bowscale and Threlkeld Tarns, brings with it the waters from the south side of Blencathra. The Greta then flows toward Keswick; receives first the small stream from Nathdale; next the Glenderaterra, which brings down the western waters of Blencathra and those from Skiddaw Forest, and making a wide sweep behind the town, joins the Derwent under Derwent Hill, about a quarter of a mile from the town, and perhaps half that distance from the place where that river flows out of the lake, but when swollen above its banks, it takes a shorter line, and enters Derwent Water.

"The Yorkshire stream was a favourite resort of Mason's, and has been celebrated by Sir Walter Scott. Nothing can be more picturesque, nothing more beautiful, than its course through the grounds at Rokeby, and its junction with the Tees;—and there is a satisfaction in knowing that the possessor of that beautiful place fully appreciates and feels its beauties, and is worthy to possess it. Our Greta is of a different character, and less known; no poet has brought it into notice, and the greater number of tourists seldom allow themselves time for seeing anything out of the beaten track. Yet the scenery upon this river, where it passes under the sunny side of Latrigg, is of the finest and most rememberable kind:

—Ambiguo lapsu, refluitque fluitque,
Occurrensque sibi venturas aspicit undas.

There is no English stream to which this truly Ovidian

description can more accurately be applied. From a jutting isthmus, round which the tortuous river twists, you look over its manifold windings, up the water to Blencathra; down it, over a high and wooded middle ground, to the distant mountains of Newlands, Cawsey Pike, and Grizedale."

GUNILDA;

OR, THE WOEFUL CHASE.

A joyful train left Lucy's halls
At morning, cheer'd with bugle calls,
That long ere eve, a mournful train,
Returned to Lucy's halls again.

They went with hound and spear and bow,
To lay the prowling wild-wolf low.
They came with hound and bow and spear—
And one fair daughter on her bier.

Her prancing palfrey starting wide,
She gallop'd from Lord Lucy's side,
A shining huntress, gay, and bold,
And fair as Dian's self of old.

The quarry cross'd her lover's view;
He led the chace with shrill halloo,
Through brake and furze, by stream and dell,
Nor stopp'd until the quarry fell.

Far off aloud rang out his horn
The triumph on the echoes borne,
Long ere the listening maid drew rein
To woo it to her ear in vain.

Bright as a phantom, far astray,
She stood where broad before her lay
Wilton's high wastes and forest rude,
And all the Copeland solitude.

Far off, and farther, rang the horn :
Farther the echoes seem'd to mourn.
" Now, my good Bay, thy frolic o'er,
Thy swiftest and thy best once more !"

By Hole of Haile she turned her steed :
Coursed gaily on by Yeorton Mead ;
Glanced where St. Bridget's hamlet show'd ;
And down into the coppice rode.

And singing on in gladness there,
She pass'd beside the she-wolf's lair ;
When furious from her startled young
The wild brute on Gunilda sprung.

From frighted steed dragg'd low to ground,
The she-wolf, with her cubs around,
Made havoc of that peerless form,
And heart with bounding life so warm.

Clearer rang out their horn, to cheer
Their lost one ; and proclaim'd them near.
Proudly they said—" Gunilda's eyes
Will brighten when she sees our prize !"—

They found her ; but their words were " Woe !
" Woe to the bank where thou liest low !
Woe to the hunting of this day,
That left thy limbs to beasts, a prey !"

With downcast faces, eyeballs dim,
They bore her up that mount—to him
A Mount of Sorrow evermore,
Too faithful to the name it bore.

They made in Bega's aisle her tomb,
And laid her in the convent gloom ;
And carved her effigy in stone,
And hew'd the she-wolf's form thereon—

In pity to this hour to wake
The pilgrim's sorrow for her sake,
And his who blew the lively horn,
Expecting her—and came to mourn.

NOTES TO "GUNILDA; OR, THE WOEFUL CHASE."

A traditional story in the neighbourhood of Egremont relates the circumstance of a lady ot the Lucy family being devoured by a wolf. According to one version this catastrophe occurred on an evening walk near the Castle ; whilst, a more popular rendering of the legend ascribes it to an occasion on which the lord of the manor, with his lady and servants, were hunting in the forest; when the lady having been lost in the ardour of the chase, was after a long search and heart-rending suspense, found lying on a bank slain by a wolf which was in the act of tearing her to pieces. The place is distinguished by a mound of earth, near the village of Beckermet, on the banks of the Ehen, about a mile below Egremont. The name of Woto Bank, or Wodow Bank as the modern mansion erected near the spot is called, is said to be derived by traditionary etymology, from the expression to which in the first transports of his grief the distracted husband gave utterance—" Woe to this bank."

Hutchinson is inclined to believe " that this place has been witness to many bloody conflicts, as appears by the monuments scattered on all hands in its neighbourhood ; and by some the story is supposed to be no more than an emblematic allusion to such conflicts during the invasion of the Danes. It is asserted that no such relation is to be found in the history of the Lucy family ; so that it must be fabulous, or figurative of some other event."

There are, however, yet to be seen in the burial ground attached to the Abbey Church of St. Bees, the remaining parts of two monumental figures which may reasonably be presumed to have reference to some such event as that recorded by tradition. The fragments, which are much mutilated, are of stone; and the sculpture appears to be of great antiquity. Common report has assigned to these remains the names of Lord and Lady Lucy.

In their original state, the figures were of gigantic size. The features and legs are now destroyed. The Lord is represented with his sword sheathed. There is a shield on his arm, which appears to have been quartered, but the bearings upon it are entirely defaced. On the breast of the Lady is an unshapely protuberance. This was originally the roughly sculptured limb of a wolf, which even so lately as the year 1806, might be distinctly ascertained. These figures were formerly placed in an horizontal position, at the top of two raised altar tombs within the church. The tomb of the Lady was at the foot of her Lord, and a wolf was represented as standing over it. The protuberance above mentioned, on the breast of the Lady, the paw of the wolf, is all that now remains of the animal. About a century since, the figure of the wolf wanted but one leg, as many of the inhabitants, whose immediate ancestors remembered it nearly entire, can testify. The horizontal position of the figures rendered them peculiarly liable to injuries, from the silent and irresistible ravages of time. Their present state is, however, principally to be attributed to the falling in of the outer walls of the priory, and more particularly to their having been used, many years since, by the boys of the Free Grammar School, as a mark to fire at. There can be little doubt that the limb of the wolf has reference to the story of one of the Ladies Lucy related above.

It may not however be unworthy of remark, that the Lucies were connected, through the family of Meschines, with Hugh d' Abrincis, Earl of Chester, who in the year 1070 is said to have borne azure a wolf's head erased argent, and who had the surname of Lupus.

The wife of Hugh Lupus was sister to Ranulph de Meschin.

The family of Meschines has been said to be descended from that at Rome called by the name Mæcenas, from which the former one is corrupted. "Certainly," says a recent writer, "it has proved itself the Mæcenas of the Priory of St. Bees, not merely in the foundation of that religious house, but also in the charters for a long course of years, which have been granted by persons of different names, indeed, but descended from, or connected with, the same beneficent stock." This is shown in the following extract from a MS. in the Harleian Collection:—

"Be y^t notid that Wyllyam Myschen son of Ranolf Lord of Egermond founded the monastery of Saint Beysse of blake monks, and heyres to the said Meschyn y^s the Lords Fitzwal, the Lord Haryngton, and the Lord Lucy, and so restyth founders of the said monastery therle of Sussex the Lord Marques Dorset, therle of Northumberland as heyres to the Lords aforesaid."

The religious house thus restored, consisting of a prior and six Benedictine monks, was made a cell to the mitred Abbey of Saint Mary, at York. And under this cell, Bishop Tanner says, there was a small nunnery situated at Rottington, about a mile from St. Bees.

At the dissolution, the annual revenues of this priory, according to Dugdale, were £143 17s. 2d. ; or, by Speed's valuation, £149 19s. 6d. ; from which it appears there were only two religious houses in the county more amply endowed, viz. the priory of Holme-Cultram, and the Priory of St. Mary, Carlisle ; which latter was constituted a cathedral church at the Reformation.

The conventual church of St. Bees is in the usual form of a cross, and consists of a nave with aisles, a choir, and transepts, with a massive tower, at the intersection, which until lately terminated in an embattled parapet. This part of the building is now disfigured by an addition to enable it to carry some more bells. The rest of the edifice is in the early English style, and has been thoroughly restored with great taste and feeling. On the south side of the nave there was formerly a recumbent wooden figure, in mail armour, supposed to have been the effigy of Anthony, the last Lord Lucy of Egremont, who died A.D. 1368. The Lady Chapel, which had been a roofless ruin for two centuries, was fitted up as a lecture-room for the College established by Bishop Law in 1817.

The priors of this religious house ranked as barons of the Isle of Man ; as the Abbot of the superior house, St. Mary's, at York, was entitled to a seat amongst the parliamentary barons of England. As such he was obliged to give his attendance upon the kings and lords of Man, whensoever they required it, or at least, upon every new succession in the government. The neglect of this important privilege would probably involve the loss of the tithes and lands in that island, which the devotion of the kings had conferred upon the priory of St. Bees.

In the library of the Dean and Chapter of Carlisle is the following curious account of the discovery of a giant at St. Bees :—

"A true report of Hugh Hodson, of Thorneway, in Cumberland, to S͏ʳ Rob Cewell (qy. Sewell) of a Gyant found at S. Bees, in Cumb'land, 1601, before X͏ᵗ mas.

"The said Gyant was buried 4 yards deep in the ground, wᶜʰ is now a corn feild.

"He was 4 yards and an half long, and was in complete armour : his sword and battle-axe lying by him.

"His sword was two spans broad and more than 2 yards long.

"The head of his battle axe a yard long, and the shaft of it all of iron, as thick as a man's thigh, and more than 2 yards long.

"His teeth were 6 inches long, and 2 inches broad ; his forehead was more than 2 spans and a half broad.

"His chine bone could containe 3 pecks of oatmeale.

"His armour, sword, and battle-axe, are at Mr. Sand's of Redington, (Rottington) and at Mr. Wyber's, at St. Bees."—
Machel MSS. Vol. vi.

16

THE SHIELD OF FLANDRENSIS.

The Knight sat lone in Old Rydal Hall,
Of the line of Flandrensis burly and tall.
His book lay open upon the board :
His elbow rested on his good sword:
His knightly sires and many a dame
Look'd on him from panel and dusky frame.
High over the hearth was their ancient shield,
An argent fret on a blood-red field—
"Peace, Plenty, Wisdom."—"Peace?" he said:
" Peace there is none for living or dead."

The Autumnal day had died away:
The reapers deep in their slumbers lay:
The harvest moon through the blazoned panes
From Scandale Brow poured in the stains :
His household train, and his folk at rest,
    he child that he loved best :

His startled ear caught up the swell
Of distant sounds he knew too well.
By his golden lamp to the shield he said,
" Peace? Peace there is none for living or dead."

The Knight he came of high degree,
None better or braver in arms than he :
Worthy of old Flandrensis' fame,
Whose soul not battle nor broil could tame.
That neighing and trampling of horses late,
That hubbub of voices round his gate,
That sound of hurry along the floors,
That dirge-like wail through distant doors,
Tempestuous in the calm, he heard :
And he looked on the shield, nor spoke, nor stirr'd.

From inmost chambers far remote
Responsive flow'd one dirge-like note :
Loud through the arches deep and wide
One little voice did sweetly glide ;
Its sad accords along the gloom
Swelled on towards that lordly room—
" We wait not long, our watch we keep,
We all are singing, and none may sleep :
When stone on stone nor roof remain,
The unresting shall have rest again."

The Knight turned listening to the door.
His little maid came up the floor.
Her nightly robe of purest white
Gleamed purer in the faded light.
The blazoned moonbeams slowly swept
The spaces round, as on she stept.
And lo ! in his armour from head to toe,
With his beard of a hundred winters' snow,
Stood old Flandrensis burly and tall, ·
With his breast to the shield, and his back to the wall.

The six score winters in his eyes
Unfroze, as on through the blazoned dyes,
Sable, and azure, and gules, she came.
Through his heaving beard low fluttered her name.
But slowly and solemnly, leading or led
By phantoms chanting for living or dead,
Pass'd on the little voice so sweet—
"We all are singing: we all must meet"—
And into the gloom like a fading ray:
And the form of Flandrensis vanished away.

The Knight, alone, in his ancient hold,
Sat still as a stone: his blood ran cold.
For his little maiden was his delight.
Then forth he strode in the face of the night.
His dogs were in kennel, his steeds in stall :
His deer were lying about his hall:

His swans beneath the Lord's Oak Tree:
The silvery Rotha was flowing free.
He set his brow towards Scandale hill:
The vale was breathing, but all was still.

He thought of the spirits the snow-winds rouse,
The Piping Spirits of Sweden Hows,
That wail to the Rydal Chiefs their fate—
That pipe as they whirl around lattice and gate,
With their grey gaunt misty forms : but now,
There was not a stir in the lightest bough :
The winds in the mountain gorge were laid;
No sound through all the moonlight stray'd.
He turned again to his ancient Keep:
'There all was silence, and calm, and sleep.

But all grew changed in the gloomy pile.
His little maiden lost her smile.
The menials fled: that knightly race
Was left alone in its ancient place:
The pride of its line of warriors quailed—
Those sworded knights once peerless hailed:
To the earth broke down from its hold their shield.
With its argent fret and its blood-red field:
And they fled from the might of the powers that
        strode
In the darkness through their old abode.

And Sir Michael brooded an autumn day,
As he looked on the slope at his child at play,
On the green by the sounding water's fall:
And often those words did he recall—
"We wait not long, our watch we keep;
We all are singing, and none may sleep.
When stone on stone nor roof remain,
The unresting shall have rest again."
And the Knight ordained, as he brooded alone—
"There shall not be left of it roof or stone."

And Sir Michael said—"I will build my hall
On the green by the sounding waterfall:
And an arbour cool at its foot, beside.
And I'll bury my shield in the crystal tide,
To cleanse it from blood perchance, that so
Peace, Plenty, and Wisdom again may flow
Round old Flandrensis' honours and name."—
And the pile arose: and the sun's bright flame
Was pleasant around it: and morn and even
It lay in the light and the hues of heaven.

And Sir Michael sat in the arbour cool,
Where the waters leapt in the crystal pool;
Saying—"Gone is yon keep to a grim decay.
And now, my little one, loved alway!
Whence came thy singing so wild and deep?"—

—" We all were singing, and none might sleep,
'Till all the Unmerciful heard their strain.
But now the unresting have rest again."—

So the keep went down to the dust and mould.
And the new pile bore the blazon of old—
The pride of the old ancestral shield—
The argent fret on the blood-red field;
        " Peace, Plenty, Wisdom "
          Beneath enscrolled.

NOTES TO "THE SHIELD OF FLANDRENSIS."

The ancient Manor house at Rydal stood in the Low Park, on the top of a round hill, on the south side of the road leading from Keswick to Kendal. But on the building of the new mansion on the north side of the highway, in what is called the High Park, the manor house became ruinous, and got the name of the Old Hall, which, says Dr. Burn, in his time, "it still beareth." Even then there was nothing to be seen but ruinous buildings, walks, and fish ponds, and other marks of its ancient consequence; the place where the orchard stood was then a large enclosure without a fruit tree in it, and called the Old Orchard. At the present day few indications of its site remain. Tradition asserts that it was deserted from superstitious fears.

The present mansion was erected by Sir Michael le Fleming in the last century. It stands on the north side of the road, on a slope facing the south, is a large old fashioned building, and commands a fine view of Windermere. Behind it rises Rydal Head, and Nab-Scar a craggy mountain 1030 feet above the level of the sea. The Park is interspersed with abundance of old oaks, and several rocky protuberances in the lawn are covered with fine elms and other forest trees. The Lord's Oak, a magnificent specimen, is built into the wall on the lower side of the Rydal Road over which it majestically towers. "The sylvan, or rather forest scenery of Rydal Park," says Professor Wilson, "was, in the memory of living men, magnificent, and it still contains a treasure of old trees." The two waterfalls, the cascades of the rivulet which runs through the lawn, are situated in the grounds. The way leads through the park meadow and outer gardens by a path of singular beauty and richness. They are in the opinion of

Gilpin and other tourists unparalleled in their kind. The upper fall is the finest, in the eyes of those who prefer the natural accessories of a cascade : but the lower one, which is below the Hall, is beheld from the window of an old summer house. This affords a fine picture frame ; the basin of rock and the bridge above, with the shadowy pool, and the over-hauging verdure, constituting a perfect picture.

The heraldic distinction, the fret, is found more than once in Furness Abbey, and is undoubtedly the ancient arms of le Fleming. An entire seal appended to a deed from Sir Richard le Fleming of Furness dated 44 Edward the Third (1371) shews a fret hung cornerwise, the crest, on a helmet a fern, or something like it. The seal annexed to another deed dated 6 Henry V. (1419) is the same as above described ; the motto, *S. Thome Flemin*, in Saxon characters.

The present crest and motto are of modern date, and explain each other : the serpent is the emblem of wisdom, as the olive and the vine are of peace and plenty. But upon what occasion this distinction was taken does not appear.

THE ROOKS OF FURNESS.

"Caw ! Caw !" the rooks of Furness cry.
"Caw ! Caw !" the Furness rooks reply.
In and about the saintly pile, ˙
Over refectory, porch, and aisle,
Perching on archway, window, and tower,
Hopping and cawing hour by hour.
Saint Mary of Furness knows them well !
They are souls of her Monks laid under a spell.
They were once White Monks ; ere the altars fell,
And the vigils ceased, and the Abbey bell
Was hush'd in the Deadly Nightshade Dell.

"Caw ! Caw !" for ever, from morn
Till night they trouble the ruins forlorn :
Roger the Abbot, parading in black,
Briand the Prior, and scores at his back

Of those old fathers cawing amain,
All robed in rooks' black feathers, in vain
Waiting again for the Abbey to rise,
For matins to waken the morning skies,
And themselves to chant the litanies.

"Caw ! Caw !"   No wonder they caw !
To see—where their vigorous rule was law—
Fair Love with his troops of youths and maids,
With holiday hearts, through greenwood shades
Come forth, and in every Muse's name,
With songs, a joyful time proclaim ;
And to hear the car-borne Demon's yell,
The Steam-Ghoul screeching the fatal knell
Of peace in the Deadly Nightshade Dell.

"Caw ! Caw !" still over the walls
You wheel and flutter, with ceaseless calls ;
Thinking, no doubt, of your cells and holes,
You poor old Monks' translated souls !
Sad change for you to be cawing here,
And black, for many a hundred year !
But haunt as you may your ancient pile,
You will never more chant in the holy aisle ;
You never will kneel as you knelt of yore ;
Nor the censer swing, nor the anthem pour ;
And your souls shall never shake off the spell
That binds you to all you loved so well,
Ere the altars fell, and the Abbey bell
Was hush'd in the Deadly Nightshade Dell.

"Caw! Caw!"   In the ages gone,
When the mountains with oak were overgrown,
Up the glen the Norskmen came,
Lines of warriors, chiefs of fame—
With Bekan the Sorcerer, earthward borne,
By toil, and battle, and tempest worn—
Crowding along the dell forlorn.
Over the rill, high on the steep,
There in his barrow wide and deep,
With axe and hoe those armed men
Buried him down, by the narrow glen,
With the flower, at his feet, ot wondrous spell :
Buried him down, and covered him well,
And left him hid by the lonely Dell.

"Caw! Caw!" O would the wise Monks had known
Who slept his sleep in that barrow alone,
When they gathered the bekan he made to grow,
And bore it to bloom in the dell below.
For they pulled at the heart of the mighty Dead ;
And they broke his peace in his narrow bed ;
And on fibre and root the Sorcerer's power
Fasten'd the spell that changed the flower ;
From sweet to bitter its juices pass'd ;
And the deadly fruit on the poisoned blast
Scattered its sorcery ages down.
And where once with cowl and gown,
Hymning the Imperial Queen of Light,
Went forth the Monks—the shade of night

Was spread more deadly than tongue can tell.
Witchery walked where all had been well :
Well with all that hymned and prayed ;
Well with Monk, and well with maid
That sought the Abbey for solace and aid.
But the lethal juices wrought their spell :
One by one was rung their knell :
One by one from choir and cell
They floated up with a hoarse farewell ;
And the altars fell, and the Abbey bell
Was hush'd in the Deadly Nightshade Dell.

NOTES TO "THE ROOKS OF FURNESS."

In the southern extremity of Furness, about half a mile to the west of Dalton, a deep narrow vale stretches itself from the north, and opens to the south with an agreeable aspect to the noonday sun ; it is well watered with a rivulet of fine water collected from the adjacent springs, and has many convenient places for mills and fish-ponds.   This romantic spot is the Vale of Deadly Nightshade, or, as it is sometimes called, Bekangs-Gill.

The solitary and private situation of this dell being so well formed and commodious for religious retreat had attracted the attention of Evanus, ¯or Ewanus, a monk, originally belonging to the monastery of Savigny in Normandy, from which he and a few associates had migrated, and had recently seated themselves at Tulket, near Preston in Amounderness, where Evanus was chosen to be their first abbot.   Accordingly, they were induced to change their residence ; and exactly three years and three days after their settling at Tulket on the fourth of the nones of July, 1124, they removed to the sequestered shades of Bekangs-Gill, and there began the foundation of the magnificent Abbey of St. Mary in Furness, in magnitude only second of those in England belonging to the Cistercian Monks, and the next in opulence after Fountains Abbey in Yorkshire, being endowed with princely wealth and almost princely authority, and not unworthy of the style in which its charter records the gifts and grants, with all their privileges, of its Royal founder, "to God and St. Mary," in the following words :—

"In the name of the Blessed Trinity, and in honour of St. Mary of Furness, I Stephen, earl of Bulloign and Mortaign, consulting God, and providing for the safety of my own soul, the soul of my wife the countess Matilda, the soul of my lord and uncle Henry king of England and duke of Normandy, and for the souls of all the faithful, living as well as dead, in the year of our Lord 1127 of the Roman indiction, and the 5th and 18th of the epact :

"Considering every day the uncertainty of life, that the roses and flowers of kings, emperors, and dukes, and the crowns and palms of all the great, wither and decay ; and that all things, with an uninterrupted course, tend to dissolution and death :

" I therefore return, give and grant, to God and St. Mary of Furness, all Furness and Walney, with the privilege of hunting ; with Dalton, and all my lordship in Furness, with the men and everything thereto belonging, that is, in woods and in open grounds, in land and in water ; and Ulverston, and Roger Braithwaite, with all that belongs to him ; my fisheries at Lancaster, and Little Guoring, with all the land thereof ; with sac [1], and soc [2], tol [3], and team [4], infangenetheof [5], and every thing within Furness, except the lands of Michael Le Fleming ; with this view, and upon this condition, That in Furness an order of regular monks be by divine permission established : which gift and offering I by supreme authority appoint to be for ever observed : and that it may remain firm and inviolate for ever, I subscribe this charter with my hand ; and confirm it with the sign of the Holy Cross.

" Signed by
    Henry, King of England and Duke of Normandy.
    Thurstan, Archbishop of York.
    Audin, } Bishops.
    Boces, }
                Robert, Keeper of the Seal.
                Robert, Earl of Gloster."

The magnitude of the Abbey may be known from the dimensions of the ruins ; and enough is standing to show the style of the architecture, which breathes the same sim-

---

1 *Saccum.*—The power of imposing fines upon tenants and vassals within the lordship.
2 *Soccum.*—The power and authority of administering justice.
3 *Tollum.*—A duty paid for buying and selling, &c.
4 *Theam, Team.*—A royalty granted for trying bondmen and villains, with a sovereign power over their villain tenants, their wives, children, and goods, to dispose of them at pleasure.
5 *Infangenetheof.*—The power of judging of thefts committed within the liberty of Furness.

plicity of taste which is found in most houses belonging to the Cistercian monks, which were erected about the same time with Furness Abbey. The round and pointed arches occur in the doors and windows. The fine clustered Gothic and the heavy plain Saxon pillars stand contrasted. The walls shew excellent masonry, are in many places counter-arched, and the ruins discover a strong cement. But all is plain : had the monks even intended, the stone would not admit of such work as has been executed at Fountains and Rieval Abbeys. The stone of which the buildings have been composed is of a pale red colour, dug from the neighbouring rocks, now changed by time and weather to a tint of dusky brown, which accords well with the hues of plants and shrubs that everywhere emboss the mouldering arches.

The church and cloisters were encompassed with a wall, which commenced at the east side of the great northern door, and formed the strait enclosure ; and a space of ground, to the amount of sixty-five acres, was surrounded with a strong stone wall, which enclosed the porter's lodge, the mills, granaries, ovens, kilns, and fish-ponds belonging to the Abbey, the ruins of which are still visible. This last was the great enclosure, now called the deer-park, within which, placed on the crown of an eminence that rises immediately from the Abbey, and seen over all low Furness, are the remains of a beacon or watch-tower, raised by the society for their further security, and commanding a magnificent prospect. The door leading to it is still remaining in the enclosure wall, on the eastern side.

During the residence of the monks at Tulket, and until the election of their fifth Abbot (Richard de Bajocis) they were of the order of Savigny under the rule of St. Benedict ; and from their habit or dress were called Grey Monks ; but at the time of the general matriculation of the Savignian monasteries with that of Citeaux, the monks of Furness also accepted of the reform, exchanged their patron St. Benedict for St. Bernard, changed their dress from grey to white, and so became White Monks, Bernardins, or Cistercians, the rule of which order they religiously observed until the dissolution of the monasteries.

The Cistercian order in its origin was devoted to the practice of penance, silence, assiduous contemplation, and the angelical functions (as Mr. West expresses it) of singing the divine praises ; wherefore it did not admit of the ordinary dissipation which attends scholastic enquiries. St. Bernard who was himself a man of learning, well knowing how far reading was necessary to improve the mind even of a recluse, took great care to furnish his monks with good libraries. Such of them as were best qualified were employed in taking copies of books in every branch of literature, many of which, beautifully written on vellum, and elegantly illuminated, are at this time to be seen in their libraries. They used neither furs nor linen, and never eat any flesh, except in time of dangerous sickness ; they abstained even from eggs, butter, milk, and cheese, unless upon extraordinary occasions, and when given to them in alms. They had belonging to them certain religious lay brethren, whose office was to cultivate their lands, and attend to their secular affairs : these lived at their granges and farms, and were treated in like manner with the monks, but were never indulged with the use of wine. The monks who attended the choir slept in their habits upon straw ; they rose at midnight, and spent the rest of the night in singing the divine office. After prime and the first mass, having accused themselves of their faults in public chapter, the rest of the day was spent in a variety of spiritual exercises with uninterrupted silence. From the Feast of the Exaltation of the Holy Cross (the 14th of September) until Easter they observed a strict fast : and flesh was banished from their infirmaries from Septuagesima until Easter. This latter class of monks was confined to the boundary wall, except that on some particular days the members of it were allowed to walk in parties beyond it, for exercise and amusement ; but they were very seldom permitted either to receive or pay visits. Much of these rigorous observances was mitigated by a bull of Pope Sixtus IV., in the year 1485, when among other indulgencies the whole order was allowed to eat flesh three times in every week ; for which purpose a particular dining-room, separate and distinct from the usual refectory, was fitted up in every monastery. They were distinguished for extensive charities and liberal hospitality ; for travellers were so sumptuously entertained at the Abbey, that it was not till the dissolution that an inn was thought necessary in this part of Furness, when one was opened for their accommodation, expressly because the Monastery could no longer receive them. With the rules of St. Bernard the monks had adopted the white cassock, with a white caul and scapulary. Their choral dress was either white or grey, with caul and scapulary of the same, and a girdle of black wool ; over that a hood and a rocket, the front part of which descended to the girdle, where it ended in a round, and the back part reached down to the

17

middle of the leg behind : when they appeared abroad, they wore a caul and full black hood.

The privileges and immunities granted to the Cistercian order in general were very numerous : and those to the Abbey of Furness were proportioned to its vast endowments. The Abbot held his secular court in the neighbouring castle of Dalton, where he presided, with the power of administering not only justice, but injustice, since the lives and property of the villain tenants of the lordship of Furness were consigned by a grant of King Stephen to the disposal of the lordly Abbot ! The monks also could be arraigned, for whatever crime, only by him. The military establishment of Furness likewise depended upon the Abbot. Every mesne lord and free homager, as well as the customary tenants, took an oath of fealty to the Abbot, to be true to him against all men, except the king. Every mesne lord obeyed the summons of the Abbot, or his steward, in raising his quota of armed men ; and every tenant of a whole tenement furnished a man and a horse of war for guarding the coast, for the border service, or any expedition against the common enemy of the king and kingdom. The habiliments of war were a steel coat, or coat of mail, a falce, or falchion, a jack, the bow, the byll, the crossbow, and spear.

What wonder, says a lively writer, that Abbot Pele, or any other man, owning such vast possessions and having such temporal and spiritual privileges as the following, should have grown proud and gross, and contumacious ! Within the limits of his own district he was little short of omnipotent. The same oath of fealty was taken to him as to the king himself ; he had no less than twelve hundred and fifty-eight able men armed with coats of mail, spears, and bows and arrows, upon the possessions of the Monastery, ready for active service, four hundred of whom were cavalry ; besides manorial rights, he had extended feudal privileges, appointment of sheriff, coroner, and constable, wreck of the sea, freedom from suit of county ; a free market and fair at Dalton, with a court of criminal jurisdiction ; lands and tenements exempt from all toll and tax whatever ; the emoluments incidental to wardship, such as the fining of young ladies who married against his will, &c. He had the patronage of all the churches save one ; no bailiff could come into his territories under any pretence whatever ; and no man was to presume in any way to molest or disturb him on pain of forfeiting ten pounds to the king. In addition to its rich home territory in the North Lonsdale, the Abbey possessed the manor of Beaumont in the south ; land and houses at Bolton, and in many other places near Lancaster ; five villages in Yorkshire, with much land and pasturage; and a mansion for the abbot, in York itself ; all beautiful Borrowdale in Cumberland was their property; houses at Boston in Lincolnshire; land in the Isle of Man ; and houses in Drogheda and two other towns in Ireland. The home lordship comprehended the rich district of Low Furness and all the district included between the river Duddon on the one side, and the Elter (beginning at the Shire Stones on the top of Wrynose), Lake Windermere and the Leven on the other ; with the isles of Walney and Foulney, and the Pile of Fouldrey. They had an excellent harbour of refuge fitted to accommodate the largest vessels of that era at any time of tide, and they had four good iron mines in their near neighbourhood, the ore of which, however, they do not seem to have exported. The total income of the society appears, at the time of its dissolution in 1537, to have been more than nine hundred pounds a-year ; which would be represented by about ten times that value in our time, or *nine thousand a-year.*

But in the reign of Edward the First, its revenues seem to have been nearly as large again. According to the late Mr. Beck, the author of *Annales Furnesienses*, to which we are indebted for much of these particulars, the tenants of the Abbey paid great part of their rents by provisioning the monks with grain, lambs, calves, &c., or bartered them for beer, bread, iron, wood, and manure. More than two hundred gallons of beer were distributed weekly among these tenants upon tunning days, accompanied with about three score of loaves of bread; the expenditure in this particular alone, per annum, must have been at least one thousand pounds of our present money : one ton of malleable iron was also given to the same people for the repair of their ploughs, and wood for that of their houses and fences. They might take, too, all the manure—amounting yearly to four or five hundred cartloads—with the exception of that from the Abbot's and high stables. The tenants paid by way of fine, or admission to their tenements, but one penny, called "God's Penny," and were sworn to be true to the king and to the convent. What alms were distributed amongst the poor by this wealthy and pious society we have no means of discovering. It was bound, upon the anniversary of Saints Crispin and Crispinian, to distribute two oxen, two cows, and

one bull among the poor folks who assembled for that purpose
at the Porter's Lodge. At the same place, ninety-nine
shillings' worth of bread, and six maze of *fresh* herrings,
valued at forty shillings, were also given in alms every Monday
and Tuesday ; the convent maintained from its very com-
mencement thirteen poor men, allowing each of them thirty-
three shillings and fourpence yearly : and eight widows
received a similar allowance of provisions to that allowed for
the same number of monks. They had five flagons of ale
weekly, and each of them a *clibanus*,* which it is supposed
must have been a certain quantity of bread. Lastly, there
were two schools held in some part of the monastery, where
the children of those tenants who paid their rent in provisions,
and who it is probable lived in the neighbourhood, received
their education gratuitously, and dined in the hall during their
attendance as well. If one of these showed symptoms of
superior intelligence, he had the privilege of being elected
into the society in preference to all others, by which step he
might rise by good fortune or *finesse* even to be Lord of
Furness.

The society numbered three and thirty monks at the time
of its dissolution, and about one hundred converts and
servants, and no convert was admitted who could not pay for
the labour of an hireling. To have been head of such a
colony at home, and to have wielded such a power abroad,
must have made even the most pious of abbots "draw too
proud a breath;" and yet with all the faults and all the vices
of that cowled priesthood, we cannot now forbear to pity their
sad fate, when bidden by the remorseless king to leave their
grand old residences and quiet ways of life wherein they had
lived so long !

It must be added, that to so much power and so great
prosperity, with all the beneficence and usefulness of the
society there had come to be allied an amount of profligacy
and irreligion proportionate to the many advantages which it
had enjoyed.

The early part of the sixteenth century found the morality
of the monastery represented in many instances by social
arrangements in direct violation of the injunctions laid upon
all monastic institutions, "in the king's behalf;" amongst
others, of that one which especially enjoins that "women of
what state or degree soever they be, be utterly excluded from

* *Clibanus*, a portable oven : the term probably represents the
quantity of bread contained in it at one baking.

entering into the limit or circuit of this monastery or place, unless they first obtain license of the King's Highness, or his visitor." It was stated, and apparently well authenticated, that Rogerus Pele (abbot) had two wives, or what amounted to the same thing, two concubines ; and amongst his subordinate monks, Johannes Groyn had one, whilst Thomas Hornsby had five. Thus, evil days in one sense had already come ; and others were fast drawing nigh. The mandate, moreover, had been prepared for their destruction independently of these and such like shortcomings ; but they afforded a powerful handle by which to wrest them to destruction.

First came the commissioners appointed by the King for visiting the monasteries in the North of England, with their searching examination into everything connected with each separate society : next, the list of crimes charged on the monks at the time of the visitation : then the devices of the Earl of Sussex "advertised" in his letter to the King, wherein "I, the said erle, devising with myselfe, yf one way would not serve, how, and by what other means, the said monks might be ryd from the said abbey ;" the summons to Whalley of the unhappy Abbot to make his proposal, in his own handwriting, according to the "ded enrolled, which A. Fitzherbert hath drawn" for the surrender of his monastery to the King : and then the final consummation of all. For come it must. On the 7th day of April, 1537, in spite of prayers to the "kynge," in spite of many a "shillinge in golde" given to the "right honerable and our singler goode Mr. Mayster Thomas Cromwell, secretarie to the Kynge's highness," the royal commissioners came down upon their prey. After hanging the Abbot of Whalley, and the royal injunction that "all monks and chanons, that be in any wise faultie, are *to be tyed uppe without further delay or ceremonie*," the Abbot of Furnesse is found "to be of a very facile and ready minde," and all hope of averting his doom being over, and his sense of peril hastening his submission, "it coming freely of himself and without enforcement," he signed the fatal deed of surrender, confessing with contrition "the mysorder and evil lyfe both to God and our prynce of the brethren of this monasterie ;" the pen passed from the hand of the Superior to each monk in succession, and the "lamp on the altar of St. Mary of Furness was extinguished for ever."

With forty shillings given to them by the King, and clad in "secular wedes" (that is, lay garments), without which they were not permitted to depart, they turned their faces from their magnificent home in the Nightshade Dell. To the degraded Abbot was given the Rectory of Dalton, valued at £33 6s. 9d. yearly, obtained with difficulty, and even of which he was not allowed undisturbed possession. But no traces of his associates at the Abbey appear to have survived their departure from it, unless we dimly discern them in the miserable record which relates that sixteen years after the period of their dissolution, fifteen pounds* were still paid in annuities out of the revenues of the late monastery; that noble possession which the hapless Thirty surrendered to the King.

Of the three and thirty monks of which the society at Furness was composed, the names of the Abbot, the Prior, and twenty-eight of the brethren, were appended to the deed: two had been committed to ward and sure custody in the King's castle of Lancaster, for being "found faultye:"† and one of the number remains unaccounted for.

---

* This sum is stated by West to be £151, which Mr. Beck says is a mistake. The deed of surrender of Bolton Priory was signed by the Prior and fourteen canons. Of the subscribers to this instrument, two, in 1553, which would be about sixteen years after their dissolution, continued to receive annuities of £6 13s. 4d.; one, £6; seven, £5 6s. 8d. each; and one, £4. The other canons were dead, or otherwise provided for.

† For treason. One of them, Henry Talley, had said that no secular knave should be head of the Church; and the other had declared that the king was not the true king, and no rightful heir to the crown.

KING DUNMAIL.

They buried on the mountain's side
King Dunmail, where he fought and died.
But mount, and mere, and moor again
Shall see King Dunmail come to reign.

Mantled and mailed repose his bones
Twelve cubits deep beneath the stones ;
But many a fathom deeper down
In Grisedale Mere lies Dunmail's crown.

Climb thou the rugged pass, and see
High midst those mighty mountains three,
How in their joint embrace they hold
The Mere that hides his crown of gold.

There in that lone and lofty dell
Keeps silent watch the sentinel.
A thousand years his lonely rounds
Have traced unseen that water's bounds.

His challenge shocks the startled waste,
Still answered from the hills with haste,
As passing pilgrims come and go
From heights above or vales below.

When waning moons have filled their year,
A stone from out that lonely Mere
Down to the rocky Raise is borne,
By martial shades with spear and horn.

As crashes on the pile the stone,
The echoes to the King make known
How still their faithful watch they hold
In Grisedale o'er his crown of gold.

And when the Raise has reached its sum,
Again will brave King Dunmail come ;
And all his Warriors marching down
The dell, bear back his golden crown.

And Dunmail, mantled, crowned, and mailed,
Again shall Cumbria's King be hailed ;
And o'er his hills and valleys reign
When Eildon's heights are field and plain.

NOTES TO "KING DUNMAIL."

The heroic king Dunmail was the last of a succession of native princes, who up to the tenth century ruled over those mountainous provinces in the north-western region of England which were chiefly peopled by the earliest masters of Britain, the Celtic tribes of Cymri, or Picts. The territories of Dunmail, as king of Cumbria, included the entire tract of country from the western limits of the Lothians in Scotland to the borders of Lancashire, and from Northumberland to the Irish Sea.

The several British kingdoms which were originally comprised within this area maintained a long and resolute resistance against the power of the first Saxon monarchs; and although in the course of time most of them were brought under the supremacy of those strangers, as tributary provinces, they still continued a sort of independent existence, electing their own kings and obeying their own laws.

On the establishment of the Heptarchy, several of these provinces were included within the Saxon kingdom of Northumbria; but although they were claimed by the Northumbrian monarchs, there was even then little admixture of their people with the fair-haired followers of Hengist and Horsa, and each continued to be governed by its own chieftain or king until the Norman conquest, and existed under what was called the Danish law. So long as the native chieftains were allowed to exercise a subordinate authority, the Northumbrian kings had no occasion to interfere with the internal government of the subject provinces. If the tribute was duly rendered, they remained unmolested; if it was withheld, payment was enforced by arms; or, in extreme cases, the refractory state (to use a modern phrase) was "annexed," and the domestic government extinguished.

Of the petty rulers of these British kingdoms no notices have been transmitted to us. These are confined to the kings of Strathclyde, or, as they are designated by our earliest informers, of Alclyde; the latter being the name of their capital, which stood on a rocky eminence, adjacent to the modern town of Dumbarton; whilst the former significantly describes the position of their territory in the great strath or valley of the Clyde. This little district (of Strathclyde), which must not be confounded with the larger territory of Cumbria, that as yet had no existence under any general government or common name, comprised the modern counties of Lanark, Ayr, and Renfrew, on the south of the Clyde, and, probably, Dumbartonshire on the north. In the series of Strathclydian kings, tradition has placed the name of the celebrated King Arthur; and the local nomenclature is said to afford many traces of his fame, especially in the case of their citadel of Alclyde, or Dumbarton, which is styled "Castrum Arthuri," in a record of the reign of David the Second. Ryderic, the successor of Arthur, died in 601, in the eighth year of the reign of Ethelfrith, king of Northumberland; and from that time onward, during the remainder of this and the succeeding reigns of Edwin and Oswald, we hear nothing of the independent existence of this people, nor do we even know the names of their chieftains; it is probable that they had been reduced to subjection. But in the very year of Oswald's disastrous death, A.D. 642, we find the Britons carrying on important military operations on their own account, in which Owen their king distinguished himself, by slaying on the battle-field of Strath-carmaic, Donal Break, king of the Scots. During the long reign of Oswi in Northumberland, we read of one king of Strathclyde, Guinet, but the record is only of his death, A.D. 657, not of any exploit which he performed. On the death of Ecgfrith, A.D. 670, the Britons of Strathclyde appear to have recovered their liberty; and thenceforward we have a tolerably complete list of their kings during the two succeeding centuries.

Ethelfrith, who had effected the conquest of the central and western portion of Northumbria, and may be regarded as the founder of the Northumbrian kingdom, "conquered," as we read in Beda, "more territories from the Britons than any other king or tribune;" but although he was thus able to overrun a vast district of country, his followers were not sufficiently numerous to colonise it. In some places, indeed, "he expelled the inhabitants, and placed Angles in their stead," but "in others," and doubtless to a much greater extent, "he allowed the vanquished to retain their lands, "on payment of tribute." In the reign of Edwine, too, the Anglo-Saxon population were under his immediate government ; the petty British States were still ruled by tributary princes. And no doubt their political condition continued more or less the same during the century and half which preceded the dissolution of the Heptarchy, and after the reconstruction of its several parts under one crown.

On Northumbria being overrun by the renowned Danish Viking Healfdene, A.D. 875, fifty years after the Heptarchal kingdoms had been dissolved, it is recorded that the indigenous inhabitants of the part called Cymriland, the Cumbrians, or Britons, being too weak to defend themselves from the hateful aggressions of the Danes, and deprived of the protection of the Saxon kings of Northumbria, who had themselves succumbed to the common enemy, turned for aid to the only neighbours who seemed sufficiently powerful to resist the invaders. They therefore implored the aid of Grig or Gregory, king of Scotland, by whose assistance in the following year the Scandinavian ravagers were expelled. These Indigenæ, or British inhabitants, must have been the people of Galloway, and of the district around Carlisle ; for the Strathclyde Britons were already under the authority of Gregory, as the guardian of Eocha, a minor, who, as the son of Hu king of Strathclyde, and nephew of the second Constantine, king of Scotland, succeeded to the crowns of both these realms. Whether the Britons subsequently quarrelled with their powerful ally, and being defeated in battle, were obliged to cede to the victor their rocky highlands and adjacent places ; or they voluntarily submitted themselves to Gregory, with their lands and possessions, thinking it preferable to be subject to the Scots, who, although enemies, were Christians, than to infidel pagans, there does not appear to be any evidence to determine.

The vigour of Gregory king of Scotland having been found, notwithstanding his prowess and the success of his arms, inadequate to support an authority which had been usurped by him as regent during the minority of Eocha, after holding the reins of government in Scotland and Strathclyde during eleven years, was expelled, together with Eocha, by Donal, son of the late King Constantine II., A.D. 893.

To Donal, who was slain by the Danes, A.D. 904, succeeded his cousin Constantine III., the son of Aodh, who had been slain by Gregory. Another Donal, brother to Constantine III., had been "elected" king of the Strathclyde Britons four years before the elevation of that monarch to the throne of Scotland. During the life of this Donal, the districts of Carlisle and Galloway were not united to Strathclyde, but remained attached to Scotland; from which, however, they were separated after his decease, and given to his son and successor, Eugenius.

To the new kingdom, thus founded by Constantine in favour of his nephew and presumptive heir, by the union of Carlisle and Galloway with Strathclyde, was given the name of Cumbria, derived from the common appellation of its inhabitants. Its extent is precisely defined in a return made by the prior and convent of Carlisle to a writ of Edward the First, requiring them, as well as other religious houses, to furnish, from chronicles or other documents in their possession, any information bearing upon the alleged right of supremacy over Scotland vested in the English crown. The return sets forth, "That district was called Cumbria, which is now included in the bishoprics of Carlisle, Glasgow, and Whitherne, together with the country lying between Carlisle and the river Duddon:" in other words, the entire tract from the Clyde to the confines of Lancashire. In the "Inquisitio Davidis," which does indeed extend to all parts of Cumbria which remained in David's possession, we are expressly told that "he had not then within his dominion the whole Cumbrian region," the present county of Cumberland, or, as it was then called, Earldom of Carlisle, having been severed from it soon after the Norman Conquest. Although Fordun is the only author who narrates the cession of Carlisle and Galloway to Gregory, and the subsequent grant of these districts to Eugenius, whereby they were united to Strathclyde, and the whole merged into a single government, we have abundant evidence of the existence of Cumbria and the intimate union of Constantine and Eugenius at this period. In the year 938, these princes, in conjunction with the Danes and Welsh, attempted to wrest the sovereign power out of the vigorous hands of Athelstane. The combined forces were signally defeated by the Anglo-Saxon monarch at Brunanburgh (supposed by some to be Bromborough, near Chester); Eugenius was slain, and Constantine escaped only by a precipitate retreat.

It is at this period that Dunmail, the second and last *sole* "king of rocky Cumberland," appears upon the historic stage. It has been thought not improbable that he was the son of Eugenius or Owen, the preceding king," and the same person who is described as Dunwallon, "the son of Owen," and who died at Rome thirty years after his memorable engagement with Edmund of England and Leoline of South Wales, in the mountain pass which is distinguished by his name. "In the annals of Ulster, indeed," say the supporters of this supposition, "this Dunwallon is described as king of Wales, but Caradoc calls him prince of Strathclyde, and his patronymic designation seems to identify him with Dunmail, if, as we assume, the latter was the son of the first king of Cumberland." But by whatever means Dunmail obtained the crown; whether by inheritance as the son of Eugenius, or by "election" as one of the native Cumbrian princes, and according to the ancient custom of the Britons; we soon find him supporting the Northumbrians in hostilities against the Saxon monarch, Edmund the First. That monarch, although victorious, was so weakened that he dared not pursue Dunmail without the assistance of the Scots. And the condition upon which Malcolm, king of Scotland, joined Edmund with his forces, was, that if they were successful, Malcolm should possess Cumbria by paying homage to Edmund and his successors. The subjection of this wild race of mountaineers was then determined upon as a necessary step towards the pacification of the kingdom; and the last record which history affords us of the Cumbrian Britons, is that of their defeat, A.D. 945, in the heart of their native mountains, between Grasmere and Keswick, and their final dispersion or emigration into Wales.

The place where Dunmail determined to hazard the battle which proved fatal to him was the famous Pass which bears his name. Edmund slew his vanquished enemy upon the spot which is still commemorated by the rude pile of stones so well known as his cairn; and, in conformity with the barbarous customs of that age, put out the eyes of his two sons; after which, having completely ravaged and laid waste the territories of Dunmail, he bestowed them on his ally Malcolm; the latter undertaking to preserve in peace the Northern parts of England, and to pay the required fealty and homage to Edmund. Upon the same conditions they were afterwards confirmed to him by one of Edmund's successors, Edgar; which monarch also divided what at that time remained of the ancient kingdom of Northumbria into Baronies, and constituted it an Earldom. Thenceforward these north western regions were held as a military benefice subject to the English sceptre by the heir to the crown of Scotland, under the title of the Principality of Cymriland or Cumbria. This Principality, which included Westmorland, continued in possession of the heirs to the Scottish crown during the reigns of Harold and Hardicanute, the last Danish Kings, and of Edward the Confessor and Harold the Second, the last Saxon monarchs of England.

The only circumstance which is recorded of it during the century which followed the defeat of Dunmail, is its total devastation by Ethelred, king of England, A.D. 1000, at which time it is represented by Henry of Huntingdon as the principal rendezvous of the marauding Danes.

In the year 1052, Macbeth held the Scottish throne, whilst Malcolm, the son of his predecessor, the murdered Duncan, sat on that of Cumbria. Siward, earl of Northumberland, was commissioned by Edward the Confessor to invade Scotland, and avenge the "murder" of Duncan. In this he succeeded, defeated and slew Macbeth, and placed the king of Cumbria, or, as some historians assert, his son, on the throne of Scotland. This Malcolm, surnamed Canmore, held at the time of the Conquest, Cumbria and Lothian, in addition to the ancient kingdom of Scotland.

In the year 1072, the Earldom of Carlisle, containing the present County of Cumberland, with the Barony of Westmorland, was wrested from Malcolm Canmore by William the Conqueror, who granted it to his powerful noble, Ranulph de Meschin, one of that numerous train of military adventurers, amongst whom he had distributed all the fair territory of Britain, to hold, with a sort of royal power, by the sword, as he himself held the kingdom by virtue of the crown,—*tenure ita libere ad gladium, sicut ipse rex tenebat Angliam per coronam.*

Thus the existing limits were established between England and Scotland. The kingdom of Cumbria was reduced to the dimensions indicated by the "Inquisitio Davidis," and was held as a principality dependent on the crown of Scotland ; until it at length became formally attached to the Scottish dominions.

Meanwhile the Barony of Westmorland having been separated from the Earldom of Carlisle, there remained the district comprised within the present limits of the County of Cumberland, to which alone that name was thenceforward applied.

The circular heap of stones which forms the pile called Dunmail-Raise, and gives its name to the mountain Pass between the vales of Grasmere and Wytheburn, is seen adjoining the high-road, where it is crossed by the wall which there marks the boundaries of Westmorland and Cumberland. The stones constituting this rude monument are thrown loosely together on each side of an earthen mound in a huge cairn or *raise*, the history of which is little known, and concerning which antiquarians are by no means agreed. It measures twenty-four yards in diameter, and rises gradually to an elevation of six feet, being flat at the top, and the centre indicated by a well defined space in rather larger stones.

Mr. Gilpin conjectures that the pile was probably intended to mark a division not between the two Counties of Cumberland and Westmorland, but rather between the two kingdoms of England and Scotland, in elder times, when the Scottish border extended beyond its present bounds. The generally received tradition, however, concerning this cairn is, that it was raised to commemorate the name and defeat of Dunmail, the last king of Cumbria, in the year 945, in his conflict with the Saxon Edmund, on the occasion above related. "But," says Mr. Gilpin, "for whatever purpose this rude pile was fabricated, it hath yet suffered little change in its dimensions ; and is one of those monuments of antiquity, which may be characterized by the scriptural phrase of *remaining to this very day.*"

The legend of the Cumbrian hero and his host, awaiting the completion of their rocky pile beneath the lonely mountain pass ; from which they are to issue in their appointed time to join "in that great battle which will be fought before the end of the world ; " is but one of the beliefs which seem to have been left behind them by our Scandinavian ancestors. It is in fact another version of the story of Woden and his host, whose winter trance is enacted by various popular heroes ; and which has not only been localised amongst ourselves, but has almost overspread all christendom. The original nature of Woden or Odin was represented as that of a storm god, who swept through the air in roaring winds, either alone or with a great retinue consisting of souls of the dead which have become winds. The whirlwind, which precedes the tempest, and has ravaged the woods and fields, is pursued to its death in the last storms of autumn. Sometimes the god is pictured as a hunter, and the winds have taken the shapes of men, dogs, etc., whilst the whirlwind figures as a boar. The achievement of its death is soon followed by that of the hunter Woden himself; who during the winter is dead, or asleep, or enchanted in the cloud mountain. From this beautiful fiction of a twilight age, the winter trance of Woden, has grown up the story of those caverned warriors, which, under whatever name they are known, and wherever they repose, are all representations of Odin and his host.

Arthur, the vanished king, our own Arthur, whose return is expected by the Britons, according to mediæval Germany, is said to dwell with his men at arms in a mountain ; all well provided with food, drink, horses, and clothes.

Charlemagne slumbers with his enchanted army in many places ; in the Desenberg near Warburg, in the Castle of Herstella on the Weser, in the Karlsburg on the Spessart, the Frausberg and the Donnersberg on the Pfalz, etc.

The Emperor Henry the Fowler is entranced in the Sudernerberg, near Goslar.

The Emperor Frederick Barbarossa is in a cavern in the Kyffhaüser mountain, in the old palatinate of the Saxon imperial house. There with all his knights around him, he sits to this day, leaning his head upon his arm, at a table through which his beard has grown, or round which, according to other accounts, it has grown twice. When it has thrice encircled the table he will wake up to battle. The cavern glitters with gold and jewels, and is as bright as the sunniest day. Thousands of horses stand at mangers filled with thorn bushes instead of hay, and make a prodigious noise as they stamp on the ground and rattle their chains. The old Kaiser sometimes wakes up for a moment and speaks to his visitors. He once asked a herdsman who had found his way into the Kyffhaüser, "Are the ravens (Odin's birds) still flying about the mountain ?" The man replied that they were. "Then," said Barbarossa, "I must sleep a hundred years longer."

The Eildon Hills, which witnessed of old the magical exploits of Michael Scott, are three in number. These were originally one : their present formation being the work of a demon, for whom the wizard, in fulfilment of some infernal contract, was obliged to find employment, and by whom the mighty task was achieved in a single night. They are nearly of the same height, changing greatly their appearance, and, as it were, their attitude, with the point of view ; at one time one of them only being visible, at another time two, and again all three. They form a peculiar and romantic feature

ıu the scenery of the Tweed : and are still to the eye of
the imagination what they once were in the common belief,—
wizard hills, the subjects of wild traditions and unearthly
adventures.   In them lay for centuries those "caverned
warriors," which Thomas the Rhymer showed at night to the
daring horse jockey, who went by appointment to the Lucken
Hare to receive the price of the black horse which he had
sold to the venerable favourite of the Fairy Queen.   His
money having been paid to him, in ancient coin ; on the
invitation of his customer to view his residence, he followed
his guide in the deepest astonishment through long ranges of
stalls, in each of which a horse stood motionless, while an
armed warrior lay equally still at the charger's feet.   "All
these men," said the prophet in a whisper, "will awaken at
the battle of Sheriffmuir."

The small mountain lake, called Grisedale Tarn, is situated
at a very considerable elevation above the surrounding vales,
in a depression formed at a point where the shoulders of
Helvellyn, Seat-Sandal, and Fairfield touch each other ; and
just below the summit of the "hause" or pass through which
winds the mountain track that leads from Grasmere into
Patterdale.

THE BRIDALS OF DACRE.

The Baron of Greystoke is laid in the quire.
Who is she that sits lone in her mourning attire?
Her maids all in silence stand weeping apart :
Or but whisper the woe that is big at her heart.

From her guardian the King the dread summons has
      come ;
And Greystoke's sweet orphan must quit her lone
      home :
With the proudest of Barons to wait on her word—
His domain for her pleasaunce, her safeguard his
      sword.

But what is to her all their homage and state,
Since the youthful Lord Dacre may pass not their
      gate?
Even now he forgets her, she thinks in her gloom;
And the Cliffords to-morrow will bear her to Brough'm.

"With him, O with him," in her sorrow she cried,
" With the gallant Lord Dacre to run by my side
"In the fields, as of old, with his hand on my rein,
"I would give all the wealth the wide world can
contain."—

Lord Dacre forget her? No! sooner the might
Of Helvellyn shall bend to the storm on its height;
He has vow'd—"Let them woo! but in spite of the
King
"The wide north with her bridal at Dacre shall ring."

As the Cliffords rode hard on that morrow to claim
The fair ward of the King, by Lord Dacre's they
came.
And they cast out their words in derision and scorn,
As they pass'd by his tower in the prime of the morn.

" Shall we greet the bright heiress of Greystock for
thee?
"Or await thee at Brough'm her rich bridal to see?"
—"In our annals," he cried, "we've a story of old,
"A fit tale for a bridal, that *twice* shall be told.

" In your Skipton's high hall, in your stateliest room
" Of Pendragon, and high through the arches of
    Brough'm,
" Have your bridals been sung, but not one to the lay
" That I'll ring through old Brough'm for the bride
    on that day.

" Your meats may be scant, and unbrimm'd the
    bright bowl ;
" But the notes of that tale through your fortress
    shall roll !
" Here I pledge me, proud Cliffords ! come friend,
    or come foe,
" With that tale of old times to her bridal I'll go !"—

Loud laugh'd they in scorn as hard onward they rode :
And the horsemen and horses all gallantly show'd.
With bright silver and gold, too, her harness did ring,
As they rode back to Brough'm with the Ward of
    the King.

And proud was the welcome, and courtly the grace,
And warm was the clasp of that stately embrace,
When the Lady of Brough'm took her home to her
    breast,
Like a lamb to the fold, a lone dove to its nest.

But in still hours of night, and mid pastimes by day,
To the wild woods of Greystoke her heart fled away,
To the fields where, as once with *his* hand on her
    rein,
She would give all the world to ride child-like again.

It was night; when the moon through her circle had
    worn;
And back into darkness her crescent was borne;
Not in fancy nor dreams came a voice to her side—
"Sweet, awake thee, Lord Dacre is come for his
    bride."

Through the lattice he bore her, and fast did he fold
In his arms the sweet prize from the wind and the
    cold;
Sprang the wall to his steed, and o'er moorland and
    plain
Bore her off to his Tower by the Dacor again.

And the Cliffords that morn in their banquetting hall
Read the legend his dagger had traced on the wall—
" In the annals of Dacre the story is old
Of Matilda the Fair and Lord Ranulph the Bold !

"The bride-meats unbaked, and the bride-cup
    unbrew'd,
Not by bridesmaid for bride even a rose to be
    strew'd,
Was the way with our sire in that story of old
Of Matilda the Fair and Lord Ranulph the Bold !

"But they woke up to fury in Warwick that morn.
For a bride from their Fortress by night had been
    borne.
And your annals in Brough'm of its sluggards shall
    ring,
That have lost for the Cliffords the Ward of their
    King."

The beard of that Baron curled fiercely with ire,
And the blood through his veins raged—a torrent of
    fire,
As he glanced from the panel by turns to his sword ;
And then strode from the hall without deigning a
    word.

They sought her through turret, by bush, and by
    stone ;
But the bower had been broken, the Beauty was
    gone ;

And the joy-bells of Dacre from Greystock to
　　Brough'm
Pealed the news through the vales that the bride
　　was brought home.

NOTES TO "THE BRIDALS OF DACRE."

Dacre Castle, one of the outermost of a chain of border fortresses stretching down the valleys of the Eamont and the Eden in Cumberland, is a plain quadrangular building, with battlemented parapets, and four square turrets, one at each corner; it is now converted into a farm house. The moat is filled up, although the site is still to be traced, and the outworks are destroyed. There are two entrances—one at the west tower, and another between the towers in the east front. The walls are about seven feet in thickness. There are two arched dungeons communicating by steps with the ground floor; and access was obtained to the roof by means of four circular staircases, one in each tower; some of which are now closed up. The staircases, however, did not conduct to the top of the towers; this was gained by means of stone steps from the roof of the Castle.

Bede mentions a monastery, which being built near the river Dacor, took its name from it, over which the religious man Suidbert presided. It was probably destroyed by the Danes, and never restored; and there are no vestiges of it remaining : the present church is supposed to have been built from the ruins.

William of Malmesbury speaks of a Congress held at Dacre in the year 934, when Constantine, king of Scotland, and his nephew Eugenius, king of Cumberland, met king Athelstan, and did homage to him at Dacre. This fact is singularly corroborated by there being in the Castle a room called to this day the "room of the three kings," while the historical fact itself is entirely forgotten in the country. This proves the antiquity of the tradition, which has survived the original building and attached itself to the present, no part of which dates from an earlier period than the fourteenth century. That Dacre was in those remote times a place of some importance is evident from the meeting aforesaid. The occasion appears to have been the defection of Guthred, with Anlaff his brother, and Inguld king of York, when Athelstan levied a great force, and entered Northumberland so unexpectedly, that the malcontents had scarcely time to secure themselves by flight. Guthred obtained protection under Constantine, king of Scotland, to whom Athelstan sent messengers, demanding his surrender, or upon refusal, he threatened to come in quest of him at the head of his army. Constantine, although greatly piqued at this message, yet afraid of the formidable arms of Athelstan, consented to meet him at Dacre; to which place he came, attended by the then king of Cumberland, where they did homage to Athelstan.

After the Conquest, if not before, Dacre was a mesne manor held of the barons of Greystoke by military suit and service. The parish, manor, rivulet, and castle, were all blended with the name of the·owners. Their arms, the pilgrim's scallop, may possibly have been taken from their being engaged in Palestine; but as the name of their place dates as far back as the time of Athelstan, the Dacres no doubt took their name, like most of the families of the district, from the place where they were settled, and with all deference to the cross-legged knight* in the church, who may or may not have battled at the siege of Acre, its present Norman spelling is more likely to have arisen from the manner in which it is entered in the Domesday Book than from any exploits of his before that famous fortress. That they were men of high spirit and enterprise, and favourites of the ladies, there exists convincing evidence. Matilda, the great heiress of Gilsland,† was by Randolph Dacre carried off from Warwick Castle, in the night-time, while she was Edward the Third's Ward, and under the custody and care of Thomas de Beauchamp, a stout Earl of Warwick ; and

---

* Cross-legs have been proved of late not to indicate Crusaders always.

† Matilda de Multon, the daughter and heir of Thomas de Multon, of Gilsland, was only thirteen years of age at the time of her father's death, when she became the ward of King Edward II. ; but in 1317 by the marriage which consummated this act of daring chivalry, the barony was transferred to the Dacre family.

Thomas Lord Dacre dashingly followed the example of his ancestor, nearly two centuries afterwards, by carrying off, also in the night time, from Brougham Castle, Elizabeth of Greystoke, the heiress of his superior lord, who was also the King's ward, and in custody of Henry Lord Clifford, who, says Mr. Howard, probably intended to marry her. Their vigour and ability displayed as wardens of the Marches must also add favourably to our estimate of them as men.

Sandford in his MS. gives the following curious account, written apparently immediately after the repair of the Castle by the Earl of Sussex:—"And from Matterdale mountains comes Daker Bek; almost at the foot thereof stands Dacker Castle alone, and no more house about it, And I protest looks very sorrowfull, for the loss of its founders, in that huge battle of Touton feild : and that totall eclips of that great Lord Dacres, in that Grand Rebellion with lords North-umberland, and Westmorland in Queen Elizabeth's time, and in the north called *Dacre's Raide*.

"—— but it seems an heroyick Chivaleir, steeles the heir of Lord Moulton of Kirkoswald and Naward and Gilsland, forth of Warwick Castle, the 5th year of King Edward the 3rd ; and in the 9th year of the same king had his pdon for marying her and Created Lord Dacres and Moulton. In King Henry the eight's time the yong Lord Dacres steels the female heir of the Lord Graistoke forth of Broham Castle besides Peareth: where the Lord Clifford had gott her of the king for his sons mariage : and thereupon was the statute made of felony to marry an heir. And thus became the Lord Dacres decorate with all the honors and Lands of the Lord Graistok a very great Baron : but the now Earle of Sussex Ancestore had married the female heir of the Lord Dacres in King Edward the 4th time, before the Lands of Graistock came to the Lord Dacre's house."

The Barony of Greystoke, which comprehends all that part of Cumberland, on the south side of the Forest of Inglewood, between the seignory of Penrith and the manor of Castlerigg near Keswick, and contains an area comprehending the parishes of Greystoke, Dacre, and part of Crosthwaite, and nearly twenty manors, was given by Ranulph de Meschines, Earl of Cumberland, to one Lyulph, whose posterity assumed the name of the place, and possessed it until the reign of Henry the Seventh, when their heiress conveyed it in mar-riage to Thomas Lord Dacre, of Gilsland, whose family ended in two daughters, who married the two sons of the Duke of Norfolk. Philip Howard, Earl of Arundel, the Duke's eldest son, had, with his wife, Lady Anne Dacre, the lands of Greystoke, which have since continued in his illustrious family.

The original fortress of Greystock was built in the reign of Edward III. by Lord William de Greystock, that nobleman having obtained the king's license to castellate his manor-house of Greystock in the year 1353. Being garrisoned for Charles I., it was destroyed by a detachment of the Parliamentary army in June, 1648, except one tower and part of another. The Castle was almost entirely rebuilt about the middle of last century by the Hon. Charles Howard, and additional extensions were subsequently made by his great-grandson, the eleventh Duke of Norfolk, who bequeathed it to the present Mr. Howard, by whom the work of renovation was continued and completed in 1846. In the night of the 3rd and 4th of May, 1868, it was very seriously damaged by fire.

Elizabeth Greystoke, Baroness Greystoke and Wemme, was a minor at the time of her father's death. She was the only daughter of Sir Robert Greystoke, knight, who died June 17th, 1483, in the lifetime of his father, Ralph, seventeenth Baron Greystoke. By an inquisition held after the death of that nobleman, it was found that he died on Friday next after the Feast of Pentecost, in the second year of King Henry VII., namely, June 1st, 1487. He was succeeded by Elizabeth, his grand-daughter and heiress, who during her minority was a ward of the crown, and had special livery of all her lands in 1506. This lady married Thomas, ninth Baron Dacre of Gillesland, and third Lord Dacre of the North; by which marriage the Barony of Greystoke became united with that of Gillesland.

The nobleman in whose custody the King had placed his ward was Henry the tenth Baron Clifford, better known as Lord Clifford the Shepherd. He had married a cousin of Henry VII., and on the accession of that monarch had been restored, by the reversal of his father's attainder, to his honours and estates. Their sons had been educated together, and brought up in habits of intimacy; and the friendship thus formed in youth was continued after the one had succeeded to the crown as Henry VIII., and the other had ceased to be "Wild Henry Clifford," and had been advanced by his royal kinsman and associate to the dignity of Earl of Cumberland.

Of the Lady Elizabeth it is stated that "lord Clifford gott

her of the king for his son's marriage ;" or for himself, "who probably intended to marry her." These suppositions lose something of their importance when we learn that a considerable disparity in years existed between Lord Clifford and the Lady, as well as between her and his son ; the former being nearly thirty years her senior, and the latter almost a dozen years her junior; and during a great portion of her minority, the first Lady Clifford, though probably residing much apart from her husband, or unhappily with him, was yet alive. He was, however, a nobleman nearly allied to the king, of great power and influence in the north of England, and had been neighbour to the old Lord Greystoke, her grandfather. Under the circumstances, the selection made by the sovereign was a natural one. Her youth, her rank, and her rich inheritance, were a prize worthy of the aspiration of the noblest among her peers, whoever may have been the suitor intended for her by the king; and they were won by one who afterwards showed that he was as gallant in war as he had proved himself to be daring and loyal in love.

Lord Dacre, after imitating the spirited bearing of his ancestor in his love affair, exhibited it in an equal degree in a more serious enterprise, when it was attended with equal success. He had a principal command in the English army in the battle of Flodden Field, which was gained on the 9th of September, 1514, over the Scots, who had invaded the kingdom during the absence of Henry VIII. at Tournay. He commanded the right wing of the army; and wheeling about during the action, he fell upon the rear of the enemy and put them to the sword without resistance, and thus contributed greatly to the complete victory which followed.

The gratitude of his sovereign for his faithful services invested him with the dignity of the most noble Order of the Garter, and with the office of Lord Warden of the West Marches. He died October 24th, 1525, and was buried with his wife, under the rich altar-tomb, in the south aisle of the choir of Lanercost.

Brougham Castle in the thirteenth century, the time of John de Veteripont, the most ancient owner that history points out, is called in instruments wherein his name is mentioned, the *house of Brougham ;* from which it is inferred that license had not then been procured to embattle it. It came to the Cliffords by the marriage of his grand-daughter Isabella, the last of the Veteriponts, with Roger, son and heir of Roger Clifford, of Clifford Castle, Herts, whom the king had

appointed guardian to her during her minority.* This Roger
de Clifford built the greater part of the Castle, and had placed
over its inner gateway the inscription—THIS MADE ROGER ;
"which," says Bishop Nicholson, "some would have to be
understood not so much of *his* raising the Castle, as of the
Castle raising *him*, in allusion to his advancement of fortune
by his marriage, this Castle being part of his wife's inherit-
ance." On the death of Roger, who was slain in the Isle of
Anglesey, in a skirmish with the Welsh, his widow, during
her son's minority, sat as sheriffess in the county of Westmor-
land, upon the bench with the judges there, "concerning the
legality of which," says the Countess of Pembroke, " I
obtained Lord Hailes his opinion."†

Her grandson Robert built the eastern parts of the Castle.
During the subsequent centuries it fell several times into
decay, having been destroyed by the Scots and by fire, and
was as often restored.

King James was magnificently entertained at Brougham
Castle, on the sixth, seventh, and eighth days of August,
1617, on his return from his last journey out of Scotland.
After this visit it appears to have been again injured by fire,
and to have lain ruinous until 1651 and 1652, when it was
repaired for the last time, by Anne, Countess of Pembroke,
who tells us, "After I had been there myself to direct the
building of it, did I cause my old decayed Castle of Brougham
to be repaired, and also the tower called the *Roman Tower*,
in the said old castle, and the court house, for keeping my
courts in, with some dozen or fourteen rooms to be built in it

---

* The King committed these ladies (Isabella and Idonea de Veteripont),
being then young, to the guardianship of Roger de Clifford, of Clifford
Castle, Herefordshire, and Roger de Leybourne. According to the
custom of the times, and the real intent of the trust, as soon as the
heiresses were of proper age. they were married to the sons of their
guardians.—*Pennant.*

† It has again and again been stated, that the Countess herself in the
seventeenth century repeated this exhibition of her ancestress in the
thirteenth : and not merely as an assertion of her right, but frequently
and habitually. No evidence has been found, that she ever did so at
all. She was, however, recognized as sheriff, and she exercised the
authority of the office by deputy. Thus we have her recording that she
appointed such a deputy sheriff in 1651. The office appears to have been
regarded as attached to the estate of Brougham Castle, or the other lands
which had originally belonged to the Veteriponts ; it descended with
those estates to the Earls of Thanet : but in 1850 a sheriff was appointed
by the crown, under the authority of an Act passed in the previous
session of Parliament, entitled "An Act to provide for the execution for
one year of the Office of Sheriff in the County of Westmorland."

upon the old foundation." The *tower of leagues* and the *Pagan tower* are mentioned in her Memoirs ; and also a state room called *Greystocke Chamber.* But the room in which her father was born, her "blessed mother" died, and King James lodged in 1617, she never fails to mention, as being that in which she lay, in all her visits to this place. After the death of the Countess, the Castle appears to have been neglected, and has gradually gone to decay.

THRELKELD TARN:

OR, TRUTH FROM THE DEEPS.

By doubts and darkest thoughts oppress'd,
From cheerful hope out-driven,
A sceptic laid him down to rest
Mid regions earthquake-riven.

And scanning Nature's awful face,
And all the glorious sky,
He cried—"To perish, and no trace
Survive us when we die,—

"This, spite of hope, is man's forlorn
And unremitting lot ;
No realm awaits the heart out-worn ;
Earth fades, and heaven is not.

" For Reason's ray, like yon bright sun,
   Rebukes the feebler light
Of hope from star-eyed Fable won,
   And old Tradition's night.

" We shall no more to life arise,
   Nor reassume our breath,
Nor light revisit these dim eyes
   Once closed in endless death.

" As soon shall stars at noontide beam
   While burns the sun's bright ray,
As stand before high Truth the dream
   That Thought survives the clay."—

He turned : beside him yawning wide
   Lay Mountains' hugely rent :
Whence far within their depths espied,
   A little gleam was sent.

One star the blackened pool below
   Reflected bright and clear,
While earth was revelling in the glow
   And sunshine of the year.

Then starting, cried he—" Heaven ! thou art
   Above our powers to know.
Take thou this blindness from my heart,
   And let me, trusting, go."

NOTES TO "THRELKELD TARN; OR TRUTH FROM THE DEEPS."

Threlkeld or Scales Tarn is a small lake lying deeply secluded in a recess on the north eastern side of Saddleback, or Blencathra, between that mountain and Scales Fell. From the peculiarity of its situation it has excited considerable curiosity: but the supposed difficulty of access to it, its insignificant size, and the peculiar nature of its attractions, cause it to be seldom visited except by those who take it on their way to the top of Linethwaite Fell, the most elevated point of the Saddleback range.

Having gained, by a toilsome and rugged ascent from the south-east, the margin of the cavity in which the Tarn is imbedded, let the traveller be supposed to stand directly facing the middle of the mountain, the form of which gives its name to Saddleback. From the high land between its two most elevated points before him, and jutting right out to the north-east, depends an enormous perpendicular rock called Tarn Crag; at the base of which, engulphed in an immense basin or cavity of steeps, above and on the left lofty and precipitous, and gradually diminishing as they curve on the right, lies Threlkeld Tarn, described as a beautiful piece of circular transparent water, covering a space of from thirty to thirty-five acres, and surrounded with a well defined shore. From the summit, elevated upwards of two hundred yards above it, its surface is black, though smooth as a mirror; and it lies so deeply imbedded, that it is said, the reflection of the stars may be seen therein at noonday. It is generally sunless; and when illuminated, it is in the morning, and chiefly through an aperture to the east, formed by the running waters in the direction of Penrith. "A wild spot it is," says Southey, "as ever was chosen by a cheerful party where to rest, and take

19

their merry repast upon a summer's day. The green mountain, the dark pool, the crag under which it lies, and the little stream which steals from it, are the only objects ; the gentle voice of that stream the only sound, unless a kite be wheeling above, or a sheep bleats on the fell side. A silent solitary place ; and such solitude heightens social enjoyment, as much as it conduces to lonely meditation."

Southey adds, in a note—"Absurd accounts have been published both of the place itself, and the difficulty of reaching it. The Tarn has been said to be so deep that the reflection of the stars may be seen in it at noon-day—and that the sun never shines upon it. One of these assertions is as fabulous as the other—and the Tarn, like all Tarns, is shallow."

Its claim to this singularity need not be wholly rejected, however, on the ground of shallowness, if, to be deeply imbedded, rather than to be deep, be the essential condition. Several of the most credible inhabitants thereabouts have affirmed that they frequently see stars in it at mid-day ; but it is also stated that in order to discover that phenomenon, there must be a concurrence of several circumstances, viz : the firmament must be perfectly clear, the air and the water unagitated ; and the spectator must be placed at a certain height above the lake, and as much below the summit of the partially surrounding ridge.

The impression produced upon travellers a century ago by the features of Blencathra at a considerable elevation, will excite a smile in tourists of the present day. The *Southern* face of the mountain is "furrowed with hideous chasms." One of these "though by far the least formidable," is described as "unconceivably horrid :" "its width is about two hundred yards, and its depth at least six hundred." Between two of these horrible abysses, and separated from the body of the mountain on all sides by deep ravines, a portion of the hill somewhat pyramidal in shape stands out like an enormous buttress. "I stood upon this," says the narrator, whose account is quoted, "and had on each side a gulf about two hundred yards wide, and at least eight hundred deep ; their sides were rocky, bare, and rough, scarcely the appearance of vegetation upon them : and their bottoms were covered with pointed broken rocks." Again he "arrived where the mountain has every appearance of being split ; and at the 'bottom' he 'saw hills about forty yards high and a mile in length, which seem to have been raised from the rubbish that had fallen from the mountain.'" From the summit he "could not help observing that the back of this mountain is as remarkably smooth, as the front is horrid."

Over this front of Blencathra, the bold and rugged brow which it presents when seen from the road to Matterdale, or from the Vale of St. John's, the view of the country to the south and east is most beautiful. The northern side is, as has been said, remarkably smooth, and in striking contrast to that so ruggedly and grandly broken down towards the south, where every thing around bears evident marks of some great and terrible convulsion of nature.

Mr. Green with his companion, Mr. Otley, was among the early adventurers who stood on the highest ridge of Blencathra. This accurate observer, whose descriptions of this, and other unfrequented and unalterable places, will never be old, describes without exaggeration the difficulties of the ground about the upper part of this mountain. Describing the neighbourhood of the Tarn, he says, "From Linthwaite Pike on soft green turf, we descended steeply, first southward, and then in an easterly direction to the tarn,—a beautiful circular piece of transparent water, with a well defined shore. Here we found ourselves engulphed in a basin of steeps, having Tarn Crag on the north, the rocks falling from Sharp Edge on the east, and on the west, the soft turf on which we made our downward progress. These side grounds, in pleasant grassy banks, verge to the stream issuing from the lake, whence there is a charming opening to the town of Penrith ; and Cross Fell seen in the extreme distance. Wishing to vary our line in returning to the place we had left, we crossed the stream, and commenced a steep ascent at the foot of Sharp Edge. We had not gone far before we were aware that our journey would be attended with perils ; the passage gradually grew narrower, and the declivity on each hand awfully precipitous. From walking erect, we were reduced to the necessity either of bestriding the ridge or of moving on one ol its sides, with our hands lying over the top, as a security against tumbling into the tarn on the left, or into a frightful gully on the right, both of immense depth. Sometimes we thought it prudent to return ; but that seemed unmanly, and we proceeded ; thinking with Shakespeare, that "dangers retreat when boldly they're confronted." Mr. Otley was the leader, who, on gaining steady footing, looked back on the writer, whom he perceived viewing at leisure from his saddle the remainder of his upward course."

ROBIN THE DEVIL'S COURTESY.

While the vales of the North keep the Philipsons'
    fame,
Calgarth and Holm-Isle will exult at their name !
Ever true to the rights of the King, and his throne,—
Now hearken how Robin was true to his own !

" Ride, brother ! ride stoutly, ride in from Carlisle !
For the Roundheads from Kendal beleaguer Holm-
    Isle.
On land and on mere I have fifty at bay ;
And I speed on mine arrow this message away ! "—

The arrow struck truly the henchman's far door ;
And swift from the arrow that message he tore.
Then, booted and spurr'd, over mountain and plain
He rides as for life, and he rides not in vain.

He has reached the fair City, has sought through
    the crowd
The bold form of his master, and thus spoke aloud—
"The Roundheads beleaguer my lord in his Isle,
And he bids thee for life to ride in from Carlisle."—

He rode with his men, and he came to the Mere,
When a shout for the Philipsons burst on his ear;
And his errand sped well; for the Whigs to a man,
At the sight of his horsemen, all mounted and ran.

" Now listen, my Brother !—I stay'd by the Isle,
Whilst thou for the King wert array'd at Carlisle ;
I have stood by thy treasure ; I've guarded thy store;
I have kept our good name ; and now this I'll do
    more !

" Yon braggart, that thief-like came on in the dark,
And thought to catch Robin—but miss'd his good
    mark !
I'll repay him his visit ; and, by the great King !
I'll be straight with the varlet, and make his casque
    ring."—

With a half-score of horsemen, next Sunday at morn,
While the sound of the bells o'er the meadows was
    borne,
To the Kent he rode easily—on to the town—
And along the dull street—with clenched hand and
    dark frown.

"Is there none of this Boaster's fanatical crew
In all Kendal to give me the welcome that's due?
Not a blade of old Noll's, or in street or in porch?
By the Rood, then I'll look for such grace in the
    church!"

He spurr'd his wild horse through the open church
    door;
He spurr'd to the chancel, and scann'd it well o'er;
Then turned by the Altar, and glanced at each one
Of the Roundheads that leapt from their knees, and
    look'd on.

But their Leader, the trooper, his foe at the Mere,
His eye could not 'light on—" He cannot be here!"
So he rushed at the portal; but not ere arose
From the panic-loosed swordsmen harsh words and
    hard blows.

He dashed at the doorway, unstooping; a stroke
From the arch rent his helmet, his saddle-girths
    broke;
Half-stunn'd from the ground he strove up to his
    steed,
And ungirth'd has he mounted, and off with good
    speed.

With his men at his back, that stood keeping true
    ward
By each gate, when he entered alone the churchyard,
Soon left he the rebel rout straggling behind;
And was off to his Mere like a hawk on the wind.

And there with his half-score of horsemen once more
He cross'd to his calm little Isle, from the shore;
And then said bold Robin—"I've miss'd him, tis
    true;
But I paid back his visit—so much was his due!

"Had I caught but a glance of the low canting
    knave,
The next psalm that they sung had been over his
    grave!"—
And they guess'd through all Westmorland whose
    was the hand
That would dare such a deed with so feeble a band.

Saying—"Robin the Devil, who man never fear'd,
Would have dared to take Satan himself by the
      beard;
Then why not a troublesome Whig at his prayers !
—He'll not try to catch Robin again unawares."

NOTES TO "ROBIN THE DEVIL'S COURTESY."

Holm Isle, Belle Isle, or Curwen's Island, as it is some-times called from the name of its present proprietor, formerly belonged to the Philipsons of Calgarth, an ancient family in Westmorland. It is the largest island in Windermere, lying obliquely across the lake, just above its narrowest part called the Straits, and opposite to Bowness. It is of an oblong shape, distant on one side from the shore about half a mile, on the other considerably less, while at its northern and southern points there is a large sheet of water extending four or five miles. It is about one mile and three-quarters in circumference, and contains nearly thirty acres of land. Its shores are irregular, occasionally retiring into bays, or breaking into creeks. A circular structure surmounted by a dome-shaped roof was erected upon it in 1776, which is so planned as to command a prospect of the whole lake. The plantations, consisting of Weymouth pines, ash and other trees, are disposed so as to afford a complete shelter to the house, without intercepting the view. The grounds are tastefully laid out; and the island is surrounded by a gravel walk, which strangers are permitted to use. In the middle are a few clumps of trees; and a neat boat-house has been erected contiguous to the place of landing.

When the ground underneath the site of the house was excavated, traces of an ancient building were discovered at a considerable depth below the surface; among which were a great number of old bricks, and a chimney-piece in its perfect state. Several pieces of old armour, weapons, and cannon balls were also found embedded in the soil. In levelling the ground on the north part of the building, a beautiful pave-ment formed of a small kind of pebbles, and several curious gravel walks were cut through. These were probably some remains of "the strong house on the island," in which Huddleston Philipson is said to have left the family treasure under the care of his brother "Robin," while he was absent in the Royal cause at the siege of Carlisle.

During the civil wars these two members of the Philipson family served the king. Huddleston, the elder, who was the proprietor of this island, commanded a regiment. Robert held a commission as major in the same service. He was a man of great spirit and enterprise ; and for his many feats of personal valour, had obtained among the Oliverians of those parts the appellation of *Robin the Devil.*

After the war had subsided, and the more direful effects of public opposition had ceased, revenge and private malice long kept alive the animosities of individuals. Colonel Briggs, a distant kinsman of the Philipsons, of whom, notwithstanding, he was a bitter enemy, and a steady friend to the usurpation, resided at this time at Kendal ; and under the double character of a leading magistrate and an active commander, held the county in awe. This person having heard that Major Philipson was at his brother's house, on the island in Windermere, resolved, if possible, to seize and punish a man who had made himself so particularly obnoxious. With this view he mustered a party which he thought sufficient, and went himself on the enterprise. How it was conducted the narrator does not inform us—whether he got together the navigation of the lake, and blockaded the place by sea, or whether he landed, and carried on his approach in form. It is probable, as he was reduced to severe privation, that Briggs had seized all the boats upon the lake, and stopped the supplies. Neither do we learn the strength of the garrison within, nor of the works without, though every gentleman's house was at that time in some degree a fortress. All we learn is, that Major Philipson endured a siege of eight or ten days with great gallantry ; till his brother the Colonel, hearing of his distress, raised a party, and relieved him ; or, as another account says, till his brother returned from Carlisle, after the siege of that city was raised.

It was now the Major's turn to make reprisals. He put himself therefore at the head of a little troop of horse, and rode to Kendal. Here being informed that Colonel Briggs was at prayers (for it was on a Sunday morning), he stationed his men properly in the avenues, and himself, armed, rode directly into the church. It is said he intended to seize the Colonel and carry him off; but as this seems to have been totally impracticable, it is rather probable that his intention was to kill him on the spot ; and in the midst of the confusion, to escape. Whatever his intention was, it was frustrated, for Briggs happened to be elsewhere.

The congregation, as might be expected, was thrown into great confusion on seeing an armed man, on horseback, make his appearance amongst them ; and the Major, taking advantage of their astonishment, turned his horse round, and walked quietly out. But having given an alarm, he was presently assaulted as he left the assembly; and, being seized, his girths were cut, and he was unhorsed.

Another account says, that having dashed forward down the principal aisle of the church, and having discovered that his principal object could not be effected, he was making his escape by another aisle, when his head came violently in contact with the arch of the doorway, which was much lower that that through which he had entered ; that his helmet was struck off by the blow, his saddle girth gave way, and he himself, much stunned, was thrown to the ground.

At this instant his party made a furious attack on the assailants, who taking advantage of his mishap, attempted to detain him ; and the Major killed with his own hand the man who had seized him, clapped the saddle, ungirthed as it was, upon the horse, and vaulting into it, rode full speed through the streets of Kendal, calling his men to follow him, and with his whole party made a safe retreat to his asylum on the lake, which he reached about two o'clock.

The action marked the man. Many knew him; and they who did not, knew as well from the exploit, that it could be nobody but *Robin the Devil.*

In the Bellingham Chapel, in Kendal Church, is suspended high over an ancient altar tomb, a battered helmet, through whose crust of whitewash the rust of ages is plainly to be discerned. Whether this antique casque belonged to Sir Roger Bellingham, who was interred A.D. 1557 in the tomb beneath, and was exalted as a token of the distinction he had received, when made a knight banneret by the hand of his sovereign on the field of battle, or was won by the puissant burgesses of Kendal from one of the Philipsons, and elevated to its present position as a trophy of their valour, it is, strangely enough, called the "Rebel's Cap," and forms the theme of the bold and sacreligious action recorded of Robert Philipson.

As for "Robin" (who has also, though unjustly, been

calumniated and accused of having murdered the persons to whom the skulls at Calgarth belonged, and who figures, it is said, in many other desperate adventures), after the final defeat at Worcester had, by depressing for a time the hopes of the royalists, in some degree restored a sort of subdued quiet to the kingdom, finding a pacific life irksome to his restless spirit, he passed over into the sister country, and there fell in some nameless rencontre in the Irish wars, sealing by a warrior's fate a course of long tried and devoted attachment to his king ; in his death, as in his life, affording a memorable illustration of the fine sentiment embodied in these proud lines—

"Master ! lead on and I will follow thee
To the last gasp, with truth and loyalty."

During the Protectorate of Cromwell, Briggs ruled in the ascendancy ; but on the accession of Charles the Second, he was obliged for a long period to hide in the wilds of Furness.

Two hundred years have rolled away, since the generation that saw those events has vanished from the earth, and every tangible memorial of the island hero has been thought to have perished with him.   Nevertheless, time has spared one fragile, though little noticed relic ; for in the library of that most interesting of our northern English fanes, the Parish Church of Cartmel, whose age-stricken walls, so rich in examples of each style of Gothic architecture, rise but a few miles from the foot of the lake, in the centre of a vale of much beauty of a monastic character, there is retained upon the shelves a small volume in Latin, entitled "Vincentii Lirinensis hæres, Oxoniæ, 1631," on one of the blank leaves of which is this inscription in MS., the signature to which has been partly torn off :—

" For Mr Rob. Phillipson.
    Inveniam, spero, quamvis Peregrinus, amicos :
    Mite peto tecum cominus hospitium. R——"

It is pleasing to dwell on this enduring testimony of regard for a man, whose portrait, as limned on the historic canvas, has hitherto been looked upon as that only of a bold unnurtured ruffler in an age of strife.   Seen under the effect of this touch by the hand of friendship, a gentler grace illumes the air of one, whose unwavering principles and firm temper well fitted him to encounter the troubles of a stormy epoch, while, as long as the island itself shall endure, his heroic shadow rising over its groves, will cast the enthralling interest of a romantic episode upon a scene so captivating by its natural loveliness.

That the individual so addressed, was our Robin of Satanic notoriety, there cannot reasonably be a doubt, as the pedigree of the Crook Hall Philipsons does not recognise any other member of the family of that name, living between the time of the publication of the book, and the death of their last male heir. Neither is the genealogical tree of the Calgarth branch enriched with the name between that and 1652, when Christopher Philipson (of the house of Calgarth) who, amid the bitter struggle of parties, seems to have been devoted to the cultivation of letters, and who is supposed to have presented the book, along with others, to the library at Cartmel, died. Therefore to the successful soldier, whose actions gave to himself and his cause so chivalrous a colouring, alone, must the inscription be applied, the evidence it affords furnishing another illustration of the saying that "the Devil is not always as black as he is painted." But whether it be questionable that it was directed to the royalist Robin, or not, the probability is sufficiently great to justify what has been said on the subject.

Recent research through public archives has ascertained that the family of the Philipsons was established in Westmorland at least as far back as the reign of Edward III., for in an inquisition relative to the possessions of the chantry on Saint Mary's Holme, taken in 1355, the name of John Philipson is recorded as tenant to certain lands belonging to that religious foundation.

This family owned not only Calgarth Hall and extensive domains which reached along the shores of Windermere, from Low Wood to Rayrigg, consisting of beautiful woods and rich pastures, but also Crook and Holling Halls, with much of the surrounding country, as well as the large island in the centre of the lake, opposite to Bowness, in documents of the 13th century especially designated "Le Holme," but the earliest name of which was Wynandermere Isle, afterwards changed to the "Long Holme," which latter word signifies, in the old vernacular, "an island or plain by the water side," and in which they had a mansion of the old fashioned Westmorland kind, strongly fortified, called the Holme House.

Their alliances having connected them with many of the chief families of the county, they fixed their principal dwelling places at Holling, and at Crook or Thwatterden Halls; which latter abode in the time of Queen Elizabeth again became the seat of a younger branch of the house at Calgarth.

With Sir Christopher Philipson, the last heir male of the

family of Crook Hall, who, according to Mr. West, lived in the Holme in 1705, and who died in that year, the race was extinguished. Their mouldered dust lies beneath the pavement in Windermere Church, and their homes, for the most part but grey and naked ruins, know them no more.

THE LAY OF LORD LUCY OF EGREMOND.

On that Mount surnamed "of Sorrow"
  Glass'd in Enna's winding flood,
Looking forth through many a morrow
  Both the warriors, Lucies, stood ;
Stood beside the ramparts hoary,
  Brothers, vow'd their brows to wreathe
In the Holy Land with glory,
  Or its sands to rest beneath.

Quietly the vale was lying,
  Farm and meadow, forge and mill,
As the day-star faintly dying
  Paled above the eastern hill.
But beneath the cullis'd portal
  Press'd the pent-up throng of war,
Eager for the strife immortal
  With the Soldan's hosts afar.

Fame has all his soul's embraces—
  Clasps Lord Lucy maid nor wife,
As the warriors' vizor'd faces
  Turn towards the land of strife.
Through the gate beneath the towering
  Pile they wind in shining mail.
Soon afar the fortress lowering
  Sinks beneath them in the vale.

Scawfell saw them take the billow,
  Man by man on Cumbria's shore ;
Carmel's foot was first their pillow
  When again to land they bore.
And in holy fight they bound them
  To their Saviour's service true;
Fought and bled, through hosts around them,
  Till their ranks were faint and few.

Then beneath the foe contending,
  Faithful, fearless, but in vain,
Lo, the brothers bound and bending
  Drag the hopeless captive's chain.
In the Moslem dungeon wasting,
  England's bravest, both they lie ;
No sweet hope nor solace tasting,
  Only blank captivity.

Months have rolled ; and moons are waning ;
  Then stood Lucy forth and said,—
" Emir, over millions reigning !
  We are two in dungeon laid.

I, who bore a noble's banner,
I have halls and realms afar,
Wealth which many a lordly manor
Yields, beneath the western star.

" Let the Emir's heart be gracious !
Free my brother at my side ;
And a ransom rich and precious
We will bring o'er ocean wide.
So we two, whose arms avail'd not
Here our freedom to sustain,
But whose constant courage fail'd not,
May be Freedom's sons again."

Greed for gain o'er wrath prevailing
Softened soon the tyrant's mind.
Homewards one is swiftly sailing ;
Calmly one will wait behind.
For a twelve-months thus they parted.
Weary months, the year, went o'er.
But that brother, evil-hearted,
From the West return'd no more.

Then the Emir's soul no longer
Would its vengeance stern forego ;
All his rage suppress'd the stronger,
Burn'd, and burst upon his foe.
And he bade his hair be knotted
Into cords around a beam,
There to chain him till he rotted,
Where no light of heaven could gleam.

20

And in hunger sore he wasted;
    And his nails grew like a bird's;
Day's sweet blesséd airs untasted,
    And no sound of human words!
Changed in soul, and form, and feature,
    Ah! how changed from that fair mould,
In which heaven had stamped its creature
    Man and warrior, mild as bold!

Yet one heart whose daily gladness
    Once had been, from latticed bower
To look down on him in sadness
    Walking forth at evening hour;
She, the Emir's fairest daughter,
    Sees brave Lucy now no more,—
Till unresting love has brought her
    Trembling to his dungeon's floor.

There, with one mute form attending,
    Swift her arm the faulchion drew
Through his locks; the hatterel rending*
    From him, as it cleaved them through.
And with words of woman-kindness
    Whisper'd she—"To light and air,
Life and love, from dungeon blindness,
    Are we come the brave to bear."

And for love of him she bore him
    To a ship, wherein he rode
Seaward till the bright sky o'er him
    Circled round his own abode.

* The scalp with the hair attached.

Then his castle-horn he sounded,
　Which none other's skill could sound,
Where the traitor sat, confounded,
　With his bold retainers round.

But brave Lucy's soul forgave him
　All that wrong so foully done;
Him who went not back to save him
　With the ransom he had won.
Yea, and more : " From Duddon's borders
　Far as Esk, and from the sea
To where Hard-knott's ancient warders
　Sleep," he said, " I give to thee.

" Here once more by vale and mountain,
　On these ramparts side by side,
Wells up from my heart a fountain
　Wastes and dungeons have not dried."
And his stately halls he entered,
　Borne mid cheers and warriors' clang ;
While a thousand welcomes, centred
　In one shout of triumph, rang.

High the feast and great the story
　Then that fill'd his ancient halls.
Healths to Lucy's House and glory
　Shook the banners on the walls.
And their deep foundations hail'd him
　With such echoes as were born
When his own true breath avail'd him
　On the faithful Castle-horn.

And 'twas joy again to wander
　On his own fair fields, and chase
There the wild wolf, and bring under
　The strong deer in deadly race.
And if sometimes more the forest
　Won him, museful and alone;
'Twas when secret thoughts were sorest,
　Turn'd upon the past and gone.

But that lone and lordly bosom
　Sought no mate of high degree;
Wooed no fair and beauteous blossom
　From a noble kindred tree,—
As might have beseem'd, to wear her
　Throned within a warrior's breast;
Evermore to bloom, the sharer
　Of its love, its life, its rest.

So in field, and hall, and tourney,
　As he lived—upon a day,
Wearied with a toilsome journey,
　Came a guest from far away;
Feebly at his gate and humbly
　Asking, "Dwells Lord Lucy here?"
But all question parried dumbly,
　Till the voice she sought was near.

Then indeed the sorrow-laden,
　Travel-stricken form sunk down;
Slow the hatterel forth the maiden
　Drew; he knew her! 'twas his own!

Knew her, as she stood before him
    On that barren Syrian shore,
When from wrath and death she bore him
    Where no wrong might touch him more.

Bear her in! he tells them of her,
    Tells them all with eye-balls dim.
Cannot be but he must love her,
    For she bears such love to him.
She has left her father's mansion,
    Left her country, faith, and name,
Travell'd o'er the sea's expansion,
    Him to find in life and fame.

Was there ever like devotion?—
    Is he husband, father; she
Who has braved the boundless ocean
    Will his serving maiden be.
No! she shall abide in honour,
    One for ever at his side;
Every gift and grace upon her
    That beseems a warrior's bride.

Then again his days were gladden'd
    With more joys than e'er of yore.
And if thought at times was sadden'd
    With the memories which it bore,
Clasping oft his wife with true love,
    He would say with whispering breath—
" Love is life indeed! for through love
    I am here, reprieved from death!"

And his soul's allegiance fail'd not
    That fair consort, all his days.
And their blissful love—avail'd not
    Chance or time to quench its rays.
Love unto his gate had brought her
    O'er the seas from far beyond.
And with love the Emir's daughter
    Ruled the halls of Egremond.

But that kinsman, far divided
    From them by remorse and shame,
Round his courts in secret glided
    Ghost-like—nevermore the same :
Conscience-torn, repentant, weary,
    Burning, longing for the close
Of that pilgrimage so dreary.
    Power had come, but not repose.

Shadows the rebuked and chastened,
    Worn-out warrior lowly laid.
And from Bega's cloisters hastened
    Thrice the prior with his aid :
Thrice : And ere the leaves had faded,
    Brave Lord Lucy clasped his breast;
*Kiss'd him; and the convent shaded
    One more spirit into rest.

---

* In the early and middle ages kissing was the common form of salutation, and the *osculum pacis* was a sign of reconciliation and charity. Examples will occur to every reader of Scripture and the classics.

303

NOTES TO "THE LAY OF LORD LUCY OF EGREMOND."

The name of Egremont seems to be derived from its ancient possessors, the Normans, and being changed by a trifling corruption of their language, carries the same meaning, and signifies the Mount of Sorrow.

The charter of Richard de Lucy, granted to the burgesses in the time of King John, declares it to be given and confirmed "burgensibus meis de *Acrimonte*," &c.

William the Conqueror having established himself on the throne of England, and added the county of Cumberland, which he wrested from Malcolm, king of Scotland, to his northern possessions ; he gave it, together with the barony of Westmorland, to Randolph or Ranulph du Briquesard, also surnamed le Meschin, Vicomte du Bessin, elder brother of William le Meschin.   This nobleman was allied to the Conqueror by marriage with his niece, and was one of his numerous train of military adventurers.   He was the first Norman paramount feudatory of Cumberland.   When Ranulph granted out to his several retainers their respective allotments ; reserving to himself the forest of Inglewood, he gave to his brother, William le Meschin, the great barony of Copeland, bounded by the rivers Duddon and Derwent, and the sea. The latter seated himself at Egremont and there erected a castle ; and in distinction of this his baronial seat, he changed the name of the whole territory to that of the barony of Egremont.   After possessing this estate with great power for several years, and dying without male issue, it devolved to his daughter Alice, married to Robert de Romili, Lord of Skipton.

They having no male issue, these two great baronies descended to their only daughter Alice, who married William Fitz-Duncan, Earl of Murray, nephew to David, King of Scots. By this marriage there was issue a son, who died in infancy, and three daughters who divided the vast inheritance. To Amabil, the second daughter, the barony of Egremont came in partition ; and by her marriage with Reginald Lucy, passed to that family. William Fitz-Duncan was Lord of the adjoining Cumbrian seigniory or honor of Cockermouth, and of the barony of Allerdale below Derwent, which large estates had descended to him from his mother Octreda, who inherited them from her grandfather Waldeof, first lord of Allerdale, to whom they had been granted by Ranulph de Meschin. Waldeof was the son of Gospatrick, Earl of Dunbar.

Particular mention is made of two only of the name of Lucy in succession : Reginald de Lucy, who was governor of Nottingham for the King, in the rebellion of the Earl of Leicester, and who also attended the coronation of Richard I. among the other Barons ; and Richard de Lucy, his son, who, in the reign of King John, paid a fine of three hundred marks for the livery of all his lands in Coupland and Canteberge, *and to have the liberty of marrying whom he pleased*, &c. He married Ada, one of the two daughters and co-heiresses of Hugh de Morville ; and obtained a grant from King John, by which he claimed and held the whole property of his father-in-law, without partition to the other daughter, Joane. He died before or about the 15th year of King John, leaving two daughters, between whom the estates were divided, and who both married into the Multon family.

At that time, and long after, it was a part of the King's prerogative to interfere in the marriages of his nobility.*

The subsequent acts of the widowed Ada de Lucy afford us a fine illustration of the exercise of this prerogative on the part of the sovereign in the matters of widows and heiresses. Ada paid a fine of five hundred marks for livery of her inheritance ; as also for dowry of her late husband's lands ; and that she might not be compelled to marry again. She espoused, however, without compulsion, and without the king's licence, Thomas de Multon ; in consequence of which, the Castle of Egremont, and her other lands, were seized by the Crown. But upon paying a compensation, they were restored, and she had livery of them again. Her second husband, on his payment of one thousand marks to the crown,

---

* Dr. Whitaker. Vide notes to the "Bridals of Dacre," for instances.

was made guardian over the two daughters, and co-heiresses, of her first husband, de Lucy : and as a necessary consequence, and, in fact, in accordance with the permission implied by the arrangement, he married them to his two sons by his first wife.

These two daughters and co-heiresses of Lucy having married the two sons of Thomas de Multon, the elder carried with her the lordship of Egremont ; while the son of the younger assumed the surname of his maternal family, and was ancestor of the barons Lucy of Cockermouth. The infant daughter of Anthony, the third and last baron Lucy, dying in the year following his own demise, the barony was carried by the marriage of his sister Maude with the first Earl of Northumberland to the Percy family : thence to the Seymours, Dukes of Somerset ; and through them to Wyndham, Earl of Egremont, by whose descendant, the first Lord Leconfield, it is at present enjoyed.

Egremont was anciently a borough, sending two members to parliament ; but was disfranchised on the petition of the burgesses, to avoid the expense of representation. The burgesses possessed several privileges, but all records of them are lost. The ordinances of Richard de Lucy for the government of the borough is a curious record, in which several singularities are to be observed, which point out to us the customs of that distant age. By this burgage tenure, the people of Egremont were obliged to find armed men, for the defence of the Castle, forty days at their own charge. The lord was entitled to forty days' credit for goods, and no more ; and his burgesses might refuse to supply him, till the debt which had exceeded that date was paid. They were bound to aids for the redemption of the lord and his heir from captivity ; for the knighthood of one of the lord's sons, and the marriage of one of his daughters. They were to find him twelve men for his military array. They were to hold watch and ward. They could not enter the forest with bow and arrow. They were relieved from cutting off the dogs' feet within the borough, as being a necessary and customary defence : on the borders, the dogs appointed to be kept for defence, were called *slough dogs :* this privilege points out, that within the limits of forests, the inhabitants keeping dogs for defence were to lop off one foot or more, to prevent their chasing the game ; which did not spoil them for the defence of a dwelling. A singular privilege appears in the case of a burgess committing fornication with the daughter of a rustic, one who was not a burgess ;

that he should not be liable to the fine imposed in other cases for that offence, unless he had seduced by promise of marriage. The fine for seducing a woman belonging to the borough was three shillings to the lord. By the rule for inspecting dyers, weavers, and fullers, it seems those were the only trades at that time within the borough under the character of crafts-men. The burgesses who had ploughs were to till the lord's demesne one day in the year, and every burgess to find a reaper : their labour was from morning *ad nonam*, which was three o'clock, as from six to three.

Egremont was probably a place of strength, and the seat of some powerful chief, during the Heptarchy, and in the time of the Danes. The ruins of the Castle, on the west of the town, stand on an eminence, the northern extremity of which forms a lofty mound, seventy-eight feet in perpendicular height above the ditch which surrounds the fortress. On the crown of this hill, it is believed, there formerly stood a Danish fortification. The mound is said to be artificial. Tradition goes so far as to assert that it is formed of soil brought by St. Bega from Ireland, as ballast for her ship. The miraculous power of the Saint must have been largely exercised to increase it to its present proportions. It still, however, retains the virtue given to Irish earth by the blessing of St. Patrick, and no reptile can live upon it.

This fortress is not of very great extent, but bears singular marks of antiquity and strength. The approach and grand entrance from the south, has been kept by a draw-bridge over a deep moat. The entrance to the castle is by a gateway vaulted with semi-circular arches, and guarded by a strong tower. The architecture of this tower, which is the chief part of the fortress now standing, points out its antiquity to be at least coeval with the entry of the Normans. The outward wall has enclosed a considerable area of a square form ; but it is now gone so much to decay, that no probable conjecture can be made as to the particular manner in which it was fortified. On the side next the town a postern remains. To the westward, from the area, there is an ascent to three narrow gates, standing close together, and on a straight line, which have communicated with the outworks : these are apparently of more modern architecture, and have each been defended with a portcullis. Beyond these gates is the lofty mount, which has already been referred to, and on which anciently stood a circular tower, the western side of which endured the rage of time till within the last century. The whole fortification is surrounded by a moat, more properly so called than a ditch, as it appears to have been walled on both sides. This is strengthened with an outward rampart of earth, which is five hundred paces in circumference. A small brook runs on the eastern side of the Castle, and it may be presumed, anciently filled the moat. The mode of building which appears in part of the walls, is rather uncommon, the construction being of large thin stones, placed in an inclined position, the courses lying in different directions, so as to form a kind of feathered work, the whole run together with lime and pebbles, impenetrably strong. It seems to have been copied from the filling parts of the Roman wall.

An old tradition connects the lords of this Castle with the Crusades. One version of it given in the histories of Cumberland, for it is variously related, is to this effect :—"The Baron of Egremont being taken prisoner beyond the seas by the infidels, could not be redeemed without a great ransom, and being for England, entered his brother or kinsman for his surety, promising with all possible speed to send him money to set him free ; but upon his return home to Egremont, he changed his mind, and most unnaturally and unthankfully suffered his brother to lie in prison, in great distress and extremity, until the hair was grown to an unusual length, like to a woman's hair. The Pagans being out of hopes of the ransom, in great rage most cruelly hanged up their pledge, binding the long hair of his head to a beam in the prison, and tied his hands so behind him, that he could not reach to the top where the knot was fastened to loose himself : during his imprisonment, the Paynim's daughter became enamoured of him, and sought all good means for his deliverance, but could not enlarge him : she understanding of this last cruelty, by means made to his keeper, entered the prison, and taking her knife to cut the hair, being hastened, she cut the skin of his head, so as, with the weight of his body, he rent away the rest, and fell down to the earth half dead ; but she presently took him up, causing surgeons to attend him secretly, till he recovered his former health, beauty, and strength, and so entreated her father for him that he set him at liberty. Then, desirous to revenge his brother's ingratitude, he got leave to depart to his country, and took home with him the hatterell of his hair rent off as aforesaid, and a bugle-horn, which he commonly used to carry about him, when he was in England, where he shortly arrived, and coming to Egremont Castle about noontide of the day, where his brother was at dinner,

he blew his bugle-horn, which (says the tradition) his brother
the baron presently acknowledged, and thereby conjectured
his brother's return ; and then sending his friends and servants
to learn his brother's mind to him, and how he had escaped,
they brought back the report of all the miserable torment
which he had endured for his unfaithful brother the baron,
which so astonished the baron (half dead before with the
shameful remembrance of his own disloyalty and breach of
promise) that he abandoned all company and would not look
on his brother, till his just wrath was pacified by diligent
entreaty of their friends. And to be sure of his brother's
future kindness, he gave the *lordship of Millum* to him and
his heirs for ever. Whereupon the first Lords of Millum gave
for their arms *the horn and the hatterell*.

Others relate that it was the baron who remained as hostage :
and that on his release from captivity by the Paynim's
daughter, and after his departure to his native country, urged
by her love towards him, she found her way across the sea,
and presenting herself at his castle-gate, with the hatterell of
his hair which she had preserved as a token, was joyfully
recognized by the Baron, who made her his wife and the
mistress of his halls.

It is, on various grounds, an anachronism to refer this
tradition to the period when the Lucies were Lords of
Egremont. For, according to Denton, the great seignory of
Millom "in the time of King Henry I. was given by William
Meschines, Lord of Egremont, to . . . de Boyvill, father
to Godard de Boyvill, named in ancient evidences Godardus
Dapifer." This accords with the tradition, which is very old,
and is given by both Denton and Sandford, and which
makes, as we have seen, the Boyvills to be very near of kin to
the Lords of Egremont. It also particularises the occasion
upon which Millom was transferred to that family ; who took
their surname from the place, and were styled de-Millom.

That some members of the family were engaged in the
crusades, we learn from the record that Arthur Boyvill or de
Millom, the third lord, and the son of Godardus Dapifer,
granted to the Abbey of St. Mary in Furness the services of
Kirksanton in Millom, which Robert de Boyvill, his cousin-
german, then held of him ; and soon after he mortgaged the
same to the Abbot of Furness, until his return from the Holy
Land.

The crest of Huddleston of Hutton John is, Two arms,
dexter and sinister embowed, vested, argent, holding in their

hands a scalp proper, the inside gules. The tradition of the Horn of Egremont Castle, which could only be sounded by the rightful lord, and which forms the subject of a fine poem by Mr. Wordsworth, is said properly to belong to Hutton-John, an ancient manor of the Huddlestons, who were descended from the Boyvills in the female line ; Joan, the daughter and heiress of the last of the de-Milloms, in the reign of Henry III., having married Sir John Hudleston, Kt., and thus transferred the seignory into that family, with whom it continued for a period of about 500 years.

The name of Egremont will remind the poetical reader of the story of the "Youthful Romili," celebrated by Wordsworth in his noble ballad "The Founding of Bolton Priory," and by Rogers in his less ambitious lines "The Boy of Egremond." It seems to be by no means certain to which generation of William le Meschines' descendants the tale belongs. Denton says, "Alice Romley, the third daughter and co-heir of William Fitz-Duncan, was the fourth lady of Allerdale : but having no children alive at her death, she gave away divers manors and lands to houses of religion, and to her friends and kinsmen. She had a son named William, who was drowned in Craven coming home from hunting or hawking. His hound or spaniel being tied to his girdle by a line, (as they crossed the water near Barden Tower, in Craven) pulled his master from off his horse and drowned him. When the report of his mischance came to his mother, she answered, "*Bootless bayl brings endless sorrow.*" She had also three daughters, Alice, Avice, and Mavice, who all died unmarried, and without children ; wherefore the inheritance was after her death parted between the house of Albemarl and Reginald Lucy, Baron of Egremont, descending to her sister's children and their posterity."

This is Whitaker's statement :—"In the year 1121 William le Meschines and Cecilia his wife founded a Priory for canons regular, at Embsay, which was dedicated to St. Mary and St. Cuthbert, and continued there about thirty-three years, when it is said by tradition to have been translated to Bolton, on the following account.

"The founders of Embsay were now dead, and had left a daughter, who adopted her mother's name, Romillé, and was married to William Fitz-Duncan. They had issue a son, commonly called the Boy of Egremond (one of his grandfather's baronies, where he was probably born), who, surviving an elder brother, became the last hope of the family.

"In the deep solitude of the woods betwixt Bolton and Barden, the Wharf suddenly contracts itself to a rocky channel little more than four feet wide, and pours through the tremendous fissure with a rapidity proportionate to its confinement. This place was then, as it is yet, called the Strid, from a feat often exercised by persons of more agility than prudence, who stride from brink to brink, regardless of the destruction which awaits a faltering step. Such, according to tradition, was the fate of young Romillé, who inconsiderately bounding over the chasm with a greyhound in his leash, the animal hung back, and drew his unfortunate master into the torrent. The forester, who accompanied Romillé, and beheld his fate, returned to the Lady Aäliza, and, with despair in his countenance, enquired, 'What is good for a bootless Bene?' To which the mother, apprehending that some great calamity had befallen her son, instantly replied, 'Endless Sorrow.'

"The language of this question, almost unintelligible at present, proves the antiquity of the story, which nearly amounts to proving its truth. But 'bootless Bene' is unavailing prayer; and the meaning, though imperfectly expressed, seems to have been, 'What remains when prayer is useless?'"

The accuracy of this account, though admitted to be true so far as the death of a scion of Romili's house, is however doubted by Dr. Whitaker, who states that the son of the Lady Alice or Aäliza was a party and witness to the charter of translation to Bolton in 1154 of the Canons of the Priory of Embsay, founded in 1121 by William de Meschines and Cecilia de Romili his wife. Besides, as the Boy of Egremond was alive in 1160, and a partaker in the rebellion of the Pictish Celts of Scotland, of which the object was to set him on the throne as the rightful heir, Dr. Whitaker is of opinion that the story refers to one of the sons (both of whom died young) of Cecilia le Meschines, grandmother of Lady Alice.

There is however an oversight of some importance in Whitaker's statement. He altogether omits the second generation of the descendants of William le Meschines. Alice, the daughter of W. le Meschines, married Robert de Romili; Alice, her daughter, married Fitz-Duncan, who assumed the name of his wife, and was William le Romili. If their son was "the Boy of Egremond," he could not have been a witness to the charter of translation in 1154. If he was drowned in the Wharf, his death could not have been the occasion of the refounding of the Priory at Bolton. If the son of Cecilia le Meschines was "the Boy of Egremond"; as he might be so styled from his father's barony; he may have been drowned at the Strid, but his mother could not have been the second foundress of the Priory; for, as Whitaker says, the founders of Embsay were already dead. Tradition, moreover, clings to the name of the Lady Alice, as being that of the pious dispenser of her goods to sacred and religious uses. And however history may conflict with tradition, there will remain, that the Lady of Skipton, Cockermouth, and the Allerdales, bestowed her lands and goods most liberally upon the Abbeys of Fountains and Pomfret, and other religious confraternities; that she, the Lady Alice, seems always to have cherished those dispositions whose spiritual convictions moved in unison with the votive religious practices of the age; and although she, for the health of her dear son's soul (if he it were who perished in the Wharf) could not have founded near the scene of his untimely fate, the Priory before mentioned; its legendary history, which has so enshrined her affections and her sorrows, will continue to connect in the future, as in the past, the image of the youthful Romili with her griefs, and the stately Priory of Bolton with his imperishable name.

SÖLVAR-HOW.

Up the valley of Brathay rode Dagmar the Dane.
There was gold on her bit, there was silk on her rein.
You might see her white steed in the distance afar,
On the green-breasted hill, shining out like a star;
Where beyond her on high in his barrow lay sleeping
Old Sölvar the chief; and the shade, that sat keeping
His fame, by his tomb sang the Norseland's wild
    strain.

As the white steed of Dagmar shone, breasting the
    hill;
To the mound where old Sölvar lies lonely and still,
In the red light of evening, arresting her gaze,
Flocked the meek mountain ewes and the steers up
    the ways,

With the firstlings and yearlings, from hill top and
hollow,
Gathering far, the sweet voice of the Phantom to
follow—
To them sweeter than murmur of fountain and rill.

There was joy in their looks, in their eyes the clear
light
Glistened searchingly forth on that mystical sight.
And from far, too, the white steed of Dagmar the
Dane
Pricked his ears, stepping proudly, unheeding the
rein ;
And aside to the summit turned joyfully pacing ;
While the steers and the ewes listened wistfully
gazing,
And the Phantom sat singing of Sölvar the Bright.

O'er the pools of the Brathay, from Skelwith's lone
tower
The sire of the princess looked forth in that hour.
He beheld the white steed of his child, like a star
On the green-breasted hill, and he cried from afar—
"She has heard his wild strains on the hill-top
awaken,
And I from this hour am alone and forsaken.
—Not her voice nor her foot-fall, to come to me
more !"

21

For to Dagmar the fair, when the flocks of the field
And the herds were in motion their homage to
    yield
To the bright Norseland Boy—with the fire and
    the grace
Of his sires in his limbs and their pride in his face—
In the garb of his country, rehearsing the story
Of chiefs and of kings and the Norseland's old glory—
Was the Phantom in all his bright beauty revealed.

There entranced in that vision, enchained by his
    tongue,
As the strains through his harp-strings melodiously
    rung,
Sat the maid on White Svend mid the yearlings;
    till now
Far departing he turns from the hill's sunny brow;
And the ewes at his feet awhile falteringly follow,
Then range back bewildered to hill-top and hollow;
While the Maid on his fast-fading accents still hung.

Through the still light receding his loose tresses
    streamed;
But to fly with him still was the dream she had
    dreamed;
Side by side o'er the hills, through the valleys, and on
To the Norseland to hear his wild songs all alone;

And to chase from his lips every accent of sorrow,
As they walked through the dawn of a brighter
    to-morrow
Into sunlight that heaven upon earth never beamed.

Springing down from White Svend, swiftly Dagmar
    the Dane
Cast aside on his neck the rich silk-tassel'd rein ;
With her eyes fixed afar o'er the green mountain
    sward,
Whence the bright Norseland Boy cast a backward
    regard.
Call aloud from thy Tower, call aloud and implore her,
Hapless sire ! to return, ere the night gathers o'er her !
She can hear but the voice of the Phantom's sweet
    strain.

Light and fleet was her foot over hollow and hill ;
Till they reached the rude cleft of the deep-roaring
    Ghyll.
On the black dungeon's brink not a moment he
    stay'd ;
O'er the black roaring Ghyll glided softly the Shade.
Like a thin wreath of mist she descried him far over—
And her cry pierced the night-boding hill tops
    above her ;
When down the loose rocks plunged, and bridged
    the dark Ghyll.

Heard the eagle that shriek from his eyrie on high?
Struck his wings the poised rocks as he rushed to
    the sky?
Did the wild goat leap, startled, and press from their
    hold
With his hoof the loose crags?—that they bounded
    and roll'd
Far above, down, and on, soughing, plunging, and
    clashing,
Till they reached the dark Ghyll, and fell, wedging
    and crashing,
In the gulf's horrid jaws, there for ever to lie.

The fleet foot of Dagmar sprang light to the stone,
Where it bridged the dread gulf, in the twilight,
    alone.
For one moment she stood with her eyes straining
    o'er
Into space, for the bright one that answered no
    more.
He was gone from the hand she stretched, vainly
    imploring;
He was gone from the heart that beat, madly
    adoring:
And a voice from the waters cried wailingly—
    " Gone!"

Roar thou on, Dungeon-Ghyll! there was mourning
    in vain
In the fortress of Skelwith for Dagmar the Dane.
From their tower on the cliff they looked, tearful
    and pale,
On her riderless steed as it came down the vale.
In her bower and in hall there was wailing and
    sorrow.
And the hills shone renewed with each glorious
    to-morrow.
But their bright star, their Dagmar, they knew not
    again.

NOTES TO "SÖLVAR HOW."

While many Celtic names of places remain to attest the prolonged sovereignty of the Britons in Cumbria, by far the greater number refer to a period when the enterprising Northmen, coming from various shores, but all included under the comprehensive title of Danes, had pushed their conquests into the mountain country of Cumberland and Westmorland and those portions of the north of Lancashire, which are comprised within the district of the English Lakes. This territory had become the exclusive possession of the Norwegian settlers. Every height and how, every lake and tarn, every swamp and fountain, every ravine and ghyll, every important habitation on the mountain side, the dwelling place amidst the cleared land in the forest, the narrow dell, the open valley, every one is associated with some fine old name that belonged to our Scandinavian forefathers. Silver How is the hill of Sölvar, and Butter-lip-how, the mound of Buthar, surnamed Lepr the Nimble; Windermere and Buttermere, and Elter-water are the meres and water called after the ancient Norsemen, Windar, and Buthar or Butar, and Eldir, Gunnerskeld, and Ironkeld, and Butter-eld-keld, are the spring or marsh of Gunnar, and Hiarn, and Buthar the Old, or Elder. Bekangs-Ghyll, and Staingill, and Thortill-gill, indicate the ravines or fissures, which were probably at one time the boundaries respectively of the lands of Bekan, and Steini, and Thortil; Seatallan and Seatoller were once the dwelling places whence Elli and Oller looked on the plains below them; and in Ormthwaite, and Branthwaite, and Gillerthwaite we recognise the lands cleared amid the forests with the axe, whose several possessors were Ormr, and

Biorn, and Geller ; while Borrodale, and Ennerdale, and
Riggindale, and Bordale recall the days when these remote
valleys were subject to the lordly strangers Borrhy, and Einar,
and Regin, and Bor. All these names are Scandinavian pro-
per names, and are to be found in the language of that ancient
race, of whose sojourn amongst our hills so many traces remain
in the nomenclature of the district.

Coming from the wildest and poorest part of the Norwegian
coast, and mixing with the Celtic tribes of these regions, in
the early ages ; those hardy sons of the sea made extensive
and permanent settlements among them. They penetrated
into the remotest recesses of the mountains, carrying thither
their wild belief in the old northern gods, and their rude ideas
of a future life. Their warlike recollections, and their attach-
ment to the scenes of their valorous exploits, fostered the
notion which was not uncommon among them, that the spirits
of chieftains could sometimes leave the halls of Valhalla, and,
seated each on his own sepulchral hill, could look around him
on the peaceful land over which in life he had held rule, or
on that beloved sea which had borne him so often to war and
conquest. It was this thought that induced them to select for
their burial places high mountains, or elevated spots in the
valleys and plains. As a natural result of their long continued
dominion in the North of England, they came to be classed
in the imagination of the people with invisible and mystic
beings which haunted that district. The shadows of the
remote old hills were the abodes of enchantment and super-
stition. And the spirits of the departed were supposed to be
seen visiting the earth, sometimes in the guise of a Celtic
warrior careering on the wind, and sometimes in the form of
one of the old northern chieftains sitting solitary upon his
barrow. It is related of one being permitted to do so for the
purpose of comforting his disconsolate widow, and telling her
how much her sorrow disquieted him. Hence also the
dwellers among the hills, it is said, still fancy they hear on the
evening breeze musical tones as of harp strings played upon,
and melancholy lays in a foreign tongue ; a beautiful concert,
to which we owe the exquisite medieval legend of the cattle,
in thraldom to the potent spirit of harmony that rings through
the air, often when no musical sound is audible to the organ
of man, pricking up their ears in astonishment, as they listen
to the Danish or Norseland Boy, sadly singing the old bardic
lays over the barrows of his once mighty forefathers.

It has been conjectured that the colonization of this district by the Northmen was effected at two distinct periods, by two separate streams of emigration, issuing from two different parts of the Scandinavian shore. The first recorded invasion of Cumberland by the Danes appears to have taken place about the year 875 ; when an army under the command of Halfdene, having entered Northumberland and made permanent settlements there, commenced a series of incursions into the adjacent countries lying on the north and west, and thereby reached the borders of the lake region, first plundering them and finally settling there. The indications of the presence of the northern adventurers in that quarter are found to be more purely of a Danish character than those which abound beyond the eastern line of the district, and which may with great probability be referred to a colonization more particularly Norwegian.

Our own histories make no mention of anything bearing upon the subject, but there seem to be good reasons for concluding that Cumberland was also invaded from the sea coast. The Norwegian sea-rover Olaf, according to Snorro Sturlessen, had visited, among other countries, both Cumberland and Wales. And Mr. Ferguson supposes, from various circumstances, which concur to fix the date of the Norwegian settlements here in the interval between 945 and 1000, that his descents must have taken place somewhere about the year 990. At that period the Cumbrian Britons had been for half a century in subjugation to the Saxons, and since the death of Dunmail their country had been handed over to Malcolm to be held in fealty by the Scottish crown. The scattered remnants of the Celtic tribes were for the most part shut up amongst their hills, or had retired into Wales. The plains of Westmorland and Cumberland on the north and east were probably chiefly occupied by a mixed Saxon and Danish population ; for nearly a century had elapsed since the Danes from Northumberland had overrun them. In fifty years more the result of events was, as we are informed by Henry of Huntingdon, that one of the principal abodes of the "Danes," under which title old writers comprehend all Northmen, was in Cumberland. A stream of Northern emigrants, issuing, it may be supposed, from the districts of the Tellemark, and the Hardanger, a name signifying "a place of hunger and poverty," had descended along the north of Scotland, swept the western side of the island, fixed its head-quarters in the Isle of Man, and from thence succeeded in obtaining a firm footing upon the opposite shore of England ; a land, like their own, of mountains and valleys, waiting for a people as they were for a settlement, a wild and untamed country, always thinly populated and never cultivated, a land of rocks and forests and of desolation. These protected by their ships, having command of the coast, and being unopposed except by the apparently impenetrable mountain barriers before them, these warlike settlers cleared for themselves homes amidst the woods, began to gather tribute from the mountain sides, and laid the foundations of those "thwaites" and "seats" and "gates" and "garths," which at the end of almost nine centuries of fluctuation and change still bear testimony to their wide-spread rule and are called by their Northern names.

Not only do traces of them everywhere survive in names which indicate possession and location, or in words which particularise the multiform features of the country and describe the minor variations of its surface ; but the sites of their legislative and judicial institutions, and their places of burial, as well as their towns and villages, are preserved in that local nomenclature which lives in the language spoken by their kinsmen in the mother-land at the present day. The old Norse element has penetrated, and diffused itself, and hardened into the dialect of the Cumberland and Westmorland "fell-siders," and emphatically pronounces from whom it came. And, lastly, the physical and moral characteristics, as well as the manners and customs of the people, are those of the hardy race, whose transmitted blood gave the larger nerve and more enduring vigour which characterise their frame. Tall, bony, and firmly knit ; fair-haired, and of Sanguine complexion ; possessing strong feelings of independance, and a large share of shrewdness and mother-wit ; intolerant of oppression ; cautious, resolute, astute and brave ; these people, and the Cumbrians, especially, crown their list of claims to be of Norse descent with one more striking feature, a litigious spirit. Litigation appears to be almost as natural and necessary to their minds, as wrestling and other manly exercises are to their limbs : in respect to which, as well as to other amusements in which they are said to bear some resemblance to the old Icelanders, they bear away the palm from the rest of England.

Dungeon Ghyll in Great Langdale is a deep chasm or fissure in the southern face of the first great buttress of the Pikes. It is formed by a considerable stream from Pike o' Stickle ; which after making several fine leaps down the mountain side, tumbles at length over a lofty precipice about eighty feet between impending and perpendicular rocks into a deep and gloomy basin. A few slender branches are seen springing from the crevices in either face of the chasm near the top ; and immediately above the basin, a natural arch, made by two large stones which have rolled from a higher part of the mountain, and got wedged together between the cheeks of rock. By scrambling over some rough stones in the bed of the stream, the largest and finest chamber may be reached ; and the visitor stands underneath the arch, and in front of the waterfall. Over the bridge thus rudely formed, Wordsworth's " Idle Shepherd Boy " challenged his comrade to pass ; and even ladies have had the intrepidity or temerity to cross it, undeterred by the narrowness and awkwardness of the footing, and the threatening aspect of the dismal gulf below.

The station in the field adjoining the farm house called Skelwith-Fold, is the site where the Danish fortress is assumed to have stood.

THE CHURCH AMONG THE MOUNTAINS.

In this sweet vale where peace has found
  An undisturbed abode,
The everlasting hills surround
  A temple reared to God ;
Where one pure stream, the Gospel's sound,
  Flows as it ever flow'd.

Here never reach the angry jars
  Which break the Church's rest.
The unity that strife debars
  Is on this Branch imprest ;
Her truths of old no discord mars ;
  Here peace is in her breast.

One Book reveals the living lore
  Of prophets, saints, and kings.
One mild apostle here its store
  To every household brings ;
And on this temple's sacred floor
  The pure glad tidings sings.

Race follows race from field and home,
    And all in earth are laid :
But steadfast as the starry dome
    Above, the truth is spread
Around their feet, howe'er they roam,
    Unquestioned, ungainsaid.

How blest, to live and hope in peace
    Like these ! nor hear the knell
Of some sure promise, made tó cease
    Beneath the mystic's spell,
Or subtle casuist's caprice—
    And know that all is well.

In vainest strifes we cast away
    Too much from life's fair page.
The flock becomes the spoiler's prey,
    Because the shepherds rage.
And while the life is but a day,
    The warfare lasts an age.

But here may piety rejoice
    To tread the ancient ways :
Still make the one true part the choice
    Of even the darkest days ;
And lift àn undivided voice
    Of thankful prayer and praise.

Guard, Sovereign of the heights and rills !
  These precincts of Thy fold ;
This little Church, which thus fulfils
  Thy purpose framed of old.
And this Thy flock amidst these hills
  Still in Thy bosom hold.

NOTES TO "THE CHURCH AMONG THE MOUNTAINS."

Wordsworth in his description of the Lake Country as it was, and had been through centuries, till within about one hundred years, thus alludes to the places of worship. "Towards the head of these Dales was found a perfect Republic of shepherds and agriculturists, among whom the plough of each man was confined to the maintenance of his own family, or to the occasional accommodation of his neighbour. Two or three cows furnished each family with milk and cheese. The Chapel was the only edifice that presided over these dwellings, the supreme head of this pure commonwealth : the members of which existed in the midst of a powerful empire, like an ideal society or an organised community, whose constitution had been imposed and regulated by the mountains which protected it.

"The *religio loci* is nowhere violated by these unstinted, yet unpretending works of human hands. They exhibit generally a well proportioned oblong, with a suitable porch, in some instances a steeple tower, and in others nothing more than a small belfry, in which one or two bells hang visibly. A man must be very insensible who would not have been touched with pleasure at the sight of the former Chapel of Buttermere, so strikingly expressing by its diminutive size, how small must have been the congregation there assembled, as it were, like one family ; and proclaiming at the same time to the passenger, in connection with the surrounding mountains, the depth of that seclusion in which the people lived, that rendered necessary the building of a separate place of worship for so few. The edifice was scarcely larger than many of the single stones or fragments of rock which were scattered near it. The old Chapel was perhaps the most diminutive in all England, being incapable of receiving more than half a dozen families. The length of the outer wall was about seventeen feet. The curacy was 'certified to the Governors of Queen Anne's Bounty at £1. paid by the contributions of the inhabitants,' and it was also certified, "this Chapel and Wythop were served by Readers, except that the Curate of Lorton officiated there three or four times in the year.'"

Such cures were held in these northern counties by un-ordained persons, till about the middle of George II.'s reign ; when the Bishops came to a resolution, that no one should officiate who was not in orders. But, because there would have been some injustice and some hardship in ejecting the existing incumbents, they were admitted to deacons' orders without undergoing any examination. The person who was then Reader as it was called, at the Chapel in the Vale of Newlands, and who received this kind of ordination, exercised the various trades of Clogger, Tailor, and Butter-print maker.

How otherwise than by following secular occupations were even Readers to exist ? The Chapel of "Secmurthow" on the south side of the river Derwent, not far from the foot of Bassenthwaite lake, was certified to the Governors of Queen Anne's Bounty at £2., being the interest of £40. raised by the inhabitants for a Reader. "Before its augmentation," says Hutchinson, "the Reader of divine service had a precarious income ; but an actual custom existed for several years of allowing the poor minister a *whittle-gate.* He was privileged to go from house to house in the Chapelry, and stay a certain number of days at each place, where he was permitted to enter his *whittle* or knife with the rest of the family. This custom," he adds, "has been abolished in such modern times, that it is in the memory of many now living." (i.e. 1794.)

The inhabitants of many of the Chapelries in the north got by custom from the Rectors or Vicars the right of nominating and presenting the curate ; for this reason : before the death of Queen Anne, many of the Chapelries were not worth above two or three pounds a year, and the donees could not get persons properly qualified to serve them ; so they left them to the inhabitants, who raised voluntary contributions for them in addition to their salary, with clothes yearly and whittle-gate.

Clothes yearly, were one new suit of clothes, two pairs of

shoes, and one pair of clogs, shirts, stockings, etc., as they could bargain.

Whittlegate is, to have two or three weeks' victuals at each house, according to the ability of the inhabitants, which was settled amongst them, so that he should go his course as regularly as the sun, and complete it annually. Few houses having more knives than one or two, the pastor was often obliged to buy his own ; sometimes it was bought for him by the chapel-wardens. He marched from house to house with his whittle seeking fresh pasturage ; and as master of the herd, he had the elbow chair at the table-head, which was often made of part of a hollow ash-tree, such as may be seen in those parts at this day.

Buttermere was said to allow its priest whittle-gate, and twenty shillings yearly ; by other accounts, "clogg-shoes, harden-sark, whittle-gate, and guse-gate"—that is, a pair of shoes clogged or iron-shod, a shirt of coarse linen or hemp once a year, free-living at each parishioner's house for a certain number of days, and the right to pasture a goose or geese on the common.

The Wytheburn reader had sark, whittle-gate, and guse-gate.

The Mungrisdale priest had £6. 0s. 9d. a year.

Many worthies have appeared, nevertheless, among these unpretending ministers of the dales ; most prominently so, Robert Walker, for a long period curate of Seathwaite, and surnamed for his many virtues and industry, the Wonderful : of whose life and actions an interesting and detailed account is given in the Notes in Wordsworth's Works.

The Chapel of Martindale, a perpetual curacy under the vicarage of Barton, near Penrith, was served for 67 years by a Mr. Richard Birket. The ancient endowment was only £2. 15s. 4d. per annum, a small house, and about four acres of land. At his first coming, Birket's whole property consisted of two shirts and one suit of clothes ; yet he amassed a considerable sum of money. Being the only man except one in the parish who could write, he transcribed most of the law papers of his parishioners. Whenever he lent money, he deducted at the time of lending, two shillings in the pound for interest, and the term of the loan never exceeded a year. He charged for writing a receipt twopence, and for a promissory note fourpence; and used other means of extortion. He likewise taught a school, and served as parish-clerk ; and in both these offices he showed his wonderful turn for economy and gain ; for his quarter-dues from his scholars being small, he had from the parents of each scholar a fortnight's board and lodging ; and the Easter-dues being usually paid in eggs, he, at the time of collecting, carried with him a board, in which was a hole that served him as a guage, and he positively refused to accept any which would pass through. He got a fortune of £60 with his wife ; to whom he left at his decease the sum of £1200. Clark says, that on account of transacting most of the law affairs of his parishioners, he was called Sir Richard, or the Lawyer. But with reference to this title, Nicholson, Bishop of Carlisle, at the beginning of the 18th century says, "Since I can remember, there was not a reader in any chapel who was not called 'Sir.'" The old designation of the clergy before the Reformation was always "Sir" ; knight being added as the military or civil distinction. It has also been stated that the last curate of this parish, or of these parts at all, called "Sir," was the Reverend Richard Birket (apud 1689).

On the death of Mr. Birket no one would undertake the cure, on account of the smallness of the stipend : those there-fore of the parishioners who could read, performed the service by turns. Things remained in this situation for some time ; at length a little decrepid man, named Brownrigg, to whom Mr. Birket had taught a little Latin and Greek, was by the parishioners appointed perpetual Reader. For this they allowed him, with the consent of the Donee, the church per-quisites, then worth about £12 per annum. Brownrigg being a man of good character, and there being no clergyman within several miles to baptize their children, or bury their dead, the parishioners petitioned the Bishop to grant him deacon's orders ; this was accordingly done, and he served the cure forty-eight years.

Mr. Mattinson, the curate of Paterdale, who died about the year 1770, was a singular character. For fifty-six years he officiated at the small "chapel with the yew tree," at the foot of St. Sunday's Crag. His ordinary income was generally twelve pounds a year, and never above eighteen. He married and lived comfortably, and had four children, all of whom he christened and married, educating his son to be a scholar, and sending him to College. He buried his mother ; married his father and buried him ; christened his wife, and published his own banns of marriage in the church. He lived to the age of ninety-six, and died worth a thousand pounds. It has been alleged that this provident curate assisted his wife to card and spin the tithe wool which fell to his lot, viz. one third ; that he taught a school which brought him in about five pounds a year ; that his wife was skilful and eminent as a midwife, performing her functions for the small sum of one shilling ; but as according to ancient custom she was likewise cook at the christening dinner, she received some culinary perquisites which somewhat increased her profits. Clarke adds, "One thing more I must beg leave to mention concerning Mrs. Mattinson : On the day of her marriage, her father boasted that his two daughters were married to the two best men in Paterdale, the priest and the bag piper."

In Langdale, in Clark's time, the poor Curate was obliged to sell ale to support himself and his family ; and, he says, "At his house I have played *Barnaby* with him on the Sabbath morning, when he left us with the good old song,

'I'll but preach, and be with you again.'"

Taking all their circumstances into consideration, it is not to be wondered at that the personal failings of these men were looked upon by their neighbours with a leniency which would hardly be intelligible elsewhere. Not very long ago an excellent old dame only recently deceased, who for her intelligence and goodness was respected and esteemed by the highest and the lowest, and was one of the finest specimens of nature's gentlewomen to be found anywhere, was heard warmly upholding the character of a neighbouring clergyman in these words,—"Well, I'll not say but he may have *slanted* now and then, at a christenin' or a weddin' ; but for buryin' a corp, he is undeniable !"

In 1866 the Bishop of Carlisle consecrated a new church at Wythop on the shores of Bassenthwaite Lake. The old building which this edifice is intended to supersede is a decayed barn-like structure, supplied with a bell which hung from an adjoining tree. Some curious customs are associated with this Church. It was built in 1473. For some hundreds of years the inhabitants of the Chapelry were in the habit of dividing it into four quarters, from each of which a representative was elected yearly ; the functions of the four being set forth in a document dated 1623. They have to elect a parish minister or reader, who was generally the schoolmaster, a layman being eligible ; they had to collect "devotion money," supervise the repairs of the fabric, and look after the parish school. The stipend of the minister was 10½d. per Sunday. Here is a copy of an old receipt :—"Received of the chapel-men of Wythop the sum of 28s. 5d. for thirty-one weeks' reading wages, by me, John Fisher." The stipend was however supplemented by whittlegate; he was boarded and lodged by the inhabitants of the four quarters in turn. The value of the living at the present day is only £51 per annum.

This old church which is to remain as a curiosity, stands high on a mountain side; and not many years ago nettles grew luxuriantly beneath the seats in the pews and along the middle of the passage. A narrow board on a moveable bracket constitutes the communion table, and the vessels employed in the celebration of the Lord's Supper are a pewter cheese-plate and pewter pot. There is no font provided for baptisms, the purpose was served by a common earthenware vessel; nor is any vestry room attached to the building.

Vestries are seldom to be found in these remote chapels. And in the chapel at Matterdale, the sacramental wine used to be kept in a wooden keg, or small cask; perhaps is so still.

It is said of Whitbeck Chapel, which lies on the base of Black Combe, near the sea shore, that smugglers frequenting that exposed part of the coast, on many occasions deposited their illegal cargoes within its walls, until a convenient opportunity arose for removing them unobserved. Sunday sometimes came round when the sacred edifice was not in the most suitable condition for celebrating divine service. The parish clerk had then to advise the minister that it would be inconvenient to officiate on that day. It was not politic to scrutinize too closely the nature of the difficulty that existed: it was sufficiently understood. A substantial sample of the intruding contraband element found its way to the house of the minister; and forthwith due notice was circulated among the parishioners that the usual service would not be held until the Sunday following. Meanwhile the stores were disposed of, and the wild and desperate adventurers were in full career again towards the Manx or Scottish shore.

In 1300 the Lady of Allerdale, and of the Honour of Cockermouth, Isabel Countess of Albemarle was summoned to prove by what right she held a market at Crosthwaite (near Keswick). She denied that she held any market there, but said that the men of the neighbourhood met at the Church on Festival days, and there sold flesh and fish; and that she as lady of the Manor of Derwent Fells took no toll. This practice being persevered in, in 1306 the inhabitants of Cockermouth represented in a petition to parliament that there

was a great concourse of people every Sunday at Crosthwaite
Church, where corn, flour, beans, peas, linen, cloth, meat,
fish, and other merchandise were bought and sold, which was
so very injurious to the market at Cockermouth, that the
persons of that place who farmed the tolls of the king were
unable to pay their rent. Upon this a prohibitory proclamation
was issued against the continuance of such an unseemly usage.

Things had not got quite straight in this respect within the
sanctuary at a much later period. The Rev. Thos. Warcup,
incumbent of the parish church of Wigton, in the civil war
was obliged to fly on account of his loyalty to the sovereign.
After the restoration of Charles II. he returned to his cure ;
and tradition says, that the butcher-market was then held upon
the Sunday, and the butchers hung up their carcasses even at
the church door, to attract the notice of their customers as
they went in and came out of church ; and it was not an
unfrequent thing to see people, who had made their bargains
before prayer began, hang their joints of meat over the
backs of the seats until the pious clergyman had finished the
service. The zealous priest, after having long, but ineffectu-
ally, endeavoured to make his congregation sensible of the
indecency of such practices, undertook a journey to London,
on foot, for the purpose of petitioning the king to have the
market-day established on the Tuesday ; which favour it is
said he had interest enough to obtain.

This faithful priest long before his death caused his own
monument to be erected in the churchyard, with this inscription
in verse of his own composing :

> Thomas Warcup prepar'd this stone,
> To mind him of his best home.
> Little but sin and misery here,
> Till we be carried on our bier.
> Out of the grave and earth's dust,
> The Lord will raise me up, I trust ;
> To live with Christe eternallie,
> Who, me to save, himself did die.

Mihi est Christus et in vita et in morte lucrum.   Phil. i. 21.
Obiit anno 1653.

Thus it appears his decease did not take place until some
years after the date at which he records his death ; probably
a period marked by some important change in his life, or of
unusual solemnity reminds us that only thirty-five years ago,
at a very few miles from its base, one who served the pastoral

office more than fifty years, eking out a wretched maintenance upon a small farm; while his sons were at the plough, was of necessity compelled to send his daughters with horses and carts for coals and lime, and to lead manure to the fields and distribute it over the land; whilst the Dean and Chapter of his diocese were the patrons of his cure.

Such things can hardly be witnessed at this day. But a minister may be seen even now (1867) on the other side of the district, leading the choir in the aisle, in his surplice, with bow and fiddle in his hands, and then resuming his place at the desk, with becoming solemnity, until the course of the service requires his instrument again. His sense of harmony is acute; for in the middle of the psalm, his arms will fly apart, and the volume of sound be stopped, until an offensive note has been ejected, and the strain rectified, and renewed.

A curious discovery has recently been made in the venerable parish church of Windermere. The plaster having come away over one of the arches, a band of red and black was revealed. On the removal of more of the thick layers of whitewash, a beautiful inscription in old English characters was found. Further search was instituted, and similar inscriptions have been discovered on all the walls between the arches in the nave. It is conjectured that these inscriptions were placed in the church at the time of the Reformation, as they are mostly directed against the dogma of transubstantiation, whilst they give plain instructions in the doctrine of the Sacraments.

On the north side of the nave the following have been deciphered :—

"Howe many sacramentes are their?—Two : baptisme and the supper of the Lord.

"In baptisme which ys ye signe yt may be seene?—Water onelie.

"Whiche is the grace yt cannot be seene?—The washinge awaie of synnes by the bloode of Christe.

"In the Lordes supper which is ye signe yt may be sene?—Breade and Wyne.

"Which is ye grace yt cannot be seene?—The bodie and bloode of Christe."

On the south wall the inscriptions are as follow :—

"In goinge to ye table of the Lord, what ought a man to consider or doe pryncipalie?—T examine him selfe.

"Is the breade and wine turned into ye bodie and bloode of Christe?—No, for if you turne or take away ye signe that may be sene it is no sacrament.

"For the strengthenynge of your faith, howe many things learne yow in ye Lordes Supper?—Two : as by ye hand and mouthe, my bodie recciuth breade and wine : so by faithe, my soule dothe feade of ye bodie and blood of Christ : secondlie all ye benefittes of Christ his passion and his righteousness, are as surelye sealled up to be mine as my selfe had wrought them.

"To the strengthening of your faithe how many thinges learne you in baptisme?—Two : first, as water washeth away the filthines of ye fleshe : so ye bloode of Christ washeth awaie synne from my soull ; secondly, I am taught to rise againe to neunes of life."

G. AND T. COWARD, PRINTERS, CARLISLE.

SECOND EDITION.

Small Crown 8vo.   In neat Cloth binding, Price 3s. 6d.

THE FOLK-SPEECH OF CUMBERLAND

and some Districts Adjacent; being short Stories and
Rhymes in the Dialects of the West Border Counties.
By ALEX. CRAIG GIBSON, F.S.A.

The tales are remarkable for their spirit and humour. The
poetry, too, is marked by the same characteristics.—*West-
minster Review.*

The stories and rhymes have the freshness of nature about
them.—*Contemporary Review.*

Brimful of humour, homely wit and sense, and reflect the
character and life and ways of thought of an honest sturdy
people.—*Spectator.*

The stories, or prose pieces, are wonderfully clever and well
done.—*Saturday Review.*

This is an uncommon book, combining, as it does, in an
extraordinary degree, the recondite lore which throws anti-
quarians into ecstacies, with the shrewd humour, the descrip-
tive force, and the poetic charm which, garbed in the old
Norse-rooted vernacular which Cumbrians love so well, will
secure for it a cordial reception among all those who claim
"canny Cumberland" for their childhood's home.—*Eddowes's
Shrewsbury Journal.*

His poems are pictures in very natural colours.—*Durham
Chronicle.*

Destined to an honourable place among the choicest pro-
ductions of our native literature.—*Carlisle Journal.*

Besides being a learned antiquary, he has wit, humour, and
a true vein of poetry in him, and the literary skill, in addition
to turn all these to the best account.—*Carlisle Express.*

In its way perfectly unique.—*Carlisle Examiner.*

CARLISLE: G. AND T. COWARD. LONDON: J. RUSSELL SMITH.

Small Crown 8vo. In neat Cloth binding, Price 3s.6d.

"CUMMERLAND TALK;" being Short Tales

and Rhymes in the Dialect of that County. By JOHN

RICHARDSON, of Saint John's.

A very good specimen of its class. The ordinary subscriber to Mudie's would not for a moment dream of ever looking into it, and yet Mr. Richardson possesses far more ability than the generality of novelists who are so popular.—*Westminster Review.*

Good and pleasant.—*Saturday Review.*

There are both pathos and humour in the various stories and ballads furnished by Mr. Richardson. We congratulate Cumberland on having so many able champions and admirers of her dialect.—*Athenæum.*

Some of the rhymes are admirable. "It's nobbut me!" is a capital specimen of a popular lyric poem.—*Notes and Queries.*

He has seized on some of the most striking habits of thought, and describes them simply and naturally, without any straining after effect.—*Carlisle Patriot.*

To all lovers of the dialect literature of this county the volume will be heartily welcome.—*Whitehaven News.*

A worthy companion to Dr. Gibson's "Folk Speech." *Wigton Advertiser.*

The sketches are quite equal to anything of the kind we have seen.—*Kendal Mercury.*

A very pleasant addition to the records of the dialect of Cumberland.—*Westmorland Gazette.*

The best and most comprehensive reflex of the folk-speech of Cumberland that has been put into our hands.—*Soulby's Ulverston Advertiser.*

There is plenty of variety in the volume.—*Ulverston Mirror.*

CARLISLE: G. AND T. COWARD. LONDON: J. RUSSELL SMITH.

F. Cap 8vo.   Price 2s. 6d.

SONGS AND BALLADS

By JOHN JAMES LONSDALE,

Author of "The Ship Boy's Letter," "Robin's Return," &c.

WITH A BRIEF MEMOIR.

From the ATHENÆUM.

Mr. Lonsdale's songs have not only great merit, but they display the very variety of which he himself was sceptical. His first lay, "Minna," might lay claim even to imagination ; nevertheless, for completeness and delicacy of execution, we prefer some of his shorter pieces. Of most of these it may be said that they are the dramatic expressions of emotional ideas. In many cases, however, these songs have the robust interest of story, or that of character and picture. When it is borne in mind that by far the greater portion of these lays were written for music, no small praise must be awarded to the poet, not only for the suitability of his themes to his purpose, but for the picturesqueness and fancy with which he has invested them under difficult conditions.

From the WESTMINSTER REVIEW.

Poetry seems now to flourish more in the north than in the south of England. Not long ago we noticed an admirable collection of Cumberland ballads, containing two songs by Miss Blamire, which are amongst the most beautiful and pathetic in our language. We have now a small volume by a Cumberland poet, which may be put on the same shelf with Kirke White. Like Kirke White's, Mr. Lonsdale's life seems to have been marked by pain and disappointment. Like Kirke White too, he died before his powers were full developed. A delicate pathos and a vein of humour characterize his best pieces.

From the SPECTATOR.

"The Children's Kingdom" is really touching. The picture of the band of children setting out in the morning bright and happy, lingering in the forest at noon, and creeping to their journey's end at midnight with tearful eyes, has a decided charm.

From NOTES AND QUERIES.

A volume containing some very pleasing poems by a young Cumberland poet, who but for his early death, would probably have taken a foremost place amongst the lyrists of our day.

CARLISLE : G. AND T. COWARD. LONDON : J. RUSSELL SMITH.

Small Crown 8vo. Price 3s. 6d. Cloth Limp.

A GLOSSARY of the WORDS and PHRASES

OF FURNESS (North Lancashire), with Illustrative Quotations, principally from the Old Northern Writers. By J. P. Morris, F.A.S.L

We are thoroughly pleased with the creditable way in which Mr. Morris has performed his task. We had marked a number of words, the explanation of which struck us as being good and to the point, but space unfortunately fails us. We commend the Furness Glossary to all students of our dialects.— *Westminster Review.*

The collection of words is remarkably good, and Mr. Morris has most wisely and at considerable pains and trouble illustrated them with extracts from old writers.— *The Reliquary Quarterly Review,*

Mr. Morris is well known in the district, both as a writer and an antiquarian. His labours in the work before us evince him to be a zealous and untiring student. We trust his book will have the success which we think it well deserves.— *Ulverston Advertiser.*

The stranger who takes up his abode in Furness will find Mr. Morris's little book a capital helpmate.— *Ulverston Mirror.*

Apart from its etymological value the work is highly acceptable as a contribution to local literature.— *Carlisle Journal.*

We cordially recommend the glossary to admirers of the old writers, and to all curious philologists.— *Carlisle Patriot.*

Valuable as tracing to their source many good old forms of the Furness dialect, and as explaining not a few archaisms which have been stumbling-blocks to students of their mother tongue.— *Whitehaven News.*

CARLISLE : G. AND T. COWARD. LONDON : J. RUSSELL SMITH.

Price 3s. 6d. in Cloth ; or 5s. in Extra Gilt Binding.

POEMS. By PETER BURN.

A NEW AND COMPLETE EDITION.

If Mr. Burn's genius does not soar very high, she leads us into many a charming scene in country and town, and imparts moral truths and homely lessons. In many points our author resembles Cowper, notably in his humour and practical aim. One end of poetry is to give pleasure, and wherever these poems find their way they will both teach and delight.— *Literary World.*

If Mr. Burn will confine himself to pieces as expressive and suggestive as " The Leaves are Dying," or as sweet as "The Rivulet," he need not despair of taking a good position amongst the ever-increasing host of minor poets.— *The Scotsman.*

Throughout the volume there is a healthy, vigorous tone, worthy of the land of song from which the author hails. The book is a desirable contribution to the already rich literature of Cumberland.— *Dundee Advertiser.*

The SONGS and BALLADS of CUMBERLAND and the LAKE COUNTRY ; with Biographical Sketches, Notes, and Glossary. Edited by SIDNEY GILPIN.

(A New and Revised Edition in preparation.)

CARLISLE : G. AND T. COWARD. LONDON: J. RUSSELL SMITH.

F. Cap 8vo.   Price 2s.6d., in neat Cloth binding.

MISS BLAMIRE'S SONGS AND POEMS;
together with Songs by her friend MISS GILPIN of
Scaleby Castle.   With Portrait of Miss Blamire.

She was an anomaly in literature.   She had far too modest an
opinion of herself; an extreme seldom run into, and sometimes,
as in this case, attended like other extremes with disadvan-
tages.   We are inclined, however, to think that if we have
lost a great deal by her ultra-modesty, we have gained some-
thing.   Without it, it is questionable whether she would have
abandoned herself so entirely to her inclination, and left us
those exquisite lyrics which derive their charms from the
simple, undisguised thoughts which they contain.   The char-
acteristic of her poetry is its simplicity.   It is the simplicity
of genuine pathos.   It enters into all her compositions, and is
perhaps pre-eminent in her Scottish songs.

Carlisle Journal, 1842.

In her songs, whether in pure English, or in the Cumbrian
or Scottish dialect, she is animated, simple, and tender, often
touching a chord which thrills a sympathetic string deep in
the reader's bosom.   It may, indeed, be confidently predicted
of several of these lyrics, that they will live with the best
productions of their age, and longer than many that were at
first allowed to rank more highly.—*Chambers' Journal, 1842.*

F. Cap 8vo.   Price 2s., in neat Cloth binding.

ROBERT ANDERSON'S CUMBERLAND BALLADS.

As a pourtrayer of rustic manners—as a relator of homely
incident—as a hander down of ancient customs, and of ways
of life fast wearing or worn out—as an exponent of the
feelings, tastes, habits, and language of the most interesting
class in a most interesting district, and in some other respects,
we hold Anderson to be unequalled, not in Cumberland only,
but in England.   As a description of a long, rapid, and varied
succession of scenes—every one a photograph—occurring at a
gathering of country people intent upon enjoying themselves
in their own uncouth roystering fashion, given in rattling,
jingling, regularly irregular rhymes, with a chorus that is of
itself a concentration of uproarious fun and revelry, we have
never read or heard anything like Anderson's "Worton
Wedding."—*Whitehaven Herald.*

CARLISLE : GEO. COWARD.   · LONDON : J. RUSSELL SMITH.

Small Crown 8vo.   Price One Shilling.

FORNESS FOLK, THE'R SAYIN'S AN' DEWIN'S ;

or Sketches of Life and Character in Lonsdale North of
the Sands. BY ROGER PIKETAH.

We have been greatly entertained by these stories, which
reveal to us traits of a humoursome, shrewd, sturdy race, of
whom from their geographical isolation, very little has been
communicated to us by the compilers of guide books or by
local sketchers.—*Carlisle Patriot.*

We can honestly say the tales are not spoiled in serving
up. They come upon the reader with almost the full force of
viva voce recital, and prove conclusively that Roger Piketah
is a thorough master of the "mak o' toak" which he has so
cleverly manipulated.— *Whitehaven News.*

Whoever Roger Piketah may be, he has succeeded in
producing a good reflex of some of our Furness traditions,
idioms, and opinions ; and we venture to predict it will be a
favorite at penny readings and other places.—*Ulverston
Advertiser.*

F. Cap 8vo.   Price 3s. 6d.

POEMS BY MRS. WILSON TWENTYMAN of

Evening Hill.   Dedicated, by permission, to H. W.
LONGFELLOW.

F. Cap 8vo.   Price 2s. 6d.

ROUGH NOTES OF SEVEN CAMPAIGNS

in Spain, France, and America, from 1809 to 1815.
By JOHN SPENCER COOPER, late Sergeant in the
7th Royal Fusileers.

———

CARLISLE: G. AND T. COWARD. LONDON : J. RUSSELL SMITH.

Crown 8vo. Price 1s. in extra Cloth Binding; or 6d. in neat Paper Cover.

OLD CASTLES : Including Sketches of CARLISLE, CORBY, and LINSTOCK CASTLES; with a Poem ou Carlisle. By M. S., Author of an "Essay on Shakspeare," &c.

WISE WIFF. A Tale in the Cumberland Dialect By the Author of "Joe and the Geologist." Price Threepence.

THREE FURNESS DIALECT TALES. Price Threepence. Contains :—Siege o' Brou'ton, Lebby Beck Dobby, Invasion o' U'ston.

THE SONGS AND BALLADS OF CUMBERLAND With Music by WILLIAM METCALFE.

1. D'YE KEN JOHN PEEL? Words by John Woodcock Graves. Price 4s.

2. LAL DINAH GRAYSON ("M'appen I may"). Words by Alex. Craig Gibson. Price 4s.

3. REED ROBIN. Words by Robert Anderson. Price 2s.6d.

4. "WELCOME INTO CUMBERLAND." Words by the Rev. T. Ellwood. Price 3s.

5. THE WAEFU' HEART. Words by Miss. Blamire. Price 2s. 6d.

THE WELCOME INTO CUMBERLAND. QUADRILLE. Price 4s.

THE JOHN PEEL MARCH. Price 4s.

(To be continued.) *The above at Half-Price.*

CARLISLE : G. AND T. COWARD.

www.ingramcontent.com/pod-product-compliance
Lightning Source LLC
Chambersburg PA
CBHW021110270326
41929CB00009B/809

* 9 7 8 3 3 3 7 1 5 1 3 0 0 *